W9-ASY-556

"For more than a decade, an inhuman campaign of sanctions—the most complete ever in recorded history—has destroyed Iraq as a modern state, decimated its people, and ruined its agriculture, its educational and health care systems, as well as its entire infrastructure. All this has been done by the United States and United Kingdom, misusing United Nations resolutions against innocent civilians, leaving the tyrant Saddam Hussein more or less untouched. This remarkable book is an invaluable documentation of the tragedy in Iraq, and deserves reading by every citizen interested in the appalling reality of US and UK foreign policy."

—Edward W. Said

"This book gives us a key to understand the New World Order, and warns about how Iraq's tragedy may be a model for global bullying and global impunity in coming times."

—Eduardo Galeano

"Here is a brilliantly collated body of unrelenting, undeniable evidence of the horrors that sanctions and war are visiting upon the people, in particular the children, of Iraq. For ordinary citizens sanctions are just another kind of dictatorship. Remote-controlled, seemingly civilized, they actually, literally, squeeze the very breath from babies' bodies."

—Arundhati Roy

"The arguments for change are pretty convincing. The undecided should pay heed."

—*The Economist*

"This is a very important book and I hope it will be widely read."

—Tony Benn, MP British Parliament (in the *New Statesman*)

"*Iraq Under Siege* is a very useful weapon in our international struggle against sanctions. This is not only the horrible story of children dying as a result of sanctions, a story our papers are so reluctant to write about. It is also a well argued warning about the kind of 'globalized' world they will build for us, if we let them."

—Daniel Singer, *The Nation*

"Each page is a document of outrage."

—*Socialist Worker*, US

"A sustained, coherent, and comprehensive critique of US policy on Iraq."

—*Texas Observer*

"*Iraq Under Siege* is a remarkable collection of analytical essays, emotive calls to action, and useful 'to-do' lists for activists. It must be read. And it must be acted on."

—*Z Magazine*

"The first book to grant a glimpse behind the veil of ideology and propaganda that shrouds the contemporary official record."

—Sean Gonsalves, Common Dreams News Center

"This is a definitive and powerful indictment of one of the greatest war crimes of the last quarter of the twentieth century."

—*Bookmarks Review of Books*

"A brilliant book, which exposes the grim reality behind the US New World Order and British 'ethical foreign policy.'"

—*Socialist Worker, UK*

"Scrupulously edited for accuracy, readability, and diversity of voice, [it] works either as a good introduction to the crisis in Iraq or a resource for activists."

—*The Socialist*

Iraq Under Siege

The Deadly Impact of Sanctions and War
Updated Edition

Edited by Anthony Arnove

With essays by:

Ali Abunimah
Dr. Huda S. Ammash
Anthony Arnove
Naseer Aruri
Barbara Nimri Aziz
David Barsamian
Phyllis Bennis
George Capaccio
Noam Chomsky
Robert Fisk
Denis J. Halliday
Kathy Kelly
Rania Masri
Dr. Peter L. Pellett
John Pilger
Sharon Smith
Voices in the Wilderness
Howard Zinn

South End Press
Cambridge, Massachusetts

Cover design by Ellen P. Shapiro.
Cover photo by Karen Robinson/Format.
Page design and production by Alyssa Hassan and the South End Press collective.

Printed in Canada.

Library of Congress Control Number
2002113627

ISBN: 0-89608-697-6 (pbk.) — ISBN 0-89608-698-4 (cloth)

South End Press, 7 Brookline Street, #1, Cambridge, MA 02139-4146

southend@southendpress.org
www.southendpress.org

07 06 05 04 03 02 1 2 3 4 5 6 7 8 9

Table of Contents

Part 3: Life Under Sanctions

Part 4: Documenting the Impact of Sanctions

Part 5: Activist Responses

Acknowledgments and Note to the Updated Edition

When people have asked me if I would edit an updated edition of *Iraq Under Siege,* my answer has always been no—that I hoped the book would soon become historically obsolete and gather dust on a library shelf as a chronicle of a time that had passed. Tragically, not only for the people of Iraq but for those around the globe who hope for an alternative to the daily violence of this world, it is more relevant today than when it was first published. The drive to escalated war, even perhaps occupation, is intensifying. In October 2002, the US Congress gave President George Bush a blank check to "pre-emptively" attack Iraq, making the likelihood of war even greater. The sanctions continue. The no-fly zone bombings continue. And so do the lies used to justify the dehumanization and destruction of the Iraqi people, the lies that the authors of this book systematically challenge.

After the Bush II administration launched its war on the world (selling it as an endless "war on terrorism"), it became clear to many of the people who worked on *Iraq Under Siege* that a new edition was needed. Alexander Dwinell, Jill Petty, Loie Hayes, Tina Beyene, and Vijay Shah took part in the discussion that led to this new edition. In particular, Alexander and Tina put in long hours of editorial and production work to make the new book possible. I am especially grateful to Alexander for his valuable editorial suggestions and assistance.

I am deeply indebted to all the authors of the first edition of *Iraq Under Siege.* If time had permitted, there is no doubt that all of them could have contributed new insights to this edition. And, if space had permitted, there are many more voices I would have liked to have added. But given the urgency of the project, we chose to focus on updating six chapters: the Introduction and the chapters by Naseer Aruri, Voices in the Wilderness, Ali Abunimah and Rania Masri, Peter L. Pellett, and Sharon Smith. Denis Halliday, the former UN humanitarian coordinator for Iraq who courageously resigned that position and has been a leading anti-sanctions and anti-war activist since, kindly contributed a new afterword. I am grateful to all of the contributors who updated their chapters on unusually short notice, especially to Jeff Guntzel of Voices in the Wilderness, as well as to James A. Paul, the executive director of the Global Policy Forum, who kindly allowed Voices in the Wilderness and South End Press to use excerpts of his valuable research on oil interests in Iraq and the Middle East in "Myths and Realities Regarding Iraq and Sanctions."

South End and Pluto Press books are always intensely collaborative projects. *Iraq Under Siege* is perhaps even more so than usual. Sonia Shah deserves special thanks for originally encouraging me to edit this book; Loie Hayes and Sonia Shah provided valuable editorial advice; and Lynn Lu, Anne Beech, and Kathleen May also gave much-needed support for the first edition.

Every one of the contributors to *Iraq Under Siege* deserves special thanks for their labors not only on this book, but to build the movement to end the war against Iraq.

Robert Jensen, Rahul Mahajan, Romi Mahajan, Stacey Gottlieb, Nagesh Rao, Erica Rubin, Sandy Adler, Joe Richey, Nick Arons, and Chuck Quilty helped crucially with the preparation of several chapters.

Matthew Rothschild at *The Progressive,* Robert Fisk, *The Independent,* Mobilization for Survival in Boston, David Barsamian, and *The Link* generously allowed us to use or reprint material for this anthology.

Philippe Rekacewicz and *Le Monde diplomatique* went to great lengths to provide the map that opens this book. Nikki van der Gaag, the staff at *New Internationalist,* Alison Reed at Format, Karen Robinson, and Alan Pogue made available the powerful photographs in the book and on the cover, which was designed by Ellen P. Shapiro.

Shea Dean copyedited the first draft of *Iraq Under Siege,* providing many useful editorial suggestions. Rania Masri, Ali Abunimah, Sami Deeb, Nick Arons, Glenn Camp, Richard Pond, Kathy Kelly, Bilal El-Amine, George Capaccio, Afruz Amighi, Drew Hamre, Ellen Repalda, Gillian Russom, David Peterson, Ashley Smith, and Stacey Gottlieb provided important endnote references, as did the many people who regularly disseminate information useful to the anti-sanctions movement.

My understanding of depleted uranium was aided critically by the generous assistance of Rosalie Bertell, Beatrice Boctor, and Dan Fahey.

I have had the privilege of having family, friends, and allies who have taught me the meaning of Frederick Douglass's slogan that without struggle, there is no progress. There are too many to mention, but I would especially like to thank Nita Levison, Robert Arnove, Howard Zinn, Noam Chomsky, Edward W. Said, Jason Yanowitz, Annie Zirin, Sharon Smith, Ahmed Shawki, Gillian Russom, Elizabeth Terzakis, Bo Ekelund, Phil Gasper, Arundhati Roy, and my many comrades in the International

Socialist Organization, the Rhode Island Emergency Response Network, and the anti-sanctions movement.

I owe a special thanks to Gina Neff, who inspired me during the difficult months of this last year and who is always on my mind.

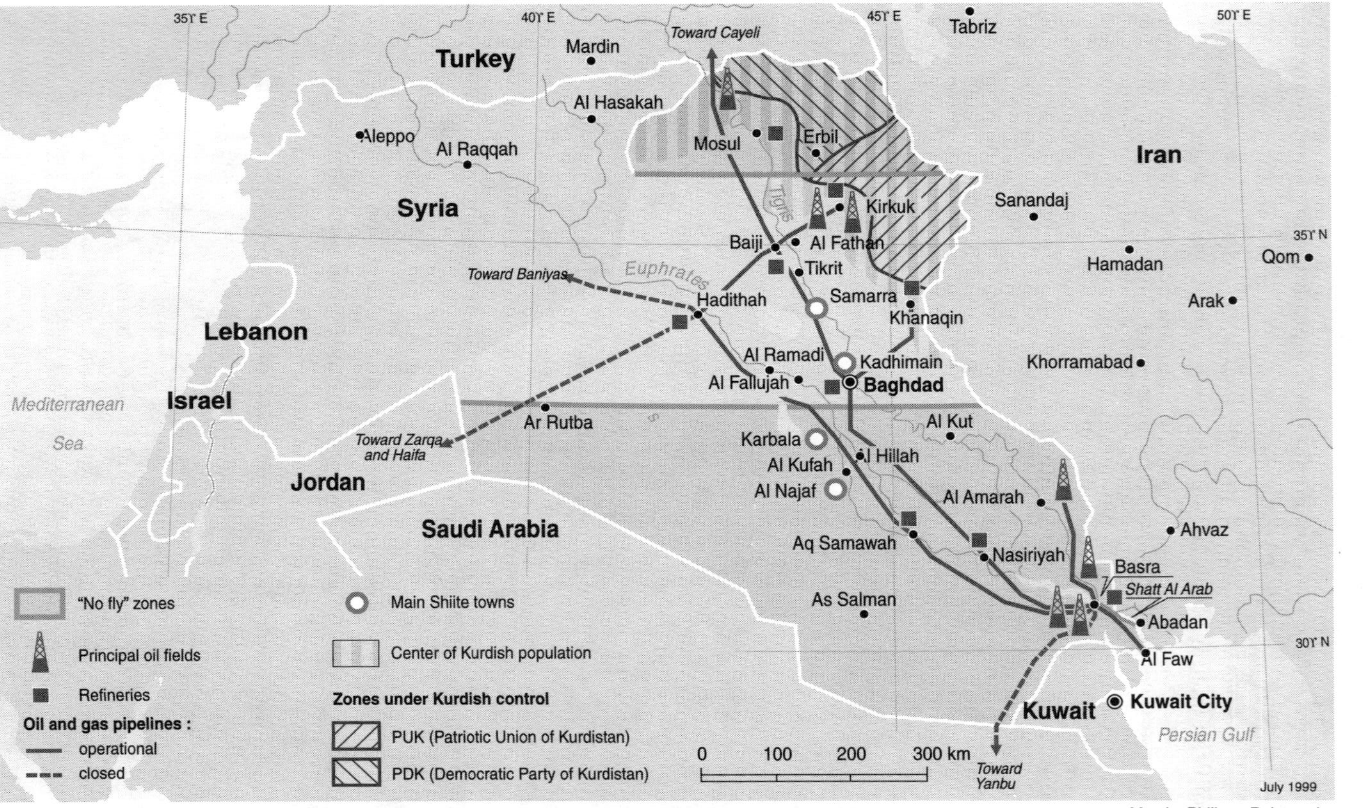

Sources : Comité professionnel du pétrole; Central Intelligence Agency 1999 Maps and Publications; United States Energy Information Administration.

Map by Philippe Rekacewicz

Introduction to the Updated Edition (2002)

Anthony Arnove

Though no connection between Iraq and the terrorist attacks of September 11 has been found, the Bush administration has significantly raised expectations that it will again invade Iraq as it extends its "war on terrorism" into new countries.

"For better or worse, a bipartisan consensus has emerged in the Bush administration and Congress alike that the United States can no longer tolerate an Iraqi regime led by Saddam Hussein," Todd S. Purdum wrote in *New York Times* "Week in Review" on February 17, 2002.[1] Since then, the rhetoric has escalated even further with several war scenarios leaked to the press; regular calls from editorial writers, politicians, and pundits to "topple Saddam Hussein"; a major address by President George W. Bush to the United Nations in which he "set stiff and immediate conditions for Saddam Hussein to meet to avoid being overthrown at the hands of US-led forces;" and a congressional vote for war.[2]

The *New York Times* noted September 7, 2002, that the Bush administration is "following a meticulously planned strategy to persuade the public, the Congress, and the allies of the need to confront the threat of Saddam Hussein." Andrew H. Card, Jr., the White House chief of staff, cynically described how the administration was stepping up its war plans for the fall, explaining, "From a marketing point of view ... you don't introduce new products in August."[3]

"We still believe strongly in regime change in Iraq," explained Secretary of State Colin Powell, whom some were mistakenly looking to as a voice of reason or moderation in the administration.[4] After some critics questioned the Bush administration's strategy for invading Iraq, Vice-President Dick Cheney said, "There is no doubt that Saddam Hussein now has weapons of mass destruction.... There is no doubt that he is amassing them to use against our friends, against our allies, and against us,"[5] despite the lack of evidence for such claims. Cheney added, "The risks of inaction are far greater than the risk of action."[6] His views were echoed by Richard A. Boucher, the spokesman for the State Department: "[T]he only way to really solve the problem [of Iraq] is through regime change."[7]

William Safire, the *New York Times* columnist, asserts that, left unchecked, Iraq will soon be able to send missiles into the streets of major US cities. According to Safire, Hussein is "gaining the power to threaten our cities with annihilation." We must therefore "liberate Iraq." The Bush administration, he assures us, is "driven not by any lust for global domination, but by out-and-out Wilsonian idealism: we want to make the Middle East safe for democracy."[8]

Safire neglected to share the fact that, as the *Times* reported the very same day, "[Bush] Administration officials do not know how many Al Hussein Scud missiles Iraq has. Estimates range from just a few to as many as 40, officials say. In addition to 390-mile-range Husseins, Iraq has made Al Samoud missiles, which have a range of 90 miles,"—a few miles short of being able to reach the United States border.[9] Nor did Safire bother to cite the March 2002 assessment of the CIA that "Most agencies believe that Iraq is unlikely to test before 2015 any [intercontinental ballistic missiles] that would threaten the United States, even if UN prohibitions were eliminated or significantly reduced in the next few years."[10]

Despite indications from European and Middle Eastern governments that they do not support US efforts to make Iraq the next target in the "war on terrorism," the debate in Washington—and internationally—is primarily about how to attack Iraq, not whether or not to do so. Despite popular opposition—expressed in a London demonstration of several hundred thousand people on September 28 and significant opposition in polls and in his own party—UK Prime Minister Tony Blair will almost certainly be by Bush's side if the US seeks to launch a major assault on Iraq. Blair told the BBC that the UK must be willing to pay a "blood price" in Iraq to "secure its special relationship with the United States."[11] The *Guardian* noted that "it is clear that some in Downing Street are determined that Britain should back America whenever it does decide to attack."[12]

In the wake of the attacks of September 11, the US government has discussed broadening its official doctrine on the "right to intervene" in Iraq to reflect its real philosophy: "The Bush administration—warning of time-bomb terrorists and the spread of deadly mass weapons—proposes a far more open-ended, sweeping use of preemptive force.... [T]he administration is making a stark argument for striking first," the *Christian Science Monitor* reported. "Twenty-first century threats may well require that we take the war to the enemy," Donald Rumsfeld, the Secretary of War, told an audience at the National Defense University.[13]

The *Boston Globe* reported that "The CIA recently received a $1 billion increase from the White House to conduct covert operations in the war on terrorism. Some of that money, according to an intelligence official who asked not to be named, will be focused on the 'Iraq problem.'"[14]

Encouraged by the war in Afghanistan, the "bomb Iraq" crew in the media and Washington have been let off their collective leash to call for the invasion of Iraq and the overthrow of Hussein by whatever means the US military has at its disposal. Drawing an untenable analogy to the war in Afghanistan, some of Bush's coterie are urging that the "Afghan model" be applied to Iraq. In this scenario, the Iraqi National Congress (the self-proclaimed "Iraqi opposition" based mostly in London, and lacking any social base in Iraq), the divided Kurdish opposition groups in the north of Iraq, and Shiite insurgents in the south would collaborate to march on Baghdad and overthrow the government, with assistance in the air and perhaps on the ground from the US military. Some 100,000 to 250,000 ground troops would be needed for such an operation, military analysts estimate, but hundreds of thousands more could potentially be involved.[15]

Many hawks within and close to the Bush administration have used Iraq as a pretext to advance an agenda that they had long before September 11, to expand US power and eliminate any threats—or potential threats—to US domination.

Richard Lowry, the editor of the *National Review,* was giving voice to the views of some in the Bush administration when he recently suggested not only overthrowing Hussein, but occupying Iraq:

> An American occupation would not last years, on the model of a MacArthur regency in Japan. Instead, the US would quickly—say, after less than a year—hand control of the country over to a UN protectorate, with some Arab input to soothe feelings and a non-American—some anodyne European, such as a Swede—running the show. He would in effect act as Iraqi dictator, but without the brace of pistols. After five years or so, as Iraq's public institutions were firmed up, the baton could be passed to an Iraqi government that one would hope would be throughly democratic—but that would at minimum be

> pro-Western and capitalist. The entire effort would represent a return to an enlightened paternalism toward the Third World, premised on the idea that the Arabs have failed miserably at self-government and need to start anew....
>
> The goal ... would not be perfection, but a pro-Western and reasonably successful regime, somewhat between the Shah of Iran and the current government of Turkey.
>
> It would guarantee the West's access to oil, and perhaps help break up OPEC.... And it would be a nice economic benefit to the United States: If the Teamsters like drilling in ANWR [the Arctic National Wildlife Refuge], they should love occupying Iraq.[16]

Lowry's asides about oil and economic benefits reveal what this strategy is really about: relegitimizing the "white man's burden" for the twenty-first century so US imperialism can continue to control the oil profits of the Middle East and the geopolitical power that stems from this. It is no accident that the repressive regimes of Iran under the Shah and Turkey serve as his model.

How will the United States, perhaps with the United Kingdom in some acceptably circumscribed role as cheerleader alongside it, get into Iraq? One increasingly likely scenario is that the Bush administration will seek to create a stand-off over sending United Nations weapons inspectors into Iraq. (Never mind that the Bush administration denied international inspectors access to US chemical and biological weapons-related facilities—almost certainly the source of the so-called Ames anthrax strain that has killed five people in the United States—because it might violate "proprietary commercial interests.")[17] This is the scenario favored by Blair, as well as by some of Bush's rightwing critics who argue, in the words of the *Financial Times,* that "a rebuff [of weapon's inspectors] by Baghdad would strengthen Washington's justification for military action."[18]

"The inspectors have to go back in under our terms, under no one else's terms," Colin Powell told the Senate Foreign Relations Committee, ignoring—as has the media—Iraq's concerns over the well-documented fact that the last inspection team in Iraq passed on intelligence information to the US government in violation of its mission.[19] Despite these concerns, when Iraq agreed "to allow the return of United Nations weapons inspectors without conditions" on September 16, 2002, the response of the White House was dismissive, with Bush spokesman Scott McClellan saying "it is a tactic that will fail."[20]

Bush can almost certainly use economic, political, and military pressure to win a vote in the Security Council to rubber stamp the US war plans. After all, the 1991 Gulf War was fought in the name of the UN, and the harsh sanctions Iraqis have suffered for the last 12 years have been UN imposed. The United States dominates the UN, especially the Security Council, but the other great powers that sit on the council have their own interests, not those of ordinary Iraqis, in mind.

Another possible scenario is that the United States will succeed in its ongoing efforts to manufacture a link between Iraq and al-Qaeda, even though no credible connection has been found. Only two days after the attacks of September 11, Paul D. Wolfowitz, the Deputy Secretary of Defense and one of the leading voices calling for a war on Iraq, said, clearly gesturing toward Iraq, "It's not just simply a matter of capturing people and holding them accountable … but removing the sanctuaries, removing the support systems, ending states [that] sponsor terrorism."[21] In March 2002, CIA director George Tenet told the Senate Armed Services Committee that "Baghdad has a long history of supporting terrorism.... [and] has also had contacts with al-Qaeda."[22] And, of course, George W. Bush named Iraq as one of the three countries, alongside Iran and North Korea, in the "Axis of Evil" confronting the United States.[23]

The background

While an invasion and occupation of Iraq would be bloody, the truth is that the war on the people of Iraq has been going on now for 12 years, since the imposition of the most comprehensive sanctions in world history on the country on August 6, 1990.

As the writers in *Iraq Under Siege* document, the people of Iraq continue to suffer the deadly impact of the sanctions, the lingering effects of the Gulf War, and continued US bombing. Under these conditions, the human impact of a renewed and intensified war is hard to imagine.

Very few people know about the aerial war against Iraq, a war that costs approximately $1 billion a year and in which "civilian casualties have become routine."[24] In a rare account of the human impact of the attacks, the *Post* described one such death:

> Suddenly out of a clear blue sky, the forgotten war being waged by the United States and Britain over Iraq visited its lethal routine on the shepherds and farmers of Toq al-Ghazalat about 10:30 a.m. on May 17.
>
> Omran Harbi Jawair, 13, was squatting on his haunches at the time, watching the family sheep as they nosed the hard, flat ground in search of grass. He wore a white robe but was bareheaded in spite of an unforgiving sun. Omran, who liked to kick a soccer ball around this dusty village, had

> just finished fifth grade at the little school a 15-minute walk from his mud-brick home. A shepherd boy's summer vacation lay ahead.
>
> That is when the missile landed. Without warning, according to several youths standing nearby, the device came crashing down in an open field 200 yards from the dozen houses of Toq al-Ghazalat. A deafening explosion cracked across the silent land. Shrapnel flew in every direction. Four shepherds were wounded. And Omran, the others recalled, lay dead in the dirt, most of his head torn off, the white of his robe stained red.
>
> "He was only 13 years old, but he was a good boy," sobbed Omran's father, Harbi Jawair, 61. What happened at Toq al-Ghazalat, 35 miles southwest of Najaf in southern Iraq, has become a recurring event in the Iraqi countryside. A week of conversations with wounded Iraqis and the families of those killed, around Najaf and in northern Iraq around Mosul, showed that civilian deaths and injuries are a regular part of the little-discussed US and British air operation over Iraq.[25]

The US military has also bombed Iraq with deadly cluster-bombs, "a weapon which has unique civilian impact," according to military analyst William Arkin. Arkin's damning account of the cluster bombs appeared on the website of the *Washington Post,* but not in its print edition:

> U.S. jets used cluster bombs [in Iraq] that have no real aimpoint and that kill and wound innocent civilians for years to come.
>
> This is not merely some insider detail. The choice of cluster bombs, still unnoticed by the American media, is likely to prove controversial....
>
> The 1,000 pound, 14-foot-long weapon carries 145 anti-armor and anti-personnel incendiary bomblets which disperse over an area that is approximately 100 feet long and 200 feet wide. In short, this weapon ... rains down deadly bomblets on an area the size of a football field with six bombs falling in every 1,000 square feet. So much for precision....
>
> Once ejected, the bomblets, each the size of soda can, simply fall freely at the mercy of local winds. A few almost always land outside of the center point of the football field size main concentration. On average 5 percent do not detonate. These unexploded bomblets then become highly volatile on the ground.[26]

In October 1999, the United States government noted that it faced a "dilemma" in its aerial campaign against Iraq. "After eight years of enforcing a 'no-fly zone' in northern [and southern] Iraq, few military targets remain," explained the *Wall Street Journal.* "We're down to the last outhouse," one unnamed US official protested. "There are still some things left, but not many," noted another Pentagon source.[27] Yet the bombing has continued, and in early September 2002, US and UK jets bombed Western Iraq for the first time since the major December 1998 bombing ("Operation Desert Fox").[28]

The fact that the United Kingdom and United States have been unilaterally bombing Iraq—at times as often as almost every other day—since December 1998 has generally merited only one-paragraph notices in the *New York Times'* "World Briefing" section. In a rare instance when the bombing made the front page, the *Times* acknowledged:

> American warplanes have methodically and with virtually no public discussion been attacking Iraq. In the last eight months, American and British pilots have fired more than 1,100 missiles against 359 targets in Iraq. This is triple the number of targets attacked in four furious days of strikes [on Iraq] in December [1998]....
>
> By another measure, pilots have flown about two-thirds as many missions as NATO pilots flew over Yugoslavia in seventy-eight days of around-the-clock war there [in 1999].[29]

By the end of 1999, US and UK forces had flown more than 6,000 sorties, dropped more than 1,800 bombs, and hit more than 450 targets.[30] The Pentagon alone spent more than $1 billion in 1999 to maintain its force of 200 airplanes, nineteen warships, and 22,000 troops which are part of the operation.[31] In 2000, the US and UK flew even more sorties than in 1999. These numbers dropped in 2001 and early 2002, but started to escalate significantly in summer 2002.[32]

The war on Iraq is "the longest sustained US air operation since the Vietnam War."[33]

The no-fly zone patrols are also clearly a part of the US effort to maintain its ability to mount a more serious assault on Iraq. In August 2002, the *Washington Post* reported that:

> The Pentagon's continued enforcement of "no-fly" zones over northern and southern Iraq has taken on added importance as the Bush administration weighs whether to invade Iraq, giving defense officials a wealth of intelligence and a means of degrading Iraqi air defenses.
>
> Some Air Force officers recommended ending the combat patrols in the spring of 2001, but senior defense officials now consider the missions ... a bulwark of military engagement with Saudi Arabia and Turkey, key allies in the region....
>
> [One Pentagon official] said that enforcing the no-fly zones "keeps our skills high on knowledge of the area and keeps our competency high in flying over the area. The benefits you get from that—should you decide to do something militarily—are great." Indeed, one officer who recently returned

> from the region said enforcing the no-fly zones buys the United States extra "battle space."...
>
> Defense officials say enforcing the no-fly zones for more than a decade also has provided invaluable intelligence as military planners plot strategies for launching a possible military campaign against Iraq.[34]

Why Iraq?

Iraq has the world's second-largest proven oil reserves, after Saudi Arabia, containing some 11 percent of the world's oil.[35]

The US and UK have devoted so much effort to dominating the region not out of concern for democracy but with the aim of controlling the profits associated with this essential resource, which is critical to the functioning of capitalism globally.

As early as 1945, the US State Department noted that oil "has historically played a larger part in the external relations of the United States than any other commodity."[36] Since World War II, the Middle East has been of unparalleled strategic importance to Anglo-American planners. In the 1950s, Iraq became a central part of this equation. At that time, Samira Haj writes, "conditions changed dramatically. Production rates increased, royalties rose sharply, and oil became the leading sector of the [Iraqi] economy."[37]

The US quickly edged out Britain, which was reduced to the role of junior partner, not only in Iraq but throughout the region.[38]

State Department planner George Kennan set out the basic framework for understanding US foreign policy in the Middle East in 1948:

> [W]e have about 50 percent of the world's wealth, but only 6.3 percent of its population.... In this situation, we cannot fail to be the object of envy and resentment. Our real task in the coming period is to devise a pattern of relationships which will permit us to maintain this position of disparity without positive detriment to our national security. To do so, we will have to dispense with all sentimentality and day-dreaming; and our attention will have to be concentrated everywhere on our immediate national objectives.[39]

New York Times columnist Thomas Friedman put this same argument in more contemporary terms when he wrote in 1999: "The hidden hand of the market will never work without a hidden fist. McDonald's cannot flourish without McDonnell Douglas.... And the hidden fist that keeps the world safe for Silicon Valley's technologies to flourish is called the US Army, Air Force, Navy, and Marine Corps."[40]

In the Middle East, the "pattern of relationships" described by Kennan has included ties to several client regimes that served Western interests in the region—especially Israel, Egypt, and Saudi Arabia. Iraq also served Western interests before its invasion of Kuwait in 1990, which turned President Hussein from an ally and friend of London and Washington into "the new Hitler." Hussein is a tyrant, but the US and UK were allied with Hussein for years while he brutalized his population; and both countries supported equal or greater thugs, including Suharto in Indonesia, Mobutu Sese Seko in Zaire, and a long list of dictators in Latin America.

In fact, when Kurds and Shiites posed a democratic challenge to Saddam Hussein's regime at the end of the Gulf War in 1991, the US government preferred that Hussein violently crush the uprising rather than risk a popular revolution. As Noam Chomsky points out in Chapter 3, quoting Thomas Friedman, Washington wanted "an iron-fisted Iraqi junta" to remain. "Our policy is to get rid of Saddam [Hussein], not his regime," explained Richard Haass, the former director of Middle East affairs on the National Security Council.[41]

As one indication of US concern for democracy in Iraq, one need only look at White House plans for the US to occupy Iraq and "install an American-led military government."[42]

Indeed, sanctions and bombing have shored up the strength of Hussein's Baathist government in many respects, as several contributors to *Iraq Under Siege* observe. The sanctions have decimated the Iraqi people, driven most Iraqis into a dependent relationship to the government, shattered institutions that could sustain opposition, and increased nationalism. One Iraqi told *USA Today*, "Any doubts I had about Saddam [Hussein] are gone.... Now I want him to stand up to the US for taking away my power, my running water, and my daughter's childhood."[43]

"Weapons of mass destruction"

Anglo-American policy in Iraq is repeatedly defended as a measure to stop arms proliferation, in particular to prevent the use of "weapons of mass destruction." Yet London and Washington have no particular trouble with countries developing or proliferating weapons of mass destruction, as long as they are friendly to the UK and the US. Israel has not only been allowed to develop the world's sixth-largest nuclear program, it also collaborated in the nuclear program of apartheid South Africa.[44]

The *Bulletin of the Atomic Scientists* recently revealed that the United States "stored 12,000 nuclear weapons and components in twenty-three countries and five American territories during the cold war," making it by far the world's greatest proliferator of nuclear weaponry.[45]

The US and UK supply arms to violent regimes throughout the world, including Saudi Arabia, Colombia, and Turkey—which is engaged in massive repression against the Kurds (allegedly the people British and US planes are defending in the northern "no-fly" zone of Iraq).[46]

Turkey's campaign against the Kurds is acceptable, however, since it "plays a critical role in protecting American security interests in the region."[47] The jets flying over Iraq regularly take off from Incirlik, Turkey, as well as from those other beacons of democracy—Kuwait and Saudi Arabia.

Invading smaller countries and threatening neighbors is also acceptable, as long as the parties in question serve strategic Anglo-American aims. Indonesia's brutal invasion and twenty-three-year occupation of East Timor, which claimed more than 200,000 lives, was supported until the very last moment by both governments. Even the much-demonized Slobodan Milosevic of Yugoslavia "was indispensable to the United States for regional security" before he displeased his Western patrons.[48]

The claim that the US and UK want to see a representative government in Iraq would be laughable if the legacy of their support for repression in the region were not so disastrous. Author Saïd K. Aburish notes:

> The existing division of the Arab Middle East into friendly and unfriendly governments has little to do with their true nature. Historically, legitimate nationalist regimes were rejected when they were considered a threat to Western interests while friendly illegitimate ones were supported regardless. Perpetuating Western hegemony and protecting economic interests from real or imagined threats takes precedence [over all other concerns].[49]

In Aburish's apt phrase, "America ... [has] made the Middle East unsafe for democracy," since democracy carries the threat of ordinary people, rather than London, Washington, and the multinational oil corporations, controlling the resources of the region.[50]

Anti-Arab and anti-Muslim racism

It is largely because the West needs to justify its control over "its" Middle Eastern oil resources that, as Edward W. Said writes, an " 'Islamic threat' furor ... [has] dominated Western policy and journalistic commentary" for years.[51]

> [T]he notion of Arab people with traditions, cultures, and identities of their own is simply inadmissible in the United States. Arabs are dehumanized, they are seen as violent irrational terrorists always on the lookout for murder and bombing outrages.... This morbid, obsessional fear and hatred of the Arabs has been a constant theme in US foreign policy since World War Two.[52]

The views of the conservative pundit Samuel Huntington—who writes regularly about "the contemporary global struggles between Muslim and non-Muslim peoples"—gained a new hearing after the attacks of September 11, 2001.[53]

New York Times columnist Nicholas Kristof chronicled some of the worst examples of this anti-Islamic hatred, but he could have added many more:

> "Islam is, quite simply, a religion of war," Paul Weyrich and William Lind, two leading American conservatives, write in a new booklet titled "Why Islam Is a Threat to America and the West." Mr. Lind said of American Muslims: "They should be encouraged to leave. They are a fifth column in this country."
>
> Ann Coulter, the columnist, suggested that "we should invade their countries, kill their leaders and convert them to Christianity."
>
> The Rev. Franklin Graham, son of the Rev. Billy Graham and a prominent evangelist in his own right, said of Islam: "I believe it's a very evil and wicked religion." The Rev. Jerry Vines, past president of the Southern Baptist Convention, declared that the Prophet Muhammad was "a demon-obsessed pedophile."[54]

As Ali Abunimah and Rania Masri point out in their chapter, the media and politicians speak as if only one lone madman—"Saddam"—lived in Iraq. News coverage of Iraq is often indistinguishable from the latest press release from the State Department, the British Foreign Ministry, or the Pentagon.

No one better embodies the depths of this convergence between military and governmental interests than *New York Times* columnist Thomas Friedman.

Friedman, for example, has advocated "bombing Iraq, over and over and over again."[55] In an article titled "Craziness Pays," Friedman explains that "the US has to make clear to Iraq and US allies that … America will use force, without negotiation, hesitation, or UN approval."[56]

Sounding like a character from *Dr. Strangelove,* he states, "Saddam Hussein is the reason God created cruise missiles. Cruise missiles are simply the only way to deal with him." In another column, he writes: "[I]f and when Saddam pushes beyond the brink, and we get that one good shot, let's make sure it's a head shot."[57]

But this pales compared with Friedman's column "Rattling the Rattler":

> With Saddam rattled, now is the time to really rattle his cage: Turn up the volume on Radio Free Iraq to extra loud and call for his ouster twenty-four hours a day: "All Saddam, all the time." Take steps to have Saddam declared a war criminal by the UN. *Blow up a different power station in Iraq every week, so no one knows when the lights will go off or who's in charge.* Offer a reward for removing Saddam from office. Use every provocation by Saddam to blow up another Iraqi general's home.[58]

That Friedman can openly advocate committing war crimes such as targeting power stations (a strategy that he advocated again during the bombing of Kosovo) indicates how debased mainstream reportage of Iraq has become.[59] Every power station that is targeted means more food and medicine that will not be refrigerated, hospitals that will lack electricity, water that will be contaminated, and people who will die. All of this is done, we are supposed to believe, in the name of democracy and human rights.

More recently, Friedman has urged Bush to refine his message on Iraq. "If the Bush team is serious about Iraq, it needs to zero in on one clear objective, produce a tightly focused war plan around it, and then sell it—with a simple bumper sticker—to America and the world."[60] Iraqi lives should be reduced to a catch phrase. Such is the nature of the "debate" about a pre-emptive attack on Iraq: the primary topic elites are discussing today is not whether to attack Iraq, but how to "sell" the war (or, in the words of Andrew Card, how to "introduce [a] new product").

Shifting blame

Evidence of the human toll of sanctions has been repeatedly confirmed and has even been publicly acknowledged on repeated occasions by top government officials, most notably Madeleine Albright, who said "[W]e think the price is worth it" when asked whether the deaths of 500,000 Iraqi children as a result of the sanctions could possibly be justified.[61]

The US and UK have repeatedly sought to frame the debate so that the sanctions are wholly the responsibility of Saddam Hussein. The main tactic they have pursued has been to make it seem that London and

Washington have done everything in their power to lift the sanctions (if only President Hussein would just agree to the reasonable terms of weapons inspections offered to him), while actually doing everything in their power to maintain the sanctions and the status quo.

As the economist and critic Edward S. Herman observes:

> One of the tricks of imperialism is to pretend that a targeted enemy has been offered a negotiating option, quickly claim that that option has been rejected, and then ruthlessly attack or continue sanctions that may be taking a heavy human toll. The beauty of this system is that no matter how many are killed by bombs, and how numerous are the children who die as a result of the sanctions, it is not our fault; they refused our (by definition) reasonable offer to "negotiate." They brought it on themselves.[62]

The highly touted "smart sanctions" are a clear illustration of this strategy. On May 14, 2002, with encouragement from the Bush II administration, the Security Council adopted Resolution 1409. The resolution allegedly lifted restrictions on Iraq's ability to import civilian goods, focusing narrowly on preventing Iraq from importing or building weapons of mass destruction. Speaking in Reykjavik, Iceland, Colin Powell said "the resolution demonstrates the [Security] Council's continued determination to meet the needs of the Iraqi people."[63]

But the real impact of the resolution is to continue the Iraqi people's suffering. The resolution represents a symbolic, rather than a substantive, change in the sanctions regime. It allows the US government, using the cover of the UN, to continue the sanctions, which have been growing more unpopular internationally, and to build ideological support for a massive military assault on Iraq.

"The resolution was intended to blunt any drive to end the sanctions altogether and to deflate criticism that the measures are hurting ordinary Iraqis more than their leader," Somini Sengupta reported in the *New York Times*. "It also seemed part of the diplomatic groundwork the Bush administration is seeking to lay as it presses its case that Mr. Hussein should be removed from power, perhaps by force."[64]

"This is all about the propaganda war of who is to blame for the humanitarian problems in Iraq. Everything in the [UN] resolution aims to shift the blame" from Washington to Baghdad, one senior official told the *Financial Times*.[65]

In the "propaganda war" with Iraq, the goal is to deny the simple fact that the sanctions—which have now been in place for more than 12 years—have had a devastating impact on the civilian population, while, in the words of the *Wall Street Journal,* "actually tightening [Saddam Hussein's] grip on power."[66] After years of hearing from Clinton, Blair, Bush, and Co. that the sanctions were designed to target the Iraqi regime and not the people, we are now supposed to believe that the new sanctions (does this sound familiar?) will target the regime and not the people.

But under the proposed smart sanctions, the United States is still able to use its power in the UN to block essential goods by citing "dual use" concerns. And the economy continues to suffer. As the US Mission to the United Nations emphasized after the vote, the "UN escrow account for Iraqi oil revenue and restrictions on items of potential military and military-related use are maintained."[67]

After the US put pressure on Russia, the UN approved a list of several hundred pages of items that fall into the dual-use category and must be reviewed for approval before Iraq can use its oil revenue (held in escrow by the UN) to purchase them.

In the past, the US government, using its veto power on the UN sanctions committee, has blocked contracts for ambulances, chlorinators, vaccines, and even pencils citing "dual use" concerns. As of May 2002, $5 billion in contracts were "on hold" because of the United States—completely undermining the claim of John D. Negroponte, the US Permanent Representative to the UN, that "under the Oil for Food Program it has always been possible to get humanitarian and civilian goods into Iraq" and that "the principal obstacle has been the refusal of the Iraqi regime to spend its own resources for the importation of those items."[68]

Negroponte's claim is further undermined by the views of UN officials working in Iraq. Adnan Jarra, a UN spokesperson in Iraq, recently praised the oil-for-food distribution network, telling the *Wall Street Journal*, "They [the Iraqis] are very efficient. We have not found anything that went anywhere it was not supposed to."[69]

According to Tun Myat, the administrator of the UN oil-for-food program, "[T]he Iraqi food-distribution system is probably second to none that you'll find anywhere in the world. It gets to everybody whom it's supposed to get to in the country." But Myat stressed, "People have become so poor in some cases that they can't even afford to eat the food that they are given free, because for many of them [selling] the food ration represents the major part of their income."[70]

Smart sanctions have done nothing to help revive the badly damaged Iraqi economy. As the Campaign Against Sanctions on Iraq (CASI) points out, "There [is still] a prohibition on foreign investment into Iraq, necessary to rebuild the shattered infrastructure of the country.... [and] Iraq will not be allowed to export any goods other than oil."[71] Even the Security Council's own humanitarian panel reported in March 1999 that for Iraq to recover, "the oil for food system alone would not suffice and massive investment would be required in a number of key sectors, including oil, energy, agriculture, and sanitation."[72]

Challenging sanctions

The consequences of another invasion of Iraq would be disastrous, not only for the people of Iraq who would suffer the impact of the attacks, but the people of the region. The effects of an invasion are impossible to predict, though the threat of the attack sparking a broader war in the Middle East, possibly involving nuclear weapons, is real.

Any strike on Iraq would also embolden other states seeking to emulate Bush's pre-emptive strike doctrine. Already Israel, Pakistan, India, Russia, Malaysia, and Colombia have started to justify expansion of their military rules of engagement in the name of following Bush and advancing the "war on terrorism." Around the globe, we are seeing a massive expansion of state terrorism masked as a defense against terrorism.

Regardless of whether or not it is fought "alone" or under the banner of the United Nations, a war in Iraq would represent an even further expansion of US hegemony in the Middle East and in the world. Its aim would not be to bring about democracy, but to control the balance of power in a geopolitically critical region and to "maintain stability," a euphemism for ordering the world capitalist system to maximize the power and profits flowing to the US empire.

It is urgent that we do everything in our power to stop Bush's brutal drive toward war on Iraq. The "war on terrorism" is unfolding on many fronts, with significant consequences for millions of people abroad, those at home who will be asked to pay the ever growing bill, and the future of the entire planet. Antiwar work has taken on a new urgency internationally. It's hard to exaggerate the stakes. As Noam Chomsky observed in his talk at the 2002 World Social Forum in Porto Alegre, "Either we will have a world without wars, or we will not have a world."[73]

The circumstances for organizing today are challenging. Patriotism has been used to marginalize criticism of the government, and civil liberties have been threatened. But the fact remains that the public could quickly turn against the broadening of the war on terrorism to include a pre-emptive strike on Iraq, as Sharon Smith notes in her chapter, especially if the antiwar movements in the US, UK, in Europe, and in the Middle East grow. The *New York Times* nervously reported that Blair is "facing mounting domestic opposition to the prospect of an American invasion of Iraq."[74] A Channel 4 poll found that a majority in Britain oppose the UK supporting a US war on Iraq.[75] A CNN poll showed that only a "slight majority of Americans still favors sending US forces into Iraq to overturn the regime of Saddam Hussein," while a *New York Times* poll found that many questioned Bush's stated war aims and that 70 percent wanted congressional candidates to talk more about the economic crisis than about Iraq.[76]

The tide can be turned. As Bush trys to build patriotic unity historian Howard Zinn notes:

> the "war on terrorism" has obscured the fact that many people in this country are still in need....
>
> We need to dig under the rubble of war and point out that the Bush administration is using the war as a cover for worsening the income gap in this country, while paying no attention to the problems of most of the American people, while enriching corporations. I think concentrating on the class issue, concentrating on the benefits being given to corporations, is critical. ....
>
> Seymour Melman of Columbia University ... [has] made an important point about the tactics of the antiwar movement. He said that the left is in a position of continually opposing war after war after war, without getting at the root of the problem—which is the economic system under which we live, which needs war and makes war inevitable. His point is that it's really an uphill struggle to concentrate on war in an atmosphere of such intense patriotism, whereas a greater concentration on economic issues—not neglecting the war, of course—and on the failure of this system to take care of human needs would give us a much stronger bond with the American people. In fact, it would make them more likely to listen to what we have to say about the war.[77]

Speaking against the Vietnam War at New York City's Riverside Church in April 1967, Martin Luther King, Jr., referred to "the greatest purveyor of violence in the world today—my own government" and declared that the US government consistently acted "on the side of the wealthy and the secure" to "create a hell for the poor."[78]

King's insight that social justice and inequality at home are linked to militarism and human rights abuses abroad is essential for the movement against sanctions and against a renewed war. As all of the contributors to this anthology point out, there is an urgent need to lift the sanctions and end the war against the people of Iraq. The struggle of activists in the US, UK, Canada, and other countries can help bring an end to the nightmare of sanctions and war in Iraq. Such efforts, if successful, can also help provide more political space for those fighting within the Middle East for a truly democratic alternative, one in which the people of the region—rather than Western and local elites—would control the region's resources and direct them to meeting human need.

Notes

1 Todd S. Purdum, "After Saddam: Now What?" *New York Times*, February 17, 2002, p. 4: 1.
2 James Harding and Carola Hoyos, "Bush Throws Down Gauntlet to Saddam," *Financial Times*, September 13, 2002, p. 1. Alison Mitchell and Carl Hulse, "Congress Authorizes Bush to Use Force Against Iraq, Creating a Broad Mandate," *New York Times*, October 11, 2002, p. A1.
3 Elisabeth Bumiller, "Bush Aides Set Strategy to Sell Policy on Iraq," *New York Times*, September 7, 2002, p. A1.
4 Purdum, "After Saddam: Now What?" p. 4: 1.
5 John Donnelly, "Cheney States Case for Action on Iraq," *Boston Globe*, August 27, 2002, p. A1.
6 Donnelly, "Cheney States Case for Action on Iraq," p. A1.
7 Richard A. Oppel, Jr., and Julia Preston, "Administration Seeking to Build Support in Congress on Iraq Issue," *New York Times*, August 30, 2002, p. A1.
8 William Safire, "Of Turks and Kurds," *New York Times*, August 26, 2002, p. A15.
9 Michael R. Gordon, "Iraq Said to Plan Tangling U.S. in Street Fighting," *New York Times*, August 26, 2002, p. A1.
10 Anthony Shadid, "CIA says Risk of Nuclear Attack Greater Than Ever," *Boston Globe*, March 12, 2002, p. A12, citing the Senate testimony of Robert Walpole, the CIA's national intelligence officer for strategic and nuclear programs.
11 Warren Hoge, "Blair Seeks to Bridge Europe Gap in U.S. Visit," *New York Times*, September 7, 2002, p. A6. BBC, "Protesters Stage Anti-War Rally," September 28, 2002 (http://news.bbc.co.uk/2/hi/uk_news/politics/2285861.stm).
12 Paul Waugh, "Blair Warned: Iraq Attack 'Illegal,'" *Guardian*, July 29, 2002, p. 1.
13 Ann Scott Tyson, "Where Antiterror Doctrine Leads," *Christian Science Monitor*, February 7, 2002, p. 1.
14 Bryan Bender, "Bush Sees Military as Option on Iraq But Covert Action May Be the Focus," *Boston Globe*, February 14, 2002, p. A1.

15 See, for example, Eric Schmitt and Thom Shanker, "American Arsenal in the Mideast Is Being Built Up to Confront Saddam Hussein," *New York Times*, August 19, 2002, p. A8.

16 Richard Lowry, "End Iraq," *National Review* 53: 20 (October 15, 2001).

17 Judith Miller, "U.S. Explores Other Options on Preventing Germ Warfare," *New York Times*, July 25, 2001, p. A4.

18 Carola Hoyos, "Cheney Pushes for Pre-emptive Strike on Iraq," *Financial Times*, August 27, 2002, p. 1.

19 Colum Lynch, "US Used UN to Spy on Iraq, Aides Say," *Boston Globe*, January 6, 1999, p. A1, and Barton Gellman, "US Spied on Iraqi Military Via UN," *Washington Post*, March 2, 1999, p. A1. See also Nicholas George, Carola Hoyos, and Roula Khalaf, "Weapons Inspections Were 'Manipulated,'" *Financial Times*, July 30, 2002, p. 7.

20 Julia Preston and Todd S. Purdam, "UN Inspectors Can Return Unconditionally," *New York Times*, September 17, 2002, p. A1; Dr. Naji Sarri, Minister of Foreign Affairs, Republic of Iraq, Letter to UN Secretary-General Kofi Annan: "A Letter to the Chief of the U.N.," *New York Times*, September 17, 2002, p. A12.

21 Elisabeth Bumiller and Jane Perlez, "Bush and Top Aides Proclaim Policy of 'Ending' States That Back Terror," *New York Times*, September 14, 2001, p. A1.

22 Richard Wolffe, "CIA Chief Accuses Iraq of Links with al-Qaeda," *Financial Times*, March 20, 2002, p. 1.

23 Julian Borger, "President Broadens War on Terrorism: Bush Pinpoints North Korea, Iran and Iraq as the 'Axis of Evil,'" *The Guardian* (London), January 31, 2002, p. 15.

24 Edward Cody, "Under Iraqi Skies, a Canvas of Death: Tour of Villages Reveals Human Cost of U.S.-Led Sorties in 'No-Fly' Zones," *Washington Post*, June 16, 2000, p. A1.

25 Cody, "Under Iraqi Skies, a Canvas of Death," p. A1.

26 William M. Arkin, "America Cluster Bombs Iraq," special to Washingtonpost.com, February 26, 2001 (http://www.washingtonpost.com /ac2/wp-dyn/A46524-2001Feb23?language=printer).

27 Ronald G. Shafer, "Washington Wire," *Wall Street Journal*, October 22, 1999, p. A21.

28 Roula Khalaf and Alexander Nicoll, "Massed Air Attack Raises the Pressure," *Financial Times*, September 7, 2002, p. 9. See also Eric Schmitt, "Air Patrols Shift Targets in Iraq, Clearing the Way for Any Attcack," *New York Times*, September 17, 2002, p. A1.

29 Steven Lee Myers, "In Intense But Little-Noticed Fight, Allies Have Bombed Iraq All Year," *New York Times*, August 13, 1999, p. A1.

30 John Donnelly and Jonathan Gorvett, "Air Campaign Over Iraq Called Growing US Risk," *Boston Globe*, November 11, 1999, p. A2, and Jamie McIntyre and James Martone, "Iraq and the Pentagon Look Back on a Confrontational Year," CNN, December 28, 1999.

31 Myers, "In Intense But Little-Noticed Fight, Allies Have Bombed Iraq All Year," p. A6.

32 Vernon Loeb, " 'No-Fly' Patrols Praised: U.S. Says Effort Pressures Iraq, Yields Intelligence," *Washington Post*, July 26, 2002, p. A23.

33 Paul Richter, "No End in Sight to US Air Campaign Over Iraq," *Los Angeles Times*, March 3, 1999, p. A1, and Jonathan S. Landay, "Who's Winning Quiet War in Iraq?" *Christian Science Monitor*, March 4, 1999, p. 1.

34 Loeb, "'No-Fly' Patrols Praised: U.S. Says Effort Pressures Iraq, Yields Intelligence," p. A23.

35 Robin Wright, "UN Will Let Iraq Sell Oil for Humanitarian Supplies," *Los Angeles Times*, May 21, 1996, p. A1; Ghassan al-Kadi, "Iraq Wants Active Oil Role," United Press International, November 15, 1999; and Dan Atkinson, "Iraq Set for No. 2 Spot in Oil Export League," *Guardian*, July 27, 1999, p. 20.

36 Gabriel Kolko, *The Politics of War: The World and United States Foreign Policy, 1943–1945* (New York: Vintage, 1968), p. 294.

37 Samira Haj, *The Making of Iraq, 1900–1963: Capital, Power, and Ideology* (New York: SUNY Press, 1997), p. 71.

38 See Mark Curtis, *The Great Deception: Anglo-American Power and World Order* (London: Pluto Press, 1998), p. 1. See especially Chapters 5 and 6. See also David Hart, "There is Nothing Moral about Our Government Sitting Like a Rabbit in Headlights," *The Times* (London), March 11, 1999. Hart argues, "[I]t is wise for the British government to share the military burden with the Americans where it can. In continuing operations against Saddam [Hussein], the government is protecting Britain's vital national interest, [and] maintaining the special relationship with America."

39 State Department Policy Planning Study, February 23, 1948, cited in Noam Chomsky, *On Power and Ideology: The Managua Lectures* (Boston: South End Press, 1987), pp. 15–16.

40 Thomas L. Friedman, *The Lexus and the Olive Tree: Understanding Globalization* (New York: Farrar, Strauss, and Giroux, 1999), p. 373. See Phil Gasper, "Fool's Paradise," *International Socialist Review* 9 (Fall 1999): 68–69.

41 Andrew Cockburn and Patrick Cockburn, *Out of the Ashes: The Resurrection of Saddam Hussein* (New York: HarperCollins, 1999), p. 37. In ABC news anchor Peter Jennings' words, "The United States did want Saddam Hussein to go, they just didn't want the Iraqi people to take over." Peter Jennings, "Showdown with Saddam," ABC, *News Saturday Night*, February 7, 1998. See Lance Selfa and Paul D'Amato, "US and Iraq: Back from the Brink?" *International Socialist Review* 4 (Spring 1998): 30–36.

42 David E. Sanger, "US Has a Plan to Occupy Iraq, Officials Report," *New York Times*, October 11, 2002, p. A1.

43 Jack Kelly, "Iraqi's Wrath Intensifies with Their Suffering," *USA Today*, January 18, 1999, p. 12A.

44 See Deborah Sontag, "Israel Eases Security Over Nuclear Whistle-Blower's Trial," *New York Times*, November 25, 1999, p. A3, and Jane Hunter, *Israeli Foreign Policy: South Africa and Central America* (Boston: South End Press, 1987), pp. 32–39.

45 Judith Miller, "US Once Deployed 12,000 Atom Arms in Two Dozen Nations," *New York Times*, October 20, 1999, p. A1. Robert S. Norris, William M. Arkin, and William Burr, "Where They Were," *Bulletin of the Atomic Scientists* 55: 6 (November–December 1999): 26–35.

46 See, for example, William Greider, *Fortress America: The American Military and the Consequences of Peace* (New York: PublicAffairs, 1998), and Tim

Webb, *The Armour-Plated Ostrich: The Hidden Costs of Britain's Addiction to the Arms Business* (London: Comerford and Miller, 1998).

47 Editorial, "Bringing Turkey into Europe," *New York Times*, December 31, 1999, p. A36.

48 Matthew Jardine and Constâncio Pinto, *East Timor's Unfinished Struggle: Inside the Timorese Resistance* (Boston: South End Press, 1996). Steven Erlanger, "Ignoring Scars, Milosevic Is Stubbornly Pressing On," *New York Times*, October 31, 1999, p. 1: 1.

49 Saïd K. Aburish, *A Brutal Friendship: The West and the Arab Elite* (London: Indigo, 1998).

50 Aburish, *A Brutal Friendship*, p. 31.

51 Edward W. Said, *The Politics of Dispossession: The Struggle for Palestinian Self-Determination, 1969–1994* (New York: Pantheon Books, 1994), p. 405.

52 Edward W. Said, "Apocalypse Now," in Noam Chomsky, Edward W. Said, and Ramsey Clark, *Acts of Aggression: Policing "Rogue" States*, ed. Greg Ruggiero and Stuart Sahulka (New York: Open Media Pamphlet Series and Seven Stories Press, 1999), pp. 8–9.

53 Samuel P. Huntington, "A Local Front of a Global War," *New York Times*, December 16, 1999, p. A31.

54 Nicholas Kristof, "Bigotry in Islam—And Here," *New York Times*, July 9, 2002, p. A21.

55 Thomas L. Friedman, "America's Multiple-Choice Quiz," *New York Times*, January 31, 1998, p. A15.

56 Thomas L. Friedman, "Craziness Pays," *New York Times*, February 24, 1998, p. A21.

57 Thomas L. Friedman, "Head Shot," *New York Times*, November 6, 1997, p. A31.

58 Thomas L. Friedman, "Rattling the Rattler," *New York Times*, January 19, 1999, p. A19; emphasis added.

59 Thomas L. Friedman, "Stop the Music," *New York Times*, April 23, 1999, p. A25. Friedman wrote: "But if NATO's only strength is that it can bomb forever, then it has to get every ounce out of that. Let's at least have a real air war. The idea that people are still holding rock concerts in Belgrade, or going out for Sunday merry-go-round rides, while their fellow Serbs are 'cleansing' Kosovo, is outrageous. It should be lights out in Belgrade: every power grid, water pipe, bridge, road and war-related factory has to be targeted.... Every week you ravage Kosovo is another decade we will set your country back by pulverizing you. You want 1950? We can do 1950. You want 1389? We can do 1389 too."

60 Thomas L. Friedman, "Fog of War," *New York Times*, August 18, 2002, p. 4: 13.

61 Leslie Stahl, "Punishing Saddam," produced by Catherine Olian, CBS, *60 Minutes*, May 12, 1996.

62 Edward S. Herman, "They Brought It on Themselves," ZNet Commentary, December 19, 1999.

63 "Powell Applauds New Export Controls for Iraq," U.S. Department of State, Office of the Spokesman, Press Release, May 14, 2002 (http://usinfo.state.gov/topical/pol/arms/02051425.htm).

64 Somini Sengupta, "U.N. Broadens List of Products Iraq Can Import," *New York Times*, May 15, 2002, p. A1.

65 Carola Hoyos, "UN Revamps Baghdad's Oil-for-Food Programme," *Financial Times*, May 15, 2002, p. 9.

66 Hugh Pope, "Iraq's Economy Shows More Vitality," *Wall Street Journal*, May 2, 2002, p. A12.

67 US Mission to the United Nations (USUN), "Fact Sheet: 'Goods Review List' for Iraq," USUN Press Release 68 (02), May 14, 2002 (http://www.un.int/usa/02_068.htm).

68 John D. Negroponte, "UN Votes New Export Control Regime for Iraq," U.S. Department of State Press Release, May 14, 2002 (http://usinfo.state.gov/regional/nea/iraq/text/0514ngpt.htm). See also Reuters, "Russia Delays U.N. Vote on Iraq Penalties," *New York Times*, May 10, 2002, p. A14.

69 Pope, "Iraq's Economy Shows More Vitality," p. A12.

70 See Christopher S. Wren, "Iraq Poverty Said to Undermine Food Program," *New York Times*, October 20, 2000, p. 16.

71 See Campaign Against Sanctions on Iraq (CASI), "CASI Disappointed at 'Mirage' of Smart Sanctions," Press Release, May 15, 2002 (http://www.cam.ac.uk/societies/casi/briefing/prscr1409.html).

72 Quoted in CASI, "CASI Disappointed at 'Mirage' of Smart Sanctions."

73 Tom Gibb, "Forum Protesters Look to Ending War," BBC News, February 1, 2002 (http://news.bbc.co.uk/1/hi/world/americas/1796105.stm).

74 Oppel, Jr., and Preston, "Administration Seeking to Build Support," p. A1.

75 Carol J. Williams, "Allies Cool to Striking Baghdad," *Los Angeles Times*, August 7, 2002, p. 1.

76 Agence France-Presse, "Slight Majority of Americans Favor Intervention Against Iraq: Poll," August 23, 2002. Adam Nagourney and Janet Elder, "Public Says Bush Needs to Pay Heed to Weak Economy," *New York Times*, October 7, 2002, p. A1.

77 Howard Zinn, *Terrorism and War*, ed. Anthony Arnove (New York and London: Seven Stories Press, 2002), pp. 37–38.

78 Martin Luther King, Jr., "Beyond Vietnam," New York, New York, April 4, 1967. Transcript available from Alternative Radio. For details, see "Resources."

Part I

The Roots of US/UK Policy

"Bush Is Criminal." An image of President George Bush at the entrance to the Al-Rashid Hotel in Baghdad. Photo by Alan Pogue (July 1998).

Chapter 1

America's War Against Iraq: 1990–2002

Naseer Aruri

With the advent of the Bush II administration, and as part of the reaction to the attacks of September 11, 2001 and President Bush's "war on terror," Iraq—which has not been linked to the September 11 attacks—has been named, together with Iran and North Korea, as one part of Bush's "Axis of Evil," hence becoming a candidate for another major invasion. If it occurs, however, such an invasion will not only be a continuation of the same war, America's war against Iraq which began in 1990–1991 and entered a new phase in January 1999, but also a war to reshape the strategic landscape in the Middle East. A number of pro-Israel, right-wing think tanks—including the Hudson Institute, the American Enterprise Institute, and the Jewish Institute for National Security (JINSA), in which Pentagon hawks are entrenched—have been urging a war that would create a pro-American regime in Iraq and enable Washington to remap the region. The war would aim to deprive Saudi Arabia of any leverage over oil prices, intimidate Syria and Hizbullah, tip the domestic balance in Iran in favor of the "reformists," dissuade Iran from developing sophisticated weapons, and settle the Arab-Israeli conflict on terms wholly agreeable to Israel.[1]

At present, the ongoing war remains a low-level, yet sustained, onslaught targeting military and economic installations that inflicts a toll on Iraqi society and civilian lives. But the situation could soon escalate.

Bush II's war on Iraq is driven by the same strategic objectives behind the mobilization of 1990–1991, irrespective of the latest rationale offered for public consumption. There are three elements of the strategic equation that have driven this ongoing war since 1991:

1. The reconstitution of an American hegemony in the Middle East that would be unquestioned, unrivaled, and in need of no legitimation. Thus the United Nations (UN) umbrella, which was so important for President George Herbert Walker Bush (Bush I) during the Gulf War in 1991, was abandoned by President Bill Clinton and is not seriously being

pursued by Bush II for fear of potential opposition from other Security Council members, a sad commentary on the US government's level of respect for international law. This lack of pursuit of even a fig leaf of respectability is a stark illustration of the manner in which the Bush II administration equates its credibility as the lone superpower with its readiness to go to war, whether or not it has any authorization at the domestic or international level.

2. The assumption that the United States is responsible for the maintenance of a stable regional security environment conducive to its own economic and strategic interests. This, in turn, is equated with "international stability," itself a self-proclaimed US responsibility in the post–cold war period.

3. Therefore, the US government must maintain an ongoing ability and willingness to project power abroad, at two or three fronts simultaneously, if necessary, to contain, if not demolish, any challenger or would-be challenger to its self-proclaimed rules. Hence, not only must Saddam Hussein be cut down to size, and perhaps eventually be overthrown, but Iraq's potential power must also be nipped in the bud and nipped again and again with every new budding. It is, therefore, the *capacity* of Iraq, and not any of its policies or current weight in the regional, order that bewildered Bush I and Clinton, and now perplexes Bush II, who keeps on threatening a war on Iraq.

American pressure against Iraq, manifested as acts of war, economic coercion, and now the threat to even use nuclear weapons, is thus likely to go on as long as the national security establishment continues to generate reports claiming the potential of Iraq to infringe on US hegemony.[2] This is likely to last until Saddam Hussein disappears from the scene or the US becomes entangled in a prolonged urban warfare in Iraq with consequences which cannot be determined now.

The rationale under Bush I and Clinton

Both presidents Bush I and Clinton invoked human rights to propel the US war machine into action, yet neither one hesitated to admit what really was at stake. Initially, the Bush arsenal delivered sorties of human rights violations: Saddam Hussein's gassing of Kurds in Iraq in 1988; babies who were allegedly torn from incubators by Iraqi soldiers; the famous Amnesty International report cited by Bush; and Iraq's illegal occupation and plunder of Kuwait. This is not to say that much of these reports (other than the completely fabricated account of the incubators peddled by a public relations firm hired by the Kuwaiti government[3]) was not true, but Washington's real concern came out when Secretary of State James Baker said that the real conflict was over "jobs" and President Bush said it was about "access to energy resources" and "our way of life." Baker even accused Iraq of having threatened a recession in the United States: "[T]his is not about increases in the price of a gallon of gas.... It is rather about a dictator who ... could strangle the global economic order, determining by fiat whether we all enter a recession or even the darkness of a depression."[4]

In fact, this statement is tantamount to the enunciation of a policy principle: that an ambitious third-world leader will not be allowed to emerge as the pacesetter in a strategic region. Thus, oil pricing and the rate of oil production in the Gulf is to be decided by the lone superpower and cannot be tampered with by any regional leader, least of all by Saddam Hussein. The latter must, therefore, be reduced to manageable proportions; hence the war not only to expel Iraqi troops from Kuwait but, more importantly, to strike at the nerve centers of Iraq.[5] In doing that, the United States established a policy objective to destroy vital parts of Iraq's infrastructure and cripple its capacity for any sort of action that might have an implied challenge to the US-imposed order.

To justify such destruction, American leaders have often placed the carnage under the rubric of preventing Iraq from threatening its neighbors. What is the origin of this justification, we may ask, and which neighbors are to be protected? Needless to say, the US government had enjoyed watching the two neighbors trying to annihilate each other during the Iran-Iraq War (1980–1988). Iraq had never been a threat to Turkey; as far as Saudi Arabia is concerned, Iraq had its best opportunity to attack that country in the summer and fall of 1990, but preferred to keep its invading troops in Kuwait. Who is left for Iraq to threaten? Israel?

Indeed, the question of Israel casts new light on US policy toward Iraq under Bush I and Clinton. According to numerous reports in the Israeli media during the summer of 1990, the Bush I administration had determined that Iraq must not be allowed to pick up the mantle of strategic deterrence vis-à-vis Israel.[6] Egypt's responsibility for deterrence was halted by its defeat by Israel's army in June 1967. Syria's subsequent assumption of that role ended with Soviet leader Mikhail Gorbachev's new policy toward the third world. Iraq would have been next in line for that role, but the Reagan-Bush administration countered by upgrading the US-Israel special relationship into a strategic alliance.

The Bush I administration, however, was intent on delivering such a knockout blow to Iraq that it would convince Israel that it had nothing to fear from Iraq and that the United States, not Israel, was responsible for regional security and for conflict resolution in the Middle East. Accordingly, since Iraq was no longer in the business of strategic deterrence, it was incumbent on Israel to join in an overall Arab-Israeli settlement under the auspices of the United States. Bush was therefore paving the road to the 1991 Madrid negotiations between the Palestine Liberation Organization and the Israeli government, but in the midst of it he lost the election, and his scheme had to await a new administration.[7]

The Bush policy of trading the destruction of Iraq for an overall settlement of the Arab-Israeli conflict—albeit one based not on the global consensus, but on a shaky Israeli-American agreement with the acquiescence of Arab officialdom—had no place in Clinton's White House. Clinton allowed the settlement component of the Bush formula to go to the sidelines to avoid a public confrontation with Israel and its US lobby. Clinton delinked Iraq policy from the issue of an Arab-Israeli settlement. Why, then, did Clinton continue the American war against Iraq? To understand Clinton's policy, we need to review the major episodes affecting US-Iraqi relations between 1993 and 1999.

The evolution of US policy under Clinton

Five major episodes sum up Clinton's policy toward Iraq.

1. On June 27, 1993, the United States launched a cruise missile attack on Iraq's intelligence headquarters, causing civilian casualties, including the death of the prominent Iraqi painter Leila Attar.[8] The savage attack ostensibly aimed to punish Iraq for having allegedly plotted to assassinate President Bush during a visit to Kuwait. Clinton's real agenda, however, was to signal a determination by the new administration to keep Iraq under the US gun and to establish a precedent for unilateral intervention. This was demonstrated in 1994 when the Clinton administration ordered Iraq to push its army away from the Kuwaiti border under the threat of force.[9] By doing so, Washington was reaffirming its role as the new protector of Kuwait and the pacesetter in the Gulf.

2. The missile attacks against Iraq on September 3 and 4, 1996, signaled that the 1991 Persian Gulf War was far from over and that the strategic imperatives that led Washington to stage the onslaught were still operable. Predictably, Clinton's rationale began with the inevitable empha-

sis on human rights. This time, however, the party that the US was purporting to defend was the Kurdish population in Iraq. But even on the first day of the missile attack, Defense Secretary William Perry was ready to admit that the issue had global and regional dimensions beyond the Kurds: "The issue is not simply the Iraqi attack on [Kurds in] Irbil [on August 31], it is the clear and present danger Saddam Hussein poses to [Iraq's] neighbors, to the security and stability of the region, and to the flow of oil in the world."[10] Nearly two weeks later, Clinton himself emphasized that US strategic interests were primarily linked to Iraq's southern neighbors, Kuwait and Saudi Arabia, rather than to the Kurds in the north. He said: "We acted in southern Iraq, where our interests are the most vital.... I ordered the attacks in order to extend the no-fly zone."[11] Clinton, who was able to extend the unilaterally established "no-fly" zone, began to speak as if the United States had manifest destiny in Iraq. He did not even attempt to offer a multilateral cover for US intervention. "I think it's important to move now," Clinton said. "We have historically ... taken the lead in matters like this, and I think this was our responsibility at this time."[12]

3. A third episode took place in October 1997, when Iraq ordered Americans on the United Nations weapons inspection team, the United Nations Special Commission (Unscom), to leave the country. On the surface, it seemed that Iraq was blatantly obstructing the work of the UN inspectors mandated by Security Council Resolution 687. But the revelations about Washington's use of the US personnel in Unscom to spy on Iraq, published sixteen months later in the *Washington Post* and *Boston Globe,* revealed that Iraq's suspicions about spying were well founded.[13] Washington's decision to rig Unscom and to utilize its personnel for espionage purposes was, to say the least, a serious threat to Iraq's security, since it enabled the Pentagon to pinpoint targets for its bombers.

The Clinton administration's reaction to Baghdad's decision to oust the Americans on the Unscom team was to threaten the use of force to "punish" Saddam, to impose more intensive sanctions, and to cancel the oil-for-food program. But that was not enough for the hawkish US media and congressional leaders, particularly in the Republican Party, who considered Clinton to be indecisive. An article by William Safire in the *New York Times* titled "Clinton's Cave-In to Saddam" was typical of this ridicule.[14]

Although the crisis was defused and the UN team was able to return to Baghdad because of Russian diplomatic efforts, a real settlement was far from being reached. For the US government, whose strategic imperatives remained unchanged from 1991, nothing short of Hussein's elimination would guarantee its undisputed hegemony. In fact, by 1997, US leaders were openly admitting the sanctions would remain regardless of whether Unscom declared that Iraq had no biological, chemical, or nuclear weapon-making capability. For example President Clinton declared (according to the *New York Times*) that the "sanctions will be there until the end of time, or as long as he [Hussein] lasts."[15] Needless to say, these unequivocally arrogant statements are in direct contradiction with Security Council Resolution 687, which states that, upon compliance, the sanctions "shall have no further force or effect."[16]

The sanctions issue is related less to Iraq's possession of weapons of mass destruction than to how the United States perceived the government in Baghdad. That was made clear by Robert Pelletreau, the former undersecretary of state for Near Eastern affairs, when he pledged that the sanctions would be lifted unilaterally by the United States if it found the next Iraqi government acceptable.[17]

Given such determination to keep the sanctions contingent on US blessings of the government in Baghdad, one wonders whether Iraq could ever have any incentive to be as diligent about compliance as the world community would like it to be. This lack of incentive was further exacerbated by the attitude and demeanor of the former head of the inspection process, Richard Butler, an accomplice in the US war against Iraq and a racist who made no attempt to hide his contempt for Arab and Islamic culture.[18]

4. A fourth major crisis was triggered on January 12, 1998, by an Iraqi decision to bar Scott Ritter, an American member of Unscom, from the inspection team. Ritter, who later became an ardent critic of US policy in Iraq, was at that time considered as extremely anti-Iraqi and as having questionable ties to US and Israeli intelligence.[19] That decision came on the heels of a stepped-up campaign by Butler to unleash his inspectors to roam around government palaces and other places considered by the Iraqis as symbols of their sovereignty. The hawkish US Secretary of Defense William Cohen, National Security Adviser Sandy Berger, Madeleine Albright, and President Clinton soon followed suit by promising more devastation as a war atmosphere began to loom on the horizon.

In the midst of what appeared to be an imminent aerial strike, UN Secretary-General Kofi Annan embarked on a very risky journey to Baghdad, designed to restore the UN inspection process. The agreement signed by Annan and Iraqi foreign minister, Tariq Aziz, on February 23, 1998, averted war, won broad approval throughout the world, and created the prospects for a transformation of Iraq's relationship with the United Nations. Under the agreement, UN diplomats would restrain the overzealous inspectors of Richard Butler, many of whom were already engaged in espionage activities for the benefit of the Pentagon; a crucial distinction was made between presidential palaces and weapons sites; and a light at the end of the tunnel was shown to Iraq by the inclusion of the following sentence: "The lifting of sanctions is obviously of paramount importance to the people and government of Iraq."[20]

The Clinton administration, which was unhappy with Annan's initiative but could hardly stand against it in public, greeted the agreement initially with characteristic skepticism and a plethora of reservations. Soon afterward, however, Washington convened the Security Council and secured the adoption of a resolution on March 2, 1998, which seemed designed to establish the kind of legal façade needed to subvert the Annan-Aziz agreement. Of particular importance was the language chosen by the United States to justify future unilateral intervention. The resolution, which threatened Iraq with "severest consequences" in the case of non-compliance, was immediately interpreted by the US as granting it an "automatic" right to intervene militarily. Absurd, shouted three permanent members of the council. The Russian ambassador, in fact, coined a new word to express his opposition to the US interpretation: there would be no "automaticity," he stated. His remarks were echoed by the Chinese and French representatives, thus leaving the US with only its dedicated yes man, Prime Minister Tony Blair of the UK, in agreement.[21]

On March 3, President Clinton hammered the last nail in the coffin of the Annan-Aziz agreement, and made a mockery of the Security Council resolution. He said, "Iraq must fulfill without obstruction or delay its commitment to open all of the nation to the international weapons inspectors—any place, any time, without any conditions, deadlines, or excuses."[22] Ignoring the consensus in the Security Council regarding the meaning and intent of Resolution 1154 of March 2, 1998, he asserted, "All the members of the [Security] Council agree that failure to do so will result in the severest consequences for Iraq."[23] That, of course, was a lie—plain and simple.

It is important to point out that the US claim is further weakened by Security Council Resolution 687 (the ceasefire resolution dated April 3, 1991), which provided for the on-site inspections. The resolution did not grant any UN member the right to use force to enforce its mandate (in contrast to claims to the contrary recently repeated by Bush II administration).[24] In fact, the resolution states that the members of the Security Council "remain seized of the matter," that is, remain in control of the situation, which negates any possibility of "automatic authorization."[25] It is the council, therefore, and not any member state or a combination of states, that should decide if and when force becomes necessary to assure compliance.

In retrospect, Kofi Annan's diplomacy had only postponed the inevitable. The United States, seeking to redefine the UN Charter and to establish precedents for unilateral bombing, would wait for an opportune moment to drum up new charges and resume the onslaught. It was not even deterred by the fact that it was openly accused of having utilized Unscom technology and the inspectors to improve the bombardment of Iraq.

5. The fifth episode, therefore, came as no surprise, but the scarcely veiled manner in which it was concocted left very little room for the imagination and resulted in the death of Unscom, hitherto a key pillar of the US interventionist strategy. Two important scenes stand out in this episode.

First, Unscom director Richard Butler, who was supposedly an international civil servant working under Kofi Annan, prepared his report for the Security Council indicting Iraq for "non-compliance" while inside the US Mission to the United Nations. And second, the Anglo-American air strikes that followed Butler's report began on December 16, 1998, before the report was considered by the Security Council, which was already in session, and after Unscom and International Atomic Energy Association (IAEA) personnel had been withdrawn from Iraq for their own safety.[26] The grand jury, judge, and executioner were one and the same. The United States not only signed the death certificate of Unscom but sapped the UN and its secretary-general of all vestiges of credibility and committed an egregious violation of the UN Charter by launching aggression against a member state.[27]

At this point, despite the nearly ten-year-long attempt by the US and UK to contain Saddam Hussein, using sanctions, "no-fly" zones, inspections, and military force, the scheme remained in tatters. Tacitly admitting that its project was collapsing, almost one year to the day since its last devastating attack, the Clinton administration decided to try diplomacy. The Security Council, at the behest of the US and UK, adopted a resolution on December 17, 1999, that would renew arms inspections and temporarily suspend some trade sanctions if Iraq complied with another set of disarmament demands. The controversial future of the resolution is nowhere better reflected than in the abstention of the three other permament members of the Security Council, France, China, and Russia.[28]

Resolution 1284 eased import restrictions on some essential items and removed the ceiling on oil exports, but it also increased the number of items considered as having "dual use." Moreover, the resolution created a new inspection requirement—the UN Monitoring, Verification, and Inspection Commission (Unmovic)—whose head has the final say on compliance. Under the most optimal conditions, which would include the appointment of someone other than a Washington or London loyalist in that post, it would take at least one year for the sanctions to be suspended. Even then, Iraq would remain on probation. Sanctions would not actually be removed, but merely suspended for 120-day renewable periods.[29] Particularly objectionable to Iraq is the unusual call for the return of the IAEA, which had already declared Iraq free of nuclear weapons years ago.[30].

Toward the end of the Clinton administration *Foreign Affairs* reported the US war against the people of Iraq resulted in "hundreds of thousands of deaths."[31] The war deprived Iraq of more than $140 billion in oil revenue by 1999 and saddled it with hyperinflation; contributed to mass poverty; unprecedented social and economic dislocation; and an intolerable rate of unemployment.[32] A nation that was on its way out of a third-world status has been forced to deal with epidemics of cholera and typhoid resulting from the dumping of raw sewage in its waterways. Its modern hospitals can hardly afford electricity or find basic medicines to treat its large malnourished and sick population. An increasing number of Iraqi professionals are being relegated to driving taxis, while the lower classes fall prey to severe exploitation. Yet the Washington and London establishments continued to argue that sanctions must remain in force to prevent Iraq from threatening its neighbors—or perhaps, as President Clinton said, "until the end of time, or as long as he [Hussein] lasts."[33] This Security Council resolution was in essence a device to continue the Anglo-American war by other means.

US policy under Bush II

In this context the Arab media and many diplomats hailed George W. Bush's election as portending a probable and salutary change in American policy towards the Middle East. It soon became clear that, despite the nuanced appearance of a change in style, the essence of the Bush II administration policy towards the region remains largely unchanged from that of the Clinton administration. The Bush II policy, however, has emphasized the linkage between Iraq and Palestine. Indeed, a carefully articulated convergence of views on the global and regional "threats" facing the United States and Israel has been confirmed by numerous statements emanating from Washington and Tel Aviv, dealing with the increased collaboration and coordination between the two countries. In particular, Secretary of Defense Donald Rumsfeld and Bush have been utilizing the cold war–like rhetoric of the Reagan administration, even though the international context is now vastly different from that of the 1980s, when the Soviet Union was intact and its threat was palpable (although vastly exaggerated). A costly anti-missile "defense" system is being justified by the administration as necessary to defend against a potential Chinese missile "threat" and the increasingly touted threat of the missile capability and the potential for production and deployment of weapons of mass destruction by Iraq and Iran.[34] Just as significant is the perceived threat to both the United States and Israel of "international terrorism." This terrorism, particularly in the aftermath of September 11, is largely associated with Islamic people in the region and elsewhere.

This convergence of perspective on the global and regional threats forms the background for the common strategic view that seems to have brought together, in mutual appreciation, America's neoconservatives, the Likudists entrenched in the Bush II administration, and the rightwing government of Israel's Ariel Sharon. Most of the trumpeting for a US attack on Iraq to unseat Saddam Hussein is coming from Israel's supporters in the administration, think tanks, media, and Congress. Richard Perle, head of the Defense Policy Board, has emerged as a leading advocate of a preemptive strike against Iraq. He told the *Washington Post* in August 2002 that "ultimately, US policy on Iraq will be set by 'civilians,' that it will involve a 'political judgment,' rather than one by the military leaders in the Pentagon who were more skeptical about the need for a war."[35] Another Bush administration proponent of war is Deputy Defense Secretary Paul Wolfowitz, who is concerned about Iraq's capacity to deliver "weapons of mass destruction," even though it does not have long-range missiles.[36] There is also John Bolton, US Under Secretary for Arms Control, who admitted that the aim in Washington was to topple Hussein, regardless of whether or not he allowed UN inspectors back in to complete the disarmament process. Bolton told BBC Radio 4's *Today* program that he "certainly hoped" Saddam would be deposed within the year, adding, "Let there be no mistake—while we also insist on the reintroduction of the weapons inspectors, our policy at the same time insists on regime change in Baghdad and that policy will not be altered, whether inspectors go in or not."[37]

Other administration hawks include Vice-President Dick Cheney, Donald Rumsfeld, and National Security Adviser Condoleezza Rice. Besides being pillars of the civilian national security establishment, the members of this cabal are partisans of Israel and are very close to the Israeli lobby, which has been promoting Sharon's thesis about the imperative need to preemptively attack Iraq. In a BBC interview, conducted on August 15, 2002, Rice made it clear that an attack on Iraq was necessary and proper:

> This [Saddam Hussein] is an evil man who, left to his own devices, will wreak havoc again on his own population, his neighbors and, if he gets weapons of mass destruction and the means to deliver them, all of us. [There] is a very powerful moral case for regime change ... We certainly do not have the luxury of doing nothing ... He has used chemical weapons against his own people and against his neighbors, he has invaded his neighbors, he has killed thousands of his own people ... He shoots at our planes, our airplanes, in the no-fly zones where we are trying to enforce U.N. security resolutions.[38]

Rice adheres to the Israeli strategy of preemption instead of deterrence or containment, hence the "obligation" not to sit idly by and the "moral" case she purports to find, despite the absence of any evidence that links Iraq to terrorism or proves that Iraq has weapons of mass destruction:

> History is littered with cases of inaction that led to have grave consequences for the world. We just have to look back and ask how many dictators who ended up being a tremendous global threat and killing thousands and, indeed, millions of people, should we have stopped in their tracks.[39]

Meron Benvinisti, the Israeli writer and former deputy mayor of Jerusalem, made the link between Israel's advocacy of an American war against Iraq and Israel's overall objective of ethnic cleansing in the West Bank. Such a war, being advocated by Sharon's men in Tel Aviv and in Washington, will provide the best cover for the long-time Zionist objective of expulsion of the Palestinians, known in Israel as "transfer." He wrote:

> Under the cover of George Bush getting even for his father, Ariel Sharon will be able to settle his own old accounts, going back to the days of Beirut. Maj. Gen. Yitzhak Eitan hinted at the strong connection between a war in Iraq and the war against the Palestinians when he said "an American attack on Iraq will also hurt the Palestinian Authority." Since the Israeli government is coming up with "worst case scenarios" on NBC, here's another

> one—an American assault on Iraq against Arab and world opposition, and an Israeli involvement, even if only symbolic, leads to the collapse of the Hashemite regime in Jordan. Israel then executes the old "Jordanian option"—expelling hundreds of thousands of Palestinians across the Jordan River. There has never been a better opportunity for that option.[40]

A survey in the daily *Maariv* newspaper, conducted in August 2002, revealed that 57 percent of Israelis were in favor of an American attack on Iraq to unseat Saddam Hussein, and the same percentage of Israelis actually believed Iraq would attack Israel, with 28 percent of them believing that such an attack against Israel would involve chemical or biological weapons.[41] Such a percentage is not surprising, given the official Israeli propaganda and disinformation campaign claiming that Israel's intelligence has gathered evidence that Iraq is speeding up efforts to produce biological and chemical weapons. Sharon's spokesman, Ranaan Gissin, made the following statement to the Associated Press: "Any postponement of an attack on Iraq at this stage will serve no purpose.... It will only give him [Hussein] more of an opportunity to accelerate his program of weapons of mass destruction.... Saddam's going to be able to reach a point where these weapons will be operational."[42]

Some US and UN officials are skeptical about the validity of these allegations, as are many international agencies and observers. Scott Ritter, a former Marine who was a chief UN weapons inspector in Iraq, accused Senator Joseph Biden, chair of the Senate Foreign Relations Committee, of running a "sham hearing" in August 2002 on the issue of whether or not the US military should invade Iraq. [43] In fact, he claimed that the hearings were intended to provide political cover for a massive military attack on Iraq.

> I believe that Iraq does not pose a threat to the US worthy of war. This conclusion is shared by many senior military officers. According to President Bush and his advisers, Iraq is known to possess weapons of mass destruction and is actively seeking to reconstitute the weapons production capabilities. I bear personal witness, through seven years as a chief weapons inspector in Iraq for the UN, to both the scope of Iraq's weapons of mass destruction programs and the effectiveness of the UN weapons inspectors in ultimately eliminating them. While we were never able to provide 100 percent certainty regarding the disposition of Iraq's proscribed weaponry, we did ascertain a 90–95 percent level of verified disarmament.... It is clear that Senator Biden and his colleagues have no interest in such facts.[44]

Similar doubts were expressed by a former UN Assistant Secretary-General, Hans von Sponeck, who headed the UN "oil-for-food" program from the time of Denis Halliday's resignation from that post until he himself resigned in 2000 in protest over the continued sanctions on Iraq.[45] In early July 2002, von Sponeck visited Iraqi installations purported to be weapons sites, and found them to be "defunct and destroyed."[46] He made the following statement about weapons and sanctions to the Institute for Public Accuracy in Washington on July 29, 2002:

> Evidence of al-Qaida/Iraq collaboration does not exist.... Six years of revisions to sanctions policy on Baghdad have repeatedly promised "mitigation" of civilian suffering. Yet, in 1999, Unicef confirmed an estimated 5,000 excess child deaths every month above the 1989 pre-sanctions rate. Four months ago, Unicef reported that more than 22 percent of the country's young children remain chronically malnourished. Credible opposition groups outside Iraq have called for delinking economic and military sanctions. At the March Arab summit in Beirut, all 22 Arab governments (including Kuwait) called for the same. If the economic embargo on Iraq is not in their interest, then in whose interest is it?[47]

As of the time of this writing, conflicting reports continue to be filed by different Washington constituencies predicting an imminent war, while many establishment voices express skepticism about a war and its rationale, consequences for the stability of the region, the stability of America's relations with its allies, and, in fact, the impact on the security of American military personnel and civilians. Leading Republicans from Congress, the State Department, and former administrations have expressed concern that an adequate case has not been made for war. However, none of the criticisms mention legal and moral principles. Rather, the debate is anchored over the "national interest" and whether America would become bogged down in another type of prolonged urban warfare, such as Vietnam, or "nation-building," as in Afghanistan. Hawkish politicians, such as Henry Kissinger and Brent Scowcroft, former national security advisers to presidents Nixon, Ford, and Bush I, have drawn attention to the risks of alienating allies, creating greater instability in the region, and harming long-term US interests.[48] Even the hawkish Lawrence Eagleburger told ABC News: "[Unless Hussein] has his hand on a trigger that is for a weapon of mass destruction, and our intelligence is clear, I don't know why we have to do it now, when all our allies are opposed to it."[49]

Among the rationale of these skeptics was also a concern about the negative impact of a war against Iraq on Bush's so-called war on terrorism. Scowcroft wrote the following in the *Wall Street Journal*: "There is no evidence to tie Saddam to terrorist organizations, and even less to the September 11 attacks.... [Military action] would seriously jeopardize, if not destroy, the global counterterrorist campaign we have undertaken."[50]

Meanwhile, although most Americans favored going to war against Iraq in fall of 2002, they made this endorsement contingent on congressional approval, allied support, and low casualty rates. A *Washington Post* and ABC News poll published on August 13 revealed that slightly more than three quarters of the people surveyed viewed Iraq as a threat, 69 percent supported some form of military action to unseat Saddam Hussein, but support dropped to 40 percent if it would cause "a significant number of casualties," and to 54 percent if allied support was absent. Only 22 percent opposed such action. The poll showed a lack of consensus on whether or not president Bush had a "clear policy" with 45 percent saying yes, while 42 percent said no. That division contrasts with 58 percent who said in a 1998 survey that President Clinton had a clear policy.[51]

A continuity of purpose

The division within the ranks of the establishment, including media, think tanks, and the government, together with the conditional majority in public opinion, makes it difficult to predict what will happen next in US policy toward Iraq. Meanwhile, the sanctions and the low-level steady bombing by US and British planes continue to take a heavy toll on Iraq and its people. They are suffering under one of the most ruthless regimes in the region and under the policies of the lone superpower, now run by an equally ruthless elite, whose victims are found among impoverished and disaffected third world people around the globe.

Irrespective of Saddam Hussein's policies, despicable as they are, the Bush administration has produced no evidence he has supported any terrorist groups or activities. His country's military capacity has been crippled, and he has no long-range missiles to deliver chemical and biological weapons, even if he has them. Many of the critics of a preemptive war argue that since containment has worked so far (albeit with deadly effect on Iraqis), what is the point of launching a full-scale war?

As the US and UK continue regular bombings of Iraq, amidst the continuous reports about an imminent full-scale war, the message is clear:

new rules of international conduct are being written. The war on Iraq, the aerial bombardment of Yugoslavia in 1999, and the full-scale invasion of Afghanistan in 2001 illustrate that the theater of operations for the US military and NATO now includes Eastern and Central Europe, the Middle East, North Africa, Central Asia, and parts of East Asia. Dissent and non-conformity regarding these rules will not be tolerated. America's risk-free wars are unencumbered by any counterbalances on the international scene or in the domestic arena.

The United States has a congress that might rank as the most conservative, arrogant, and war-like legislature in recent history. It has mainstream media that vacillate between serving as cheerleaders for US policy and urging tougher action against Iraq. It has a military that is trying to redefine its mission, that wants to test and show off its hardware, and that is always in search of an enemy to obtain large new budget allocations. But the United States also has a peace movement, one in need of reactivation and a reawakening.

Notes

1 For more discussion of the broad strategic objectives of a war against Iraq, see John Donnelly and Anthony Shadid, "Iraq War Hawks Have Plans to Reshape Entire Mideast," *Boston Globe*, September 10, 2002, p. A12; Robert Fisk, "Bush Is Intent on Painting Allies and Enemies in the Middle East as Evil," *The Independent*, September 10, 2002, p. 6; and Nicholas Blanford, "Syria Worries US Won't Stop at Iraq," *Christian Science Monitor*, September 9, 2002, p. 6.

2 See Michael R. Gordon, "U.S. Nuclear Plan Sees New Targets and Weapons," *New York Times*, March 10, 2002, p. 1: 1.

3 Mary McGrory, "Capitol Hill & Knowlton," *Washington Post*, January 12, 1992, p. C1. Dana Priest, "Kuwait Baby-Killing Report Disputed," *Washington Post*, February 7, 1992.

4 Jonathan Marshall, "Economists Say Iraq's Threat to US Oil Supply Is Exaggerated," *San Francisco Chronicle*, October 29, 1990, p. A14; Johanna Neuman, "Baker Resurrects an Old Line on War," *USA Today*, November 14, 1990; and "Excerpts from Baker Testimony on US and Gulf," *New York Times*, September 5, 1990, p. A14.

5 Barton Gellman, "Allied Air War Struck Broadly in Iraq: Officials Acknowledge Strategy Went Beyond Purely Military Targets," *Washington Post*, June 23, 1991, p. A1.

6 See, for example, David Krivine, "Israel Is Still the West's Best Defense," *Jerusalem Post*, August 15, 1990; Editorial, "The 'Good' Dictators," *Jerusalem Post*, August 22, 1990; and David Krivine, "For the Americans the Optimal Aim Is to Get Rid of Saddam," *Jerusalem Post*, August 26, 1990.

7 See Naseer H. Aruri, *Dishonest Broker: The United States, Israel, and the Palestinians* (Cambridge: South End Press, forthcoming), and Noam Chomsky, *Fateful Triangle: The United States, Israel, and the Palestinians,* updated ed. (Cambridge: South End Press, 1999), pp. 533–65.

8 Colman McCarthy, "Empty Words for Iraq's Civilian Casualties," *Washington Post*, July 6, 1993, p. D15.

9 Michael R. Gordon, "Threats in the Gulf: Kuwait," *New York Times*, October 11, 1994, p. A1.

10 William Perry, Defense Department Briefing, Federal News Service, September 3, 1996.

11 Bill Clinton, President's Weekly Radio Address, Federal News Service, September 14, 1996.

12 Bill Clinton, White House Briefing, Federal News Service, September 3, 1996.

13 Colum Lynch, "US Used UN to Spy on Iraq, Aides Say," *Boston Globe*, January 6, 1999, p. A1, and Barton Gellman, "US Spied on Iraqi Military Via UN," *Washington Post*, March 2, 1999, p. A1.

14 William Safire, "Clinton's Cave-In to Saddam," *New York Times*, November 23, 1997, p. 4: 15.

15 Barbara Crossette, "For Iraq, a Dog House with Many Rooms," *New York Times*, November 23, 1997, p. 4: 4.

16 See article 22 of Security Council Resolution 687.

17 Robert H. Pelletreau, "The US and Iraq: When Will the Nightmare End?" *Mideast Mirror* 11: 198 (October 13, 1997), p. 1; English version of Arabic article in *al-Hayat*, October 13, 1997.

18 See, for example, Richard Butler, "Iraqi Bombshell," *Talk* 1: 1 (September 1999), especially p. 240.

19 Dana Priest, "Inspector Has Triggered Nerves in Iraq, Pentagon," *Washington Post*, January 14, 1998, p. A13.

20 "Baghdad Agreement on Weapons Inspections," *Washington Post*, February 25, 1998, p. A22.

21 Lee Michael Katz, "UN Waffling on Threat of Force," *USA Today*, March 3, 1998, p. 9A. See also David Osborne, "How Long Until the UN's New Resolution Is Tested by Iraq," *The Independent*, March 3, 1998, p. 12, and Laura Silber, "US, UK Hit Opposition on Iraq Threat," *Financial Times*, March 3, 1998, p. 4.

22 Jonathan Peterson, "Clinton to Iraq: US 'Prepared to Act,'" *Los Angeles Times*, March 4, 1998, p. A6.

23 Barbara Crossette, "UN Rebuffs US on Threat to Iraq if It Breaks Pact," *New York Times*, March 3, 1998, p. A1.

24 See http://www.unog.ch/uncc/resolutio/res0687.pdf.

25 See article 34 of Security Council Resolution 687, cited above.

26 This is clear even from Butler's own self-serving account. See Butler, "Iraqi Bombshell," p. 240. See also Julian Borger and Ewen Macaskill, "Missile Blitz on Iraq," *Guardian*, December 17, 1998, p. 1.

27 Article 2(4) of the charter bars making a "threat to peace." The bombing also undermined Chapter 7, which empowers the Security Council to determine the "existence of any threat to the peace, breach of the peace, or act of aggression" (article 39) and to authorize the use of force under

article 42 after it determines that other measures undertaken under article 41 have proved to be inadequate to maintain peace and security.

28 Roula Khalaf, "UN Adopts New Resolution on Iraq," *Financial Times*, December 18–19, 1999, p. 1.

29 See article 33 of Security Council Resolution 1284.

30 See Mary Dejevsky, "Iraq Sanction Hope as UN Gives All-Clear on Weapons," *The Independent*, July 28, 1998, p. 14, and Editorial, "Back to Iraq," *Financial Times*, April 22, 1998, p. 25.

31 John Mueller and Karl Mueller, "Sanctions of Mass Destruction," *Foreign Affairs* 78: 3 (May/June 1999): 49.

32 Ghassan al-Kadi, "Iraq Wants Active Oil Role," United Press International, November 15, 1999.

33 Clinton, September 3, 1996.

34 See Vernon Loeb and Thomas E. Ricks, "Bush Speeds Missile Defense Plans," *Washington Post*, July 12, 2001, p. A1; William Safire, "Of Turks and Kurds," *New York Times*, August 26, 2002, p. A15.

35 Thomas E. Ricks, "Some Top Military Brass Favor Status Quo in Iraq: Containment Seen Less Risky Than Attack," *Washington Post*, July 28, 2002, p. A1.

36 See Ricks, "Some Top Military Brass Favor Status Quo," p. A1; Michael R. Gordon, "Iraq Said to Plan Tangling U.S. in Street Fighting," *New York Times*, August 26, 2002, p. A1.

37 Peter Beaumont, Gaby Hinsliff, and Paul Beaver, "Bush Ready to Declare War," *The Observer*, August 4, 2002, p. 1.

38 Jane Wardell, "Rice Calls Saddam Evil an Evil Man Who Will Wreak Havoc if Left to Own Devices," Associated Press, August 15, 2002.

39 Wardell, "Rice Calls Saddam Evil," August 15, 2002.

40 Meron Benvinisti, "Preemptive Warnings of Fantastic Sccenarios," *Ha'aretz*, August 15, 2002.

41 Jason Keyser, "Israel Urges U.S. to Attack Iraq," Associated Press, August 16, 2002.

42 Keyser, "Israel Urges U.S. To Attack Iraq," August 16, 2002.

43 Institute for Public Accuracy, "Ritter: A 'Sham Hearing' on Iraq,'" Press Release, July 29, 2002 (http://www.accuracy.org/press_release/PR072902.htm).

44 Institute for Public Accuracy, "Ritter: A 'Sham Hearing' on Iraq,'" July 29, 2002.

45 See Anthony Arnove, "Under Siege," *In These Times*, May 15, 2000, p. 16.

46 Institute for Public Accuracy, "Von Sponeck: Weapons Sites 'Defunct and Destroyed,'" Press Release, July 29, 2002 (http://www.accuracy.org/PR072902.htm).

47 Institute for Public Accuracy, "Von Sponeck: Weapons Sites 'Defunct and Destroyed,'" July 29, 2002.

48 Todd S. Purdum and Patrick E. Tyler, "Top Republicans Break with Bush on Iraq Strategy," *New York Times*, August 16, 2002; see also Henry Kissinger, "The War Option," *San Diego Union Tribune*, August 11, 2002, p. G1, and Brent Scowcroft, "Don't Attack Saddam," *Wall Street Journal*, August 15, 2002, p. A12.

49 Purdum and Tyler, "Top Republicans Break with Bush," p. A1.

50 Scowcroft, "Don't Attack Saddam," p. A12.

51 Richard Morin and Claudia Deane, "Poll: Americans Cautiously Favor War in Iraq," *Washingon Post*, August 13, 2002, p. A10. See also Adam Nagourney and Janet Elder, "Public Says Bush Needs to Pay Heed to Weak Economy," *New York Times*, October 7, 2002, p. A1.

Chapter 2

Iraq: The Impact of Sanctions and US Policy

Phyllis Bennis and Denis J. Halliday
Interviewed by David Barsamian

David Barsamian: *Noam Chomsky has called the air and missile attacks during the Gulf War on sewage treatment plants, irrigation systems, and water purification plants acts of biological warfare.*

Phyllis Bennis: I think that's a pretty accurate term. The US was very proud in announcing throughout the world that its war against Iraq in the early part of 1991 was a "clean" war, that we used "smart weapons" that only targeted what we wanted—aside from the fact that the vast majority of the bombs were not smart bombs at all, and of the so-called smart bombs many, many missed their targets. The targets that were hit included water treatment plants, sewage treatment plants, electrical generating plants, communications centers. The fact that the 22 million people of Iraq might be denied clean water was considered an acceptable consequence.

The result has been absolute devastation for the civilian population at enormous cost in the future to be repaired. During the December 1998 military strikes, at least one oil refinery in Basra was deliberately targeted on the grounds that that particular refinery's output was being used for smuggling.[1] Whether it was or not, I don't know; but it is a violation of international law to deliberately destroy an economic target, as was chosen here, meaning that everyone in the Pentagon involved in that decision is guilty of a war crime.

The inability of Iraq to make repairs means the continuation of malnutrition. The largest number of casualties today are the result of dirty, contaminated water caused by inadequate sewage-treatment and water-treatment facilities. What that means is that children are dying in Iraq of eminently treatable diseases: simple diarrhea, typhoid, and other contaminated-water-borne diseases, in a country whose advanced health-care system was so developed before the sanctions regime and before the bombings that the most important problem faced by Iraqi pediatricians was childhood obesity. We have devastated this country, so its level of childhood mortality is now worse than that of Sudan.[2]

You've also said that the oil-for-food program was highly politicized from the very beginning. What do you mean?

Denis Halliday: Firstly, oil-for-food was never intended to actually resolve the humanitarian crisis. It was designed to stop further deterioration. It was designed to build on what the Iraqi government was already doing and is still doing. They have a separate food-distribution program for those on fixed incomes, orphans, war widows, and others, which has continued throughout. The politicization is seen most conspicuously in workings of the sanctions committee of the UN Security Council in New York, which is second-guessing the contractors and the content and cost of supplies that the Iraqi government seeks with the approval of the World Food Program, Unicef, the World Health Organization, or the Food and Agriculture Organization in almost every case.

These are not just out of thin air. The young bureaucrats who sit on this committee in New York are not technical people. In fact, they don't want technical advice. They tend in the case of the UK and the US to send this material to their headquarters, where they are further politicized and second-guessed in order to hold back any area of potential dual usage, any area where they feel there is a risk factor. So, for example, when the Iraqis asked for 500 ambulances, approved by the World Health Organization as minimal under the circumstances, these were initially blocked in their entirety and then slowly, over a period of six to nine months, were released—100, 200 ambulances—really picayunish stuff, inexcusable. Likewise throughout the medical drug area—medical equipment for hospitals and clinics, refrigeration—and even in education—paper, books, pencils. This is unreal.

Why was Unscom such a focus of controversy and attention?

DH: I believed it escaped from the UN and became an entity unto its own, staffed not with UN people but with people from other entities on loan to the UN but actually loyal to their employing organizations, whether it's military intelligence or other intelligence agencies. That's very unfortunate. We've seen the results. Of course, now it's all finally come out in the open. The Iraqis have for years been saying that the Unscom inspectors were in fact spying and collecting data that was then used against them in military strikes. We've now seen Washington admit that.[3]

PB: The irony is that one of the things that's been lost in all of the attention about the controversy over Unscom is that its work, in the early years in particular, was quite successful. Whatever shreds of chemical or biological material that may have escaped are sitting in a jar in someone's refrigerator somewhere and are never going to be found. That's clear. The significant aspects of the weapons programs have been found and destroyed.

Critics of US policy in Iraq say that the US keeps moving the goalposts. Initially it was compliance with Resolution 687, the "mother of all resolutions." Most recently, it is for "regime change." Is there any credence to that?

PB: Moving the goalposts has been the name of the game for the US since sanctions were imposed. Rather than accepting UN Resolution 687, which says that sanctions will be removed after compliance with certain very specific qualifications regarding weapons of mass destruction, we've been told sanctions will remain until Saddam Hussein is overthrown, until sometime into the next century, as long as Saddam Hussein is in power, a variety of other things. Even if Iraq complies, we're not going to lift the sanctions anyway.

I must say also, though, that when we speak about 687, it's important to think about another aspect that often gets ignored. Besides the imposition of sanctions and dealing with weapons of mass destruction, 687 also calls for creation of a weapons of mass destruction–free zone, which means a nuclear weapons–free zone, throughout the Middle East.[4] That's very significant, because the US refuses still to officially acknowledge Israel's nuclear arsenal. The United States has been the party primarily responsible for providing weapons to Saudi Arabia, Turkey, and Israel.

In your contacts with Iraqi officials, did you hear any resonance of the fact that, in a sense, whatever they did it would never be enough?

DH: That is exactly the feeling among the ministers that I know and the technocrats in the ministries throughout Baghdad. They think it's a lost cause, and there's nothing they can do that will satisfy the US, which they recognize as the main proponent, so to speak, of this policy. It's a desperate plight for these people, who are well-intentioned, highly skilled technocrats doing their best for their own people. They themselves, their own families are victims. They are dependent on the oil-for-food program. I think they're very disheartened by the fact that the UN is no longer in control and it's not in fact the UN but the US that they're dealing with. It's greatly damaged the reputation of the UN not just in Iraq but in the entire Middle East. The very policies of the United Nations, as they see quite clearly, are diminishing the Iraqi people while strengthening the regime of Saddam Hussein.

Did you make your views known on the impact of sanctions to Kofi Annan?

DH: I wrote to him toward the end of October or early November 1997, pointing out very clearly the tragedy that we were overseeing and responsible for and the impact this would have on the UN. That letter, in fact, was leaked to *Le Monde* and became public information. I think it played a part, strangely, in having the Security Council acknowledge its errors and begin to agree to address the problem of humanitarian crises in Iraq, which led ultimately to an increase in the ceiling under which the Iraqis could operate.

You've been a company man. You worked for a company, the UN, for thirty-four years. You served in New York, Indonesia, Malaysia, Iran, and your last stint was in Iraq. Why didn't you stay inside the company and work from within?

DH: The company has two large components. One is that aspect of the member states, who actually own the UN and provide the decision-making within the UN, for whom we all work. That's where we have the crisis. The Secretariat has many problems common in any administration, any group of civil servants. I've had a very satisfactory and good career throughout my years. Development assistance is very satisfying. It's been a very positive experience, and I would do it again tomorrow. When we get into deep trouble is when the member states, particularly of the Security Council, manipulate the organization for their own national interests. That's where the crisis has come, and that's what hit me and very quickly in Iraq. In Iraq I think it's out of control. I think the Security Council is out of control. I think we've got to have an international review process to look at those resolutions and bring them back into line, compatible with the charter, with the Declaration of Human Rights, and various other international conventions.

What informed your choice to leave rather than to stay inside and fight?

DH: Because the issue was not within the Secretariat, where I had some influence. It was with the member states. I could not stand up as a civil servant and criticize the member states. That's not the way the game works. I needed to be free to do what I am doing with you today.

You resigned at the end of September 1998. You come to the US and start talking about these kinds of issues. What's the response been?

DH: It's been encouraging. I've discovered that both in Europe and the US there are thousands, possibly millions of individuals who are disheartened and disgusted with the policies of their respective governments, Europe included. In the US, we've met thousands of people and spoken to many more on the radio and by other means. I think there's a groundswell of Americans who are finding out for the first time what dreadful results are coming from the policy decisions in Washington. They're eager to try to have their views felt. They're not clear as to how that can best be done. They're not experienced in political activism. They need help and support. We're hoping to encourage that. That's all we can do, try to build a coalition of interested Americans who understand that the people of Iraq are suffering, and they are the same as we, Americans or Europeans. They have families, kids, elder folks. They need help and support. They don't deserve the punishment they are getting under the sanctions regime.

The US has certainly had a checkered history with Saddam Hussein, from a very favored ally in the 1980s to a demon, compared to Adolf Hitler, in the 1990s. Could you talk about that transition over almost a two-decade period?

PB: The US alliance with Saddam Hussein's government in Iraq actually goes back even into the 1970s, but it was in the 1980s that the US emerged as a primary diplomatic supporter, a provider of military intelligence and, very crucially, a provider of weapons of mass destruction. So, specifically biological weapons from one company in particular outside of Washington, the American Type Culture Collection, under contracts approved by the US Commerce Department, provided the biological weapons material to make anthrax, *E. coli,* botulism, and a host of other terrible biological diseases.[5]

Those sales continued even after the Iraqi regime actually used chemical weapons against its own Kurdish population in Halabja in northern Iraq and against Iranian troops on the border in clear violation of a host of international conventions.

There was an understanding that this was a very repressive regime, but he was our guy. It was what Franklin Roosevelt used to say about Anastasio Somoza: he's a son of a bitch, but he's "our son of a bitch." That's what Saddam Hussein was until virtually the moment that his government invaded Kuwait in August 1990. Suddenly he was no longer an unpleasant but useful ally; he was Hitler. It was as if there had been a coup in Iraq and it was a new and different government than the one that had been supported all those years.

What's so interesting is that at the time it had far more to do with the international situation than with the regional situation alone. There were regional aspects, certainly, questions of oil, of international stability, of Israel, but fundamental in my view at that time was the fact that the Soviet Union was about to collapse. The US was faced strategically with having to emerge with a new role for itself as a superpower, what the French are now calling a "hyperpower." I think that the idea that faced the US was that many countries and many people throughout the world would expect that with the collapse of the Soviet Union, which was imminent at that time, the US itself would pull in its superpower tents and begin to act like a normal country rather than appearing to be a continuing superpower without a sparring partner. The US wanted a way to make clear that, whatever happened to the Soviet Union, the US would remain the hyperpower, the dominant force in the Middle East and throughout the world. The invasion of Kuwait provided a pretext to do that.

When the invasion first took place, it was a containable regional crisis. It was a US choice to make it an international conflagration. At the moment of the invasion, the Arab League tried to deal with the crisis.[6] To no one's surprise, they failed. Whether they might have succeeded, given more time, I don't know, but when they called for more time, it was denied them. The US said that it was sending in troops.

For the same reason, later, when there were efforts to craft a diplomatic solution rather than a military solution to the Iraqi invasion, they were not allowed to go forward. In particular there was a last-minute initiative in February 1991 by Yevgeny Primakov, who was at the time the foreign minister of the Soviet Union. He had been ambassador to Iraq in the past. He went to Baghdad and negotiated a withdrawal agreement with the Iraqi government. The US would not even allow the Security Council to discuss it, because it was clear that they had made a decision in

Washington that this was going to be a military victory, a showpiece, and they were going to force the world to come to war with them.[7] That's what Resolution 678 was all about, authorizing the use of force.

The US basically bribed China, Colombia, and Ethiopia on the Security Council. It punished Yemen dramatically for refusing to vote yes. There were two countries that voted no. One was Cuba, the other Yemen, the sole Arab country on the council. When the Yemeni ambassador, Abdallah Saleh al-Ashtal, had just brought down his hand after voting no, one of the US diplomats said to him, "That was the most expensive no vote you ever cast."[8] In retaliation, the United States and other countries cancelled or cut back aid to Yemen, one of the poorest Arab states.[9] So, this was very, very high stakes for the United States.

China was bribed enormously to make sure it did not veto. It had threatened to veto. China wanted two things it had been unable to get since the massacre at Tiananmen Square. One was diplomatic rehabilitation. The second was long-term development aid. The US had blocked both. The day after the vote, the Chinese foreign minister was invited to the White House for a high-profile visit.[10] So, China got what it wanted. The US got what it wanted, which was an abstention rather than a veto. This was high stakes for the US, and they made the most of it.

In September 1980, Iraq invades its neighbor Iran, a clear violation of that country's sovereignty. What was the international community's response?

PB: Essentially, the response was, We'll sit back and watch. It was a little more Machiavellian. There was at least an aspect of it that said, We'll not only sit back and watch, but we'll cheer and sell popcorn while they deplete each other's resources. This was the era of "dual containment" by the US, when both Iraq and Iran were viewed as key potential challengers to US interests in the region. And again, there's a bit of subtlety here. The problem was not that they would take the oil away. Clearly, either country would have to sell oil on the world market to make a living. They couldn't eat the oil. But the question was going to be, who would be in control of access to that oil? For the US, the concern was far greater with its allies (but competitors, economically) in Germany and Japan, and elsewhere in Europe, as well. The US wanted to remain the guarantor of access to oil for its allies. That gave it a great deal of economic and political power vis-à-vis its allies, not particularly vis-à-vis Iran or Iraq. But those were the only two countries in the Middle East with the requisites for indigenous power: water, land, people, and wealth through oil. No other countries in the Middle East have all these. That made them contenders for regional power and therefore threats potentially to US strategic interests in the area. So, at the time of the Iran-Iraq war, the US made a decision to support Iraq tactically throughout that war by providing it with military assistance, both intelligence and weapons, but it wanted to do so to balance the imbalance. Iran was seen as the more dangerous and potentially more powerful of the two. The US wanted the fighting to continue.

Kanan Makiya, an Iraqi, in his book Republic of Fear *describes the internal terror that exists in Iraq under Saddam Hussein.*[11] *Did you have any experience of that?*

DH: I had on the UN team several hundred Iraqi staff. They were excellent people, committed to doing a good job and happy to work for the UN, although they felt uncomfortable in many respects in so doing. There was an element that they might be seen as disloyal to the Iraqi regime by serving the UN. I know also that many were under pressure to report to the intelligence authorities. So, they kept track of our activities. They were under real pressure. They were caught between their employer, the UN, and the government. So, that is a reality.

Otherwise, you do not come across Iraqis, privately or otherwise, who are very quick to give you their views on Iraq today and what's happening and the regime and Saddam Hussein. That's pretty dangerous. There is an underlying fear that if you're seen talking to foreigners, or they come to your home, you're going to be asked to explain yourself. It's there and they really do have to watch themselves. Despite that, they remain very courteous people. I never received any abuse, verbal or otherwise. I walked through the souk many Friday mornings talking to people going to the teashops, and was always received with courtesy. It's an extraordinary country where even regular Iraqis seem to be able to distinguish quite ably between individuals—whether they're American, British, Irish, whatever—and whatever activities their respective governments are being held responsible for by the same Iraqi people, such as the sanctions, of course, which are paramount in everybody's life and mind every hour of the day.

PB: I think it's important to keep in mind a kind of human rights framework. For twenty years, the Iraqi government denied pretty consistently the civil and political rights of the population. At the same time, the economic and social rights were very well respected. It was a country with a high standard of living, a terrific educational system, the best public health system in the region. Many Iraqis had access to advanced education and to training abroad for advanced degrees. Now, in the context of the sanctions regime, we still have the violations of civil and political rights for many Iraqis. There is no free press. But now they also have no economic and social rights as the result of the sanctions regime imposed by our government. So, the US response to the denial of one kind of human rights is to deny all the other human rights and do nothing about the first denial.

The northern third of Iraq is a "no-fly" zone, primarily a Kurdish so-called safe haven. You've been there. What did you see?

DH: I've been up there many times meeting with the Kurdish leadership, Massoud Barzani and Jalal Talabani, and also working with the technocrats at the two major parties, the Kurdistan Democratic Party and the Patriotic Union of Kurdistan. I advised them to meet with me together when we discussed the oil-for-food program, under which about $500 million every year goes into the three Kurdish governorates. This is a great deal of money anywhere, but perhaps particularly in that environment, where you have 3 million Kurds. We sat down and used this money as best we could, of course for the basic food needs, medical requirements, etc. We also had money in the north for beginning the process of rehabilitation of water systems, sewage systems, access roads and bridges, of schools, even some of the villages that had been destroyed during riotings or the *Anfal* operation, Baghdad's military campaign against the Kurds in northern Iraq, which cleared out many of the Kurdish villages. In the north, we had a flexibility we did not have in the rest of Iraq. We ran the program ourselves in the UN. We had a cash component that allowed us to employ Kurdish Iraqi contractors to take on the tasks of building schools, villages, and access roads. So, it was a very useful program doing a lot of very good work for the Kurdish population of the northern three governorates.

PB: I think we have to point out that the so-called no-fly zone in the Kurdish area is only partly a "no-fly" zone. The only planes that are not allowed to fly there are Iraqi planes. Just in the last few days what we've been seeing is major incursions both on the ground and in the air from Turkey into Iraqi Kurdistan carrying out bombing campaigns. The US has said nothing about this. Apparently the killing of Iraqi Kurds by Turkish planes is not considered a violation of the "no-fly" zone. So, this is a very limited definition of what *no-fly* really means.

It seems that the US in its foreign policy formulation has clearly identified Iraqi Kurds as good Kurds. We like them. We support them. We will protect them. But their brethren right across the border in Turkey have come under a different set of criteria. What's going on there?

PB: I think that the view of the US about who's a good Kurd and who's a bad Kurd is something that is determined less by the Kurds themselves than by the government under which they're forced to live. Kurdistan itself is divided between the authorities of Iran, Iraq, Syria, and Turkey. The Turkish Kurds, who are oppressed as Kurds far worse than the Iraqi Kurds or the Kurds anywhere else, are not allowed to use their own language in broadcasts and are not allowed to teach in Kurdish in the schools. It's a terribly repressive environment. But they are considered bad Kurds because their government, Turkey, however repressive, is an ally of the United States.

DH: The Kurds have found repeatedly in the last several hundred years that they are abused and misused as it suits other forces. So, for example, when Henry Kissinger and Richard Nixon were in Tehran talking to the shah, the shah very quickly changed his position on the Kurds and pulled the rug out entirely. The Kurds have been abused by the US as recently as 1991, when they were given all sorts of indications of military support if they were to rise up against Saddam Hussein, who was vulnerable after the Gulf War. When they did that and took an incredible risk, there was no support. George Bush backed down. The promises were empty. In fact, the CIA and other forces were withdrawn and the Kurds were very badly damaged by the Iraqi forces who remained armed, thanks to the Norman Schwarzkopf policy. His failure to prohibit helicopter gunships resulted in the Kurds being massacred in very large numbers.[12] That's a real tragedy. So, today, to see the US still interfering in that part of the world, in combination with the Turks, and with Israel, is a very unfortunate development. I think the Kurds really deserve much better.

You've used the term genocide *in reference to the sanctions. It's really a loaded term. Don't you feel that you're stretching the bounds by using it?*

DH: I began to use that word recently, the first time in Paris. It was picked up by *Le Monde* and Reuters and others. Some feel that it is indeed the wrong word. Few are able to give me a better word.

It certainly is a valid word in my view when you have a situation where we see thousands of deaths per month, a possible total of 1 million to 1.5 million over the last nine years. If that is not genocide, then I don't know quite what is.

There's no better word I can think of. Genocide is taking place right now, every day, in Iraq's cities. To say it's a passive thing is not correct. It's an active policy of continuing sanctions. The member states know full well what they're doing and what the impact is. To hide behind Saddam Hussein is a cop-out. It's not acceptable to me. We have got to take responsibility, we the Europeans, the North Americans, the members of the Security Council. It's our responsibility.

As you travel around the country and meet different groups, how do you know that you're not just talking to people who already agree with you? What about getting to the larger mass of Americans?

DH: There's no doubt we are singing to the choir. But the fact is, the choir has contacts, and every choir member has twenty friends and they have friends. The word gets around. I'm optimistic that if the American people were better informed as to the implications of Washington policy, they would stand up. And they will stand up, and there will be change. I'm pretty impressed by what I've seen in our speaking engagements.

PB: I would just say that the audience for this issue is potentially much bigger than the current one. There are many progressive people whose instincts are exactly in the right place. They think there's something wrong with sanctions, but don't necessarily have easy access or all the information they need to convince and win over other people they meet in their workplace, their factory, their school, in the street, in the church. We've had lots of questions from people who make clear that they don't have access to this information and they desperately want it. That's the beginning of this sea change that we're talking about as this issue is coming back to the top of the agenda.

There's a range of work going on. It's a very exciting time to get involved.

Interview conducted February 20, 1999, Denver, Colorado

Notes

1 John Davison and Andrew Marshall, "Bombs Aim to Topple Dictator," *The Independent,* December 20, 1998, p. 3.
2 United Nations Development Report, *Human Development Report 1999* (New York: Oxford UP, 1999), Table 8 ("Progress in Survival"), p. 170.
3 Colum Lynch, "US Used UN to Spy on Iraq, Aides Say," *Boston Globe,* January 6, 1999, p. A1, and Barton Gellman, "US Spied on Iraqi Military Via UN," *Washington Post,* March 2, 1999, p. A1.
4 See Article 14 of UN Security Council Resolution 687. All UN resolutions are available online at http://www.un.org.
5 Karl Vick, "Man Gets Hands on Bubonic Plague Germ, But That's No Crime," *Washington Post,* December 30, 1995, p. D1; Associated Press, "Report Links Gulf War Expert to US Supplier of Germs to Iraq," *New York Times,* November 28, 1996, p. A19; and William Blum, "Anthrax for Export," *The Progressive* 62: 4 (April 1998): 18–20.
6 See Clovis Maksoud, "The Arab World in the 'New World Order,'" in *Beyond the Storm: A Gulf Crisis Reader,* ed. Phyllis Bennis and Michel Moushabeck (New York: Olive Branch Press, 1991), pp. 173–80, and John Kifner, "Arabs to Convene on Iraqi Invasion," *New York Times,* August 4, 1990, p. 5.
7 Leonard Doyle, "Soviet Peace Plan Dies a Quiet Death," *The Independent,* February 24, 1991, p. 3.
8 Thomas L. Friedman, "How US Won Support to Use Mideast Forces," *New York Times,* December 2, 1990, p. 1: 1.
9 US Department of State, Bureau of Near Eastern Affairs, "Background Notes: Yemen, November 1995." Available online at http://www.state.gov. Interview with Ambassador Abdallah Saleh al-Ashtal, February 21, 2000.
10 David Hoffman, "Bush Policy Requires Global Tradeoffs," *Washington Post,* November 29, 1990, p. A1, and Editorial, "Buying Beijing's Vote," *Boston Globe,* December 4, 1990, p. 18.
11 Kanan Makiya, *Republic of Fear: The Politics of Modern Iraq,* updated ed. (Berkeley: University of California Press, 1998).
12 See Michel Moushabeck, "Iraq: Years of Turbulence," in Bennis and Moushabeck, ed., *Beyond the Storm,* pp. 31–32; Charles Glass, "The Emperors of Enforcement," *New Statesman* 127/4373 (February 20, 1998): 14–15; Faleh 'abd al-Jabbar, "Why the Uprising Failed," in *Iraq Since the Gulf War: Prospects for Democracy,* ed. Fran Hazelton, for the Committee Against Repression and for Democratic Rights in Iraq (CARDRI) (London: Zed Press, 1994), pp. 97–117; and Peter Jennings, "Showdown with Saddam," ABC, *News Saturday Night,* February 7, 1998. See also references cited by Noam Chomsky in Chapter 3, note 9.

Chapter 3

US Iraq Policy

Motives and Consequences

Noam Chomsky

There is a reasonable way to proceed to find out what the motives are for US Iraq policy. We can run through possibilities and see if some of them can be excluded. The one that immediately comes to mind, and the first one to pay attention to, is the one that is universally and vociferously expressed and never questioned. Let's just take one example, a *Boston Globe* editorial titled "A Just Attack." According to the *Globe,* Saddam Hussein is "a vengeful despot who has already used [chemical and biological] weapons on his own citizens," which is the "ultimate" horror.[1] Obviously, such a creature has to be destroyed. He poses an enormous threat. He can't be tolerated. So, you bomb him. You impose sanctions. That's essentially the universal explanation.

That justification does have at least one merit: it's very easily tested. You simply have to ask: what was the US-British reaction when Saddam Hussein used chemical weapons against his own people? And he certainly did. There's no doubt that he is a vengeful despot who has used chemical weapons against his own people. That's undoubtedly true. In 1988, he carried out a major gassing campaign against Kurds. He also used nerve gas and other chemical weapons in the war against Iran that was just finishing up at that time. In fact, the use of it increased toward the end. So, it happened. And there was a reaction on the part of the US and Britain. The reaction was that the US and Britain increased support for their favorite monster. They had been supporting Hussein avidly right through his worst crimes; after the gassing, they increased the support. It's not a secret. We can easily discover it.

How did they increase support? In some interesting ways. The US had been providing Iraq with all kinds of aid, but particularly at that point, the Reagan and Bush administrations increased subsidized food aid. Iraq had been an agricultural producer, one of the few countries in the region that was actually an efficient producer of food. So, what did they need US agricultural exports for? A lot of that's connected with the gassing of Kurds. Saddam Hussein, the vengeful despot, was destroying agricultural areas and the people who lived in them, so there was actually a food shortage. Therefore, we had to come to the rescue, to help out with this project of gassing Kurds in the north. And we did, by increasing the subsidized agricultural exports to Iraq, essentially for that reason. This continued. So, during the invasion of Panama in December 1989, George Bush took a moment to announce that we were going to increase the credits to Iraq to allow it to make purchases from US agricultural and other producers.[2]

Let's forget the small thing about increasing US exports, meaning increasing the profits for agribusiness and high technology industry. At that time, the line was that we were in a better position to deal with Iraqi human rights issues if we subsidized Hussein. A year later, it turned out that we were in a better position to deal with human rights issues if we starved the Iraqi people into submission. Somehow you're not supposed to notice that the line changed for some reason.

Madeleine Albright was asked on national television in 1996 what she thought about the fact that 500,000 Iraqi children had died as a result of the sanctions. She agreed that this was "a very hard choice," but she said that "we think the price is worth it."[3] So, that's the way in which we deal with Iraqi human rights violations, by killing 500,000 Iraqi children. "We're" willing to pay that price. That's nice to hear.

The subsidies for our favorite killer when he was carrying out the "ultimate" horror were not restricted to subsidized agricultural exports. They also included technical equipment, dual-use equipment that could be used for military purposes (helicopters, for example), and a lot of equipment that could even be used for production of chemical and biological weapons. This was all revealed afterward. At the time, there was suspicion that Saddam Hussein had biological warfare facilities. The US denied it. He was our friend, after all. He wouldn't do that sort of thing. But this was discovered by Charles Glass, a very good journalist who was at that time the Middle East reporter for ABC television. He was able to find high-level Iraqi defectors in London, and from information that he got from them using French commercial satellites, which are certainly nothing like what the Pentagon has, he was able to locate and identify biological warfare facilities. ABC let him run a spot on the news showing biological warfare facilities, including the evidence from a defecting Iraqi general.[4] Then they switched immediately to their Pentagon correspondent, who pooh-poohed the story and said this was nonsense. The story died. Now those same biological warfare facilities are being presented as proof that this reincarnation of Attila the Hun has to be destroyed by massacring his population. You're not supposed to remember that, either.

In April 1990, a group of high-ranking US senators went to Iraq. They met with Hussein in the Kurdish city of Mosul. Remember, the Kurds were the ones who were gassed. The delegation was headed by Robert Dole, who brought the president's greetings to Saddam Hussein. Alan Simpson was in the delegation. He told Hussein that his problems were not with the American government, which had no objections to him.[5]

That brings us to April 1990, already two years after the Halabja massacre. This continues up until the day of the invasion of Kuwait. Overwhelmingly, Saddam Hussein's crimes were committed during that period, and the US supported him all the way through, with a good deal of enthusiasm. So did Britain. That tells us that just by elementary logic the crimes can't be the reason why we have to destroy the monster.

What about the threat posed by Saddam Hussein? That's real. That threat peaked in the late 1980s, thanks to our support. That's the time when he was most threatening and most powerful. There's a measure of how great the threat was. Hussein had attacked Iran, with our support. He was unable to defeat Iran, a country that had just decimated its officer corps and top military at the time of the revolution in 1979 that led to Ayatollah Khomeini. Even with the Iranian military largely decimated, Iraq was unable to defeat them—with the support of the United States, Russia, Britain, Europe, and the Arab states. That gives you a measure of the threat at its peak. Today, in comparison, the Iraqi army is approximately back to where it was when the British established it as a means to suppress the population violently so that the rulers would be able to export oil to the West and ensure that the profits go to the West.

How did the US and Britain react to the threat at its peak? The main reaction was to increase the threat.

Bear in mind that in May 1987, Iraqi missiles struck the US destroyer *Stark*, killing thirty-seven personnel. They got a slap on the wrist, but that's it. That shows you're really committed to somebody. What was the *Stark* doing there? The US Navy at that time was being introduced into the Gulf to back up Iraq and support them in the war against Iran—and, of course, in its war against its own population. That alliance strengthened a year later, in July 1988. The US warship *Vincennes* shot down an Iranian commercial airliner just taking off from an Iranian airport, killing 290 people. The plane was clearly in a commercial air corridor. In fact, the *Vincennes* was in Iranian territorial waters. By that point, Iran recognized the reality. They might be able to fight a war with Iraq, but they could not fight a US-Iraqi alliance, with the US Navy now acting aggressively. The US claims—it's not credible or taken very seriously—that the airliner was mistaken for an Iranian military plane; but it was commonly pointed out that the US was not shooting down low-flying Iraqi planes, which were very visible and indeed were warplanes. Iran recognized that the game was over and essentially capitulated shortly after that.[6] That's the peak of the Iraqi threat, thanks in part to our contribution.

Saddam Hussein, in fact, used his increased power very quickly. Five days after the cease-fire, he turned to another major gas attack against Kurds in the north.[7] I've already described the US reaction. Just put this together, and we've now at least eliminated one candidate for what the motives were, namely the candidate that is universally presented, without question and with great vigor.

There is an event that did change Saddam Hussein from favored friend to "the beast of Baghdad," namely when he invaded Kuwait on August 2, 1990. What about that? Is that why we have to impose the sanctions that are killing people? That's pretty hard to argue. Was that a major crime? Sure. Invading another country is a war crime. It's the thing for which we hanged people at Nuremberg. Is it a serious crime? That's hard to argue. In comparison with the rest of Hussein's criminal record, which we had supported, it's like adding a toothpick to a mountain. Furthermore, it was recognized by the United States not to be a very serious crime. In fact, the great fear of US leaders at the time of the invasion was that Iraq would quickly withdraw, leaving a puppet regime in place, and then all the Arab states would be happy. That was the expectation. It was called the "nightmare scenario."[8]

Then comes February 1991, the Gulf massacre. It ended at the end of the month. Within days, Saddam Hussein turned to the next most serious crimes of his career after the use of chemical warfare against his own citizens. Immediately after the war, there was an uprising in southern Iraq in the Shiite areas, led by rebelling Iraqi generals. This was right under the nose of the US Army, which dominated the whole region. "Stormin'"

Norman Schwarzkopf was sitting there watching it, following orders from Washington. The rebelling generals did not ask for assistance. They asked for access to captured Iraqi equipment. That was supported by Saudi Arabia, which also requested the United States to allow them to at least have access to captured Iraqi equipment. The US refused. In fact, it refused to do anything to deter the vicious Iraqi government response, which was brutal and murderous. The US clearly wanted and had to say that it wanted the revolt to fail. And it failed. It was crushed with extreme violence. Right after that, a revolt took place in the Kurdish areas in the north, and the same story was re-enacted. Until public protest mounted, the Bush administration refused to give any protection to the rebels, in fear that they might succeed—that is, that they might overthrow "the beast of Baghdad." So, immediately after the war was over, the US essentially returned to support for its favorite murderer, as he again carried out really atrocious and vicious acts.[9]

That was too visible to suppress at the time, so there was an official justification for it, which remains today. True, this offended our sensibilities, but it was necessary to maintain something called "stability." To maintain stability we have to keep the "beast of Baghdad" in power, even though he was carrying out huge massacres in the north and the south, with our tacit support. The State Department line, as it was presented by *New York Times* chief diplomatic correspondent Thomas Friedman, was that "the best of all worlds" for the US would be an "iron-fisted Iraqi junta" that would rule Iraq just the way Saddam Hussein had done, but it would be nice if it didn't have Saddam Hussein's name on it, because that is kind of embarrassing. Friedman wrote that this would be "much to the satisfaction of the American allies Turkey and Saudi Arabia," which is probably true.[10] He left out the most striking case, because it's indelicate to mention it; but, as he and every other reporter following the Middle East knew, it would be much to the pleasure of our ally Israel, which is the only country I know of where there was open public support across the spectrum for the crushing of the Kurdish rebellion. The *Jerusalem Post* reported on this.[11] They had their reasons, which were that an independent Kurdish state would create a land corridor between Syria and Iran, which are their enemies. They didn't want this, so they wanted the US to allow Saddam Hussein to crush the Kurds.

Furthermore, during this very same period, the early 1990s, our favorite ally Turkey, which has one of the worst human rights records in the world, was increasing its own murderous attack against the Kurds in southeastern Turkey. As just one measure of that, about 1 million Kurds fled to Diyarbakir, the unofficial Kurdish capital in southeastern Turkey, during those years.[12] Nineteen ninety-four was a peak year in two respects. It was the year in which Turkish terror against the Kurds peaked, and it was the year in which US military aid to Turkey peaked.[13] Those are two things that typically go together. There's a close correlation between terror and violence and US military aid, not only in that region. Somehow that didn't mean that we had to impose sanctions on the people of Turkey, to kill hundreds of thousands of their children. This is good terror, terror carried out by our ally. Therefore, we have to expedite it.

It's plain that there cannot have been any moral or humanitarian motive behind anything that is going on. It cannot be Saddam Hussein's crimes that are motivating US policy in Iraq.

What about the threat of weapons of mass destruction? Again, there are a number of problems. Suppose they're concerned about weapons of mass destruction. Then one question is, how come they weren't concerned in 1988, when the threat was more serious than it is today? A second question has to do with the December 1998 bombing. Part of the justification was to reduce Hussein's capacity to produce weapons of mass destruction. But it was conceded at once that the bombing would have the opposite effect, that the major effect would be to eliminate Unscom inspections, even though the inspection regime is the only thing that has cut back weapons. It's been very successful, and could remain so.

There is indeed a way to eliminate the *capability* of producing weapons of mass destruction, only one way, and that is the Carthaginian solution: you totally destroy the society. If you do that, they won't be able to produce weapons of mass destruction. If you leave an infrastructure, if you leave educational and scientific facilities of any kind, if there's a revenue flow, then you have a capacity to produce weapons of mass destruction. So, the only way to end that capability—we talk about "terminating" it—is to wipe the place out. That's not going to happen, for a simple reason: Iraq is the second-largest oil producer in the world, and it's much too valuable to wipe out. But you can wipe out its population. In fact, it's in a way beneficial to do that. If you look at the history of oil production around the world, you find that it mostly takes place in areas where there aren't many people. Then there's little pressure to stop the profits from going to the people who really should have them: Western oil companies and the US Treasury. So, if the population of Iraq were reduced or marginalized, maybe even reduced to such a level that they're barely functional, then when the time comes—and it will—to bring Iraqi production back on line, they'll be less of an impediment. Iraq will be more like, say, Saudi Arabia, where there's a lot of oil but not many people around pressing for economic development and educational facilities and so on.

Without proceeding further, it seems to me you can eliminate the standard reasons from consideration on pretty elementary grounds. What is left? What is left is what should come to mind at once when anyone mentions the words "Middle East." When you mention those words, what comes to mind is oil. It should come to mind. Back in the 1940s, the US recognized the Arabian Peninsula and the Persian Gulf, in particular Saudi Arabia, to be what they called "a stupendous source of strategic power, and one of the greatest material prizes in world history."[14] That meant our rivals had to be removed. France was essentially kicked out and Britain was to play a secondary role, as long as they were properly obedient, as attack dog. But essentially the US was going to control the region.

So, the US has to control the Middle East. But there's a problem, which is that there are people in the region. They get out of hand and sometimes they want to benefit from their own resources. So, there's constant conflict. At the moment, there's an oil glut. That's one reason why it's beneficial to the US to keep Iraqi oil off the market. The US doesn't want the oil price to go too low. It's always wanted it to stay within a range, not too high because of the harm to US manufacturers, but not too low because that's harmful to the energy producers, which are mostly US-based, and their profits would go down. Temporarily, at least, it's a good idea to keep Iraqi oil off the market because the price would go even lower. The other problem with Iraqi oil is that the inside track on developing Iraqi oil is held currently by France and Russia, not by the US-based majors. We don't want that. So, for the moment at least, keeping Iraqi oil from being developed is a wise project. James Akins, an old oil hand who is the former US ambassador to Saudi Arabia, recently said, as only a semi-joke, that when the price per barrel of oil gets up to $30, Saddam Hussein will turn into Mother Teresa.[15] That captures the point, I think.

The Middle East is a region of a lot of crises and conflicts, many of them related to just this fact. People in the region have never accepted the fact that the profits from their sole resource should go to the West. That leads to all sorts of problems. To maintain control, it's necessary to have brutal regimes around that will suppress their own populations. The family dictatorships in the Gulf are too weak to do that. They have to be kept weak so they'll do what they're told, but they can't count on force to repress their population. There have always been what Melvin Laird, Nixon's secretary of defense, called "cops on the beat," a local police force of tough guys to keep order around the region.[16] That was the main role of Iran as long as it was under the shah. It is the main role of Israel, particularly since 1967. Turkey is another one. Pakistan another. This ring of non-Arab states is supposed to keep order.

You have to bear in mind that the United States and Britain are isolated now internationally and regionally, not only on the issue of Iraq, but also on the issue of Iran. How is the US going to handle this? The US has a comparative advantage in one area: force and violence. In force and violence, it is unparalleled. So, it makes good sense for planners to try to play that hand, shift everything into that arena, and that is exactly what we're seeing. That's what we saw when the US bombed Sudan, for example, destroying its major pharmaceutical plant.[17] It's interesting to notice how little attention was given to that in the United States.

I think that the message was understood by the people to whom it was likely sent, namely people in Saudi Arabia and Iran. Washington is saying, "Look, we're a violent, lawless state and we're going to use force to get what we want." I think that's probably the prime reason for the December 1998 bombing of Iraq, too. The one area where we have overwhelming advantage is in force, and it doesn't matter if the excuses are not credible. It doesn't matter if the effect of the bombing is the opposite of what we claim we're after. "What we say goes"—George Bush's definition of the New World Order while the bombs were dropping in 1991.[18]

I think that also accounts for the very clear and open contempt for international law. That's been pretty dramatic in the case of Iraq. Not that it's anything new, but the flaunting of it is dramatic. There's just no doubt at all that the bombing of Iraq and Sudan are outright violations of the UN Charter—war crimes. It's striking that the issue of whether this violated the UN Charter was barely discussed. It was discussed to some extent in England, and condemned there in the mainstream, but not here. Here there's much more discipline; when the issue was mentioned at all, which was rare, it was dismissed as a kind of technicality. That's important. There's an interesting record of explicit doctrine saying that we are not subject to international law.

In the Clinton years, US contempt for international law has become totally open. Madeleine Albright, when she was UN ambassador, simply told the UN, "We will behave multilaterally when we can and unilaterally when we must."[19] If you don't like it, get lost. In fact, the timing of the

December 1998 bombing was selected to make this very plain. The press reported that the bombing began while the Security Council was in a special session to deal with the issue of Iraq. The members of the Security Council weren't notified prior to the US/UK decision to launch an attack.[20] That's a message of contempt for the UN.

It's quite important for us to decide whether that's the "national persona that we [want to] project," as internal documents put it.[21] Of course, for a rogue state, international law and the UN Charter don't mean anything—especially for a rogue state that's violent and lawless and that's projecting that as its "national persona." That gains particular significance when that rogue state happens to be the most powerful state in the world.

Unless that's reversed, I think you can be pretty confident that there are ugly times ahead, particularly if the anticipated oil crisis in the Middle East becomes reality. The answer to how seriously we take that depends not on what happens in this room, but what happens afterward. That's where the important things will happen. I really urge you to participate.

Based on a talk given January 30, 1999, Cambridge, Massachusetts

Notes

1 Editorial, "A Just Attack," *Boston Globe,* December 17, 1998, p. A30.

2 See Noam Chomsky, *Deterring Democracy,* updated ed. (New York: Hill and Wang, 1992), p. 152, and "'What We Say Goes': The Middle East in the New World Order," in *Collateral Damage: The 'New World Order' at Home and Abroad,* ed. Cynthia Peters (Boston: South End Press, 1992), pp. 61–64 and references; Andrew Cockburn and Patrick Cockburn, *Out of the Ashes: The Resurrection of Saddam Hussein* (New York: HarperCollins, 1999); and Mark Phythian, *Arming Iraq: How the U.S. and Britain Secretly Built Saddam's War Machine* (Boston: Northeastern UP, 1996).

3 Leslie Stahl, "Punishing Saddam," produced by Catherine Olian, CBS, *60 Minutes,* May 12, 1996.

4 Charles Glass, "The Emperors of Enforcement," *New Statesman* 127/4373 (February 20, 1998): 14–15.

5 Peter Pringle, "Bush Plays a Delicate Game with Baghdad," *The Independent,* April 24, 1990, p. 16; Jackson Diehl, "US Maligns Him, Iraqi Tells Senators," *Washington Post,* April 12, 1990, p. A26; Dilip Hiro, *The Longest War: The Iran–Iraq Military Conflict* (New York: Routledge, 1991), pp. 237–240; Miron Rezun, *Saddam Hussein's Gulf War* (Westport, Connecticut: Praeger, 1992), pp. 58f.; and Cockburn and Cockburn, *Out of the Ashes,* p. 245.

6 See Chomsky, "'What We Say Goes,'" in *Collateral Damage,* p. 58.

7 See Saul Bloom, John M. Miller, James Warner, and Philipa Winkler, eds., *Hidden Casualties: Environmental, Health, and Political Consequences of the*

Persian Gulf War (Berkeley: Arms Control Research Center and North Atlantic Books, 1994), p. 335. See also Christopher Walker, "Saddam's Forces Seize Thousands of Kurds," *The Times* (London), March 21, 1991.

8 Editorial, "Hussein's Nightmare Scenario," *Boston Globe,* December 24, 1990, p. 12. See also Chomsky, *Deterring Democracy,* pp. 179–214; Hiro, *The Longest War;* and Michael R. Gordon and Bernard E. Trainor, "How Iraq Escaped to Threaten Kuwait Again," *New York Times,* October 23, 1994, p. 1: 1.

9 See the reports by Charles Glass for ABC News at the time, including *Nightline,* April 18, 1991; *World News Tonight,* April 16, 1991; *Nightline,* April 11, 1991; *World News Tonight,* April 2, 1991; *Nightline,* April 2, 1991; *World News Tonight,* March 29, 1991; *Nightline,* March 29, 1991; *World News Tonight,* March 26, 1991; *Nightline,* March 26, 1991; *World News Tonight,* March 22, 1991; *Weekend Report,* March 16, 1991.

10 Thomas L. Friedman, "A Rising Sense that Iraq's Hussein Must Go," *New York Times,* July 7, 1991, p. 4: 1.

11 See, for example, Moshe Zak, "Israel and the Kurdish Minefield," *Jerusalem Post,* April 4, 1991. For more from the Hebrew Press, see the afterword to Chomsky, *Deterring Democracy*, pp. 407–40.

12 Jonathan C. Randal, *After Such Knowledge, What Forgiveness? My Encounters with Kurdistan* (Boulder: Westview Press, 1999), p. 268. See also Human Rights Watch, *Forced Displacement of Ethnic Kurds from Southeastern Turkey* (October 1994) and *Weapons Transfers and Violations of Laws of War in Turkey* (November 1995); David McDowall, *The Destruction of Villages in South-East Turkey* (London: Medico International and Kurdish Human Rights Project, June 1996); John Tirman, *Spoils of War: The Human Cost of America's Arms Trade* (New York: Free Press, 1997); and Noam Chomsky, *The New Military Humanism: Lessons from Kosovo* (Monroe, Maine: Common Courage Press, 1999), pp. 52–59 and references.

13 Bruce Clark, "Nato Arms Pour Into Greece and Turkey," *Financial Times,* June 7, 1994, p. 2; Editorial, "America Arms Turkey's Repression," *New York Times,* October 17, 1995, p. A24; and Chomsky, *The New Military Humanism,* pp. 52–59 and references.

14 US State Department (1945), quoted in Joyce and Gabriel Kolko, *The Limits of Power* (New York: Harper and Row, 1972), p. 242. See Noam Chomsky, *Fateful Triangle: The United States, Israel, and the Palestinians,* updated ed. (Cambridge: South End Press Classics, 1999), pp. 17–20.

15 Joel Bleifuss, "Deadly Diplomacy," *In These Times,* February 7, 1999, p. 8.

16 See Chomsky, *Deterring Democracy,* pp. 54–55.

17 See James Risen, "Question of Evidence," *New York Times,* October 27, 1999, p. A1.

18 See Chomsky, "'What We Say Goes,'" in *Collateral Damage,* pp. 49–92.

20 Mark Tran, "US Tells Iraq to Pull Back Troops or Face Air Strikes," *Guardian*, October 17, 1994, p. 20.

20 See Richard Butler, "Iraqi Bombshell," *Talk* 1: 1 (September 1999): 240.

21 See John Diamond, Associated Press, "Military Study Prescribes Irrational, Vindictive Streak in Nuclear Policy," March 1, 1998. For further deatil, see Chomsky, *The New Military Humanism,* pp. 144–47.

Part 2

Myths and Realities

Farmer Karim Ghadar from Mirkey village in northern Iraq looks at his fields, which are suffering the worst drought in living memory. Photo by Nikki van der Gaag (May 28, 1999).

Chapter 4

Collateral Damage

John Pilger

The memories of my journey to Iraq are almost surreal. Beside the road to Baghdad from Jordan lay two bodies: old men in suits, unmarked, their arms stiffly beside them. A taxi rested upside-down beside them. The men had been walking beside the road, each with his meager belongings, which were now scattered among the thornbushes. The taxi's brakes had apparently failed and it had cut them down. Local people came out of the swirling dust and stood beside the bodies: for them, on this, the only road in and out of Iraq, it was a common event.

The road on the Jordan side of the border is one of the most dangerous on earth. It was never meant as an artery, yet it now carries most of Iraq's permissible trade and traffic to the outside world. Two narrow single lanes are dominated by oil tankers, moving in an endless convoy; cars and overladen buses and vans dart in and out in a kind of *danse macabre.* The inevitable carnage provides a gruesome roadside tableau of burnt-out tankers, a bus crushed like a tin can, an official United Nations Mercedes on its side, its once-privileged occupants dead.

Of course, brakes fail on rickety taxis everywhere, but the odds against survival here are shortened to zero. Parts for the older models are now nonexistent, and drivers go through the night and day with little sleep. With the Iraqi dinar worth virtually nothing, they must go back and forth, from Baghdad to Amman, Amman to Baghdad, as frequently and as quickly as possible, just to make enough to live. And when they and their passengers are killed or maimed, they, too, become victims of the most ruthless economic embargo of our time.

The inhumanity and criminal vindictiveness of the "sanctions" struck me one afternoon in Baghdad, in the studio of the great Iraqi sculptor Mohamed Ghani. His latest work is a three-meter figure of a woman, her breasts dry of milk, a child pleading with her for food, the small, frail body merged into her legs. Her face is dark and ill-defined, "a nightmare of sadness and confusion," as he describes it.[1] She is waiting in a line at a closed door. The line is recognizable from every hospital I visited; it is always the same, stretching from the dispensary into the heat outside as people wait for the life-giving drugs that are allowed into Iraq only when the UN sanctions committee feels like it: rather, when the Clinton administration and its sidekick, the Blair government, feel like it.

"The longer we can fool around in the [UN Security] council and keep things static, the better," an American official boasted to the *Washington Post,* explaining Washington's general strategy toward Iraq.[2]

While I was in Iraq, the list of "holds" on humanitarian supplies included eighteen on medical equipment, such as heart and lung machines. Along with water pumps, agricultural supplies, safety and fire-fighting equipment, they were "suspected dual use": Saddam Hussein might also make weapons of mass destruction from wheelbarrows, which were on the list. So was detergent.[3] In hospitals and hotels, there is the inescapable, sickly stench of gasoline, which is used to clean the floors, because detergent is "on hold."

While I was in Iraq, Kofi Annan, normally the most compliant of UN secretary-generals, complained to the Security Council about "holds" amounting to $700 million. These included food, supplies, and equipment that might restore the power grid, the water-treatment plants, and the telephones.[4]

The deliberate bombing of the civilian infrastructure in 1991 returned Iraq, a modern state, to "a pre-industrial age."[5] The strategy was: bomb now, die later. It is the new style of "humanitarian war." The statistics of those who have since died are breathtaking; for this reason, no doubt, they have been consigned to media oblivion.

In May 1996, US Secretary of State Madeleine Albright was asked on the CBS program *60 Minutes* if the death of more than half a million children was a price worth paying. "[W]e think the price is worth it," she replied.[6]

After returning from Iraq, I flew to Washington and interviewed James Rubin, an undersecretary of state who speaks for Madeleine Albright and US policy. Rubin claimed that Albright's words on *60 Minutes* were taken out of context.[7] I had with me the transcript of the program; her statement was clear, and I offered him a copy. "In making policy," he said, "one has to choose between two bad choices ... and unfortunately the effect of sanctions has been more than we would have hoped." He referred me to the "real world" where "real choices have to be made." In mitigation, he added, "Our sense is that, prior to sanctions, there was serious poverty and health problems in Iraq." The clear implication was that the children would have died anyway.

The opposite is of course true. As Unicef has reported, Iraq in 1990 had one of the healthiest and best-educated populations in the world; its child mortality rate was one of the lowest. Today, it is among the highest on earth.[8] Unicef has reported that more than 5,000 children under five have died on average every month in Iraq, in part because of "the prolonged measures imposed by the Security Council and the effects of the [Persian Gulf] war" on the population.[9] Today, foreign visitors cannot escape the sight of children dying. Doctor after doctor wrote in my notebook the names of vital drugs and equipment they needed. These arrive only sporadically and after a long journey through the arcane bureaucracy of the sanctions committee in New York. Doctors are denied even blood bags, even drugs as basic as those that defeat preventable dysentery and preventable tuberculosis, even morphine that allows the terminally ill to die with dignity. "It's like torture," said Dr. Jawad Al-Ali, a cancer specialist. "Maybe we can treat patients 20 percent of the time, but I think that's almost worse than no treatment at all, because it gives people hope, and for many, there is none."[10]

The words of the playwright Arthur Miller come to mind. "Few of us," he wrote, "can easily surrender our belief that society must somehow make sense. The thought that the state has lost its mind and is punishing so many innocent people is intolerable. And so the evidence has to be internally denied."[11]

At the United Nations in New York, this internal denial is as surreal as anything I saw in Iraq. There is a fine, subsidized buffet restaurant not far from where you can read the Universal Declaration of Human Rights, with its rights to liberty and, above all, life. I met Kofi Annan and asked him, "As secretary-general of the United Nations, which is imposing the sanctions on Iraq, what do you say to the parents of the children who are dying?" He replied that the Security Council was considering "smart sanctions." These will "target the leaders," rather than act as "a blunt instrument that impacts on children."[12] He had no details, and none have been forthcoming since, apart from a resolution that offered Iraq a partial suspension of sanctions in return for further weapons inspections, which Saddam Hussein turned down, predictably.[13] Meanwhile, the "blunt instrument ... impacts on children" at the rate of around 150 deaths every day.

Peter van Walsum is the Netherlands' ambassador to the United Nations and the current chair of the sanctions committee of the Security Council. What struck me about this diplomat with life-and-death powers over millions of people half a world away was that, like James Rubin, he seemed to associate Iraq, the civilized society, with Saddam Hussein, the murderer, as if they were one and the same. He also seemed to believe in holding innocent people hostage to the compliance of a dictator over whom they have no control. Such moral and intellectual contortion is common in United Nations Plaza, the State Department, and the Foreign Office in London, as a justification for the "genocidal destruction of a nation," as Denis Halliday described the effects of sanctions after he resigned in protest as the UN humanitarian coordinator in Baghdad.[14]

I had the following conversation with Ambassador van Walsum:

Why should the civilian population, innocent people, be punished for Saddam's crimes?

It's a difficult problem. You should realize that sanctions are one of the curative measures that the Security Council has at its disposal ... and obviously they hurt. They are like a military measure.

But who do they hurt?

Well, this, of course, is the problem ... but with military action, too, you have the eternal problem of collateral damage.

So an entire nation is collateral damage? Is that correct?

No, I am saying that sanctions have [similar] effects.... I ... you see ... you understand, we have to study this further.

Do you believe that people have human rights no matter where they live and under what system?

Yes.

Doesn't that mean that the sanctions you are imposing are violating the human rights of millions of people?

It's also documented the Iraqi regime has committed very serious human rights breaches....

There is no doubt about that. But what's the difference in principle between human rights violations committed by the regime and those caused by your committee?

It's a very complex issue, Mr. Pilger.

What do you say to those who describe sanctions that have caused so many deaths as a "weapon of mass destruction," as lethal as chemical weapons?

I don't think that's a fair comparison.

Aren't the deaths of half a million children mass destruction?

I don't think you can use that argument to convince me.... It is about the invasion of Kuwait in 1990.

Let's say the Netherlands was taken over by a Dutch Saddam Hussein, and sanctions were imposed, and the children of Holland started to die like flies. How would you feel about that?

I don't think that's a very fair question.... We are talking about a situation which was caused by a government that overran its neighbor, and has weapons of mass destruction.

Then why aren't there sanctions on Israel [which] occupies much of Palestine and attacks Lebanon almost every day of the week. Why aren't there sanctions on Turkey, which has displaced 3 million Kurds and caused the deaths of 30,000 Kurds?

Well, there are many countries that do things that we are not happy with. We can't be everywhere. I repeat, it's complex.

How much power does the United States exercise over your committee?

We operate by consensus.

And what if the Americans object?

We don't operate.[15]

On my last night in Iraq, I went to the Rabat Hall in the center of Baghdad to watch the Iraqi National Orchestra rehearse. I had wanted to meet Mohammed Amin Ezzat, the conductor, whose personal tragedy epitomizes the punishment of his people. Because the power supply is so intermittent, Iraqis have been forced to use cheap kerosene lamps for lighting, heating, and cooking; and these frequently explode. This is what happened to Mohammed Amin Ezzat's wife, Jenan, who was engulfed in flames. "It was devastating," he said, "because I saw my wife burn completely before my eyes. I threw myself on her in order to extinguish the flames, but it was no use. She died. I sometimes wish I had died with her."[16]

He stood on his conductor's podium, his badly burned left arm unmoving, the fingers stuck together. The orchestra was rehearsing Tchaikovsky's *Nutcracker Suite,* and there was a strange discord. Reeds were missing from clarinets and strings from violins. "We can't get them from abroad," he said. "Someone has decreed they are not allowed." The musical scores are ragged, like ancient parchment. They cannot get paper. Only two members of the original orchestra are left; the rest have gone abroad. "You cannot blame them," he said. "The suffering in our country is too great. But why has it not been stopped? That is the question for all civilized people to ask."

Notes

1 Author interview, Baghdad, October 13, 1999.

2 Barton Gellman, "UNSCOM Losing Role in Iraqi Arms Drama," *Washington Post,* January 28, 1999, p. A19.

3 UN Office of the Iraq Program, "Status of Humanitarian Contracts Under Phase V as of October 29, 1999." For a current list of holds, see the UN Office of the Iraq Program wesbite: http://www.un.org/Depts/oip/.

4 Kofi Annan, Letter to the President of the Security Council, October 22, 1999 (S/1999/1086), p. 1; and Benon V. Sevan, Annex, Note to the Secretary-General from the Executive Director of the Iraq Program, October 22, 1999 (S/1999/1066), pp. 2–4.

5 Martti Ahtisaari, *The Impact of War on Iraq: Report to the Secretary-General on Humanitarian Needs in Iraq in the Immediate Post-Crisis Environment, March 20, 1991* (Westfield, New Jersey: Open Magazine Pamphlet Series 7, 1991), p. 5.

6 Leslie Stahl, "Punishing Saddam," produced by Catherine Olian, CBS, *60 Minutes,* May 12, 1996.

7 Author interview, Washington, DC, November 29, 1999.

8 See United Nations Development Program, *Human Development Report 1999* (New York and Oxford: Oxford UP, 1999), Table 8, "Progress in Survival," pp. 170–171.

9 Unicef and Government of Iraq Ministry of Health, *Child and Maternal Mortality Survey 1999: Preliminary Report* (Baghdad: Unicef, 1999); Unicef press release, "Iraq Survey Shows 'Humanitarian Emergency,'" August 12, 1999 (Cf/doc/pr/1999/29), p. 2; and Unicef, "Questions and Answers for the Iraq Child Mortality Surveys" (August 1999). Available online at http://www.unicef.org. Unicef estimates that "if the substantial reduction in child mortality throughout Iraq during the 1980s had continued through the 1990s, there would have been half a million fewer deaths of children under-five in the country as a whole during the eight year period 1991 to 1998" (p. 2), or an average of 5,200 preventable under-five deaths per month during this period.

10 Author interview, Baghdad, October 13, 1999.

11 Arthur Miller, "Why I Wrote 'The Crucible': An Artist's Answer to Politics" *New Yorker,* October 21–28, 1996, pp. 163–64.

12 Author interview, New York, December 2, 1999.

13 Waiel Faleh, Associated Press, "Iraq Rejects U.N. Weapons Inspection Plan," *Washington Post,* December 19, 1999, p. A54.

14 Author interview, October 15, 1999.

15 Author interview, New York, December 3, 1999.

16 Author interview, Baghdad, October 24, 1999.

Chapter 5

Myths and Realities Regarding Iraq and Sanctions

Voices in the Wilderness

Myth 1: The sanctions have produced temporary hardship for the Iraqi people but are an effective, nonviolent method of containing Iraq.

Sanctions target the weakest and most vulnerable members of the Iraqi society—the poor, elderly, newborn, sick, and young. Many equate sanctions with violence. The sanctions, coupled with pain inflicted by US and UK military attacks, have reduced Iraq's infrastructure to virtual rubble. Water sanitation plants and hospitals remain in dilapidated condition. Surveys by the United Nation's Children's Fund (Unicef) and the World Health Organization (WHO) note a marked decline in health and nutrition throughout Iraq.[1]

While estimates vary, many independent authorities assert that hundreds of thousands of Iraqi children under five have died since 1990, in part as a result of the sanctions and the effects of the Gulf War. An August 1999 Unicef report found that the under-five mortality rate in Iraq has more than doubled since the imposition of sanctions.[2]

In 1999, the United Nations observed:

> In addition to the scarcity of resources, malnutrition problems also seem to stem from the massive deterioration in basic infrastructure, in particular in the water-supply and waste disposal systems. The most vulnerable groups have been the hardest hit, especially children under five years of age who are being exposed to unhygienic conditions, particularly in urban centers. The World Food Program estimates that access to potable water is currently 50 percent of the 1990 level in urban areas and only 33 percent in rural areas.[3]

The UN sanctions committee, based in New York, continues to deny Iraq billions of dollars worth of computer equipment, spare parts, medical equipment and medicines, books and periodicals, all necessary elements to sustaining human life and society.[4] Agricultural and environmental studies show great devastation, in many cases indicating long-term and possibly irreversible damage.[5]

Others have argued that, from a North American perspective, sanctions are more economically sustainable than military attacks, since sanctions cost the United States less. In fact, hundreds of millions of US tax dollars are spent each year to sustain economic sanctions. Expenses include monitoring Iraqi import-export practices, patrolling the "no-fly" zones, and maintaining an active military presence in the Gulf region.[6]

Sanctions are an insidious form of warfare, and have claimed hundreds of thousands of innocent lives.

Myth 2: Iraq possesses or seeks to build, weapons of mass destruction. If unchecked, and without economic sanctions, Iraq could, and certainly would, threaten its neighbors.

The final report of the UN Special Commission (Unscom) in 1999 stated that Unscom succeeded to a remarkable degree in finding and destroying Iraq's chemical and nuclear weapons programs.[7] There are, however, still unanswered questions regarding Iraq's biological program. What is certain is that no government has produced any hard evidence proving a biological weapons program exists, or if it does, that Saddam Hussein is planning to use biological warfare on his neighbors or the United States.

Hans Blix, head of the United Nations Monitoring, Verification, and Inspection Commission (Unmovic), the new UN weapons inspection agency that has replaced Unscom, has said he "does not accept as fact the US and UK's repeated assertions that Baghdad has used the time to rebuild its weapons of mass destruction," adding, "It would be inappropriate for me to accept and adopt this position, but it would also be naïve of me to conclude that there may be no veracity—of course it is possible, I won't go as far as saying probable."[8]

Scott Ritter, a former chief Unscom weapon's inspector, has also said that, based on his extensive work in Iraq, he sees no evidence that Iraq currently possesses the capability to produce or deploy chemical, biological, or nuclear weapons.[9]

The United States only became concerned with Iraq's military potential in 1990, after the invasion of Kuwait. In fact, the United States supplied Iraq with many of its weapons. The United States and Britain were the major suppliers of chemical and biological weapons to Iraq in the 1980s during the Iran–Iraq War, in which the United States supported both sides with weapons sales.[10]

Moreover, the United States possesses, and keeps on alert, more nuclear weapons than the rest of the world combined. Many Iraqis feel that it is disingenuous of the United States—sitting atop the world's largest nuclear arsenal, refusing to comply with international treaties or allow its weapons programs to be inspected by international experts, and being the only nation in the world ever to drop an atomic bomb—to tell Iraq what weapons it can and cannot possess.[11]

Myth 3: Iraq has acted in violation of UN resolutions, while the United States has not.

While the US singles out Iraq for its failure to comply with UN resolutions and human rights standards, Washington maintains profitable relationships with almost all of Iraq's neighbors. In recent years, the United States supplied Saudi Arabia, Turkey, and Israel with billions of dollars in weapons.[12] The United Nations, Amnesty International, and even the State Department have condemned all of those countries for serious violations of human rights and UN resolutions.

UN Resolution 687, paragraph 14, calls for regional disarmament as the basis for reducing Iraq's arsenal. By arming Iraq's neighbors in the Middle East, the US government is contravening the same UN resolution that it cites to justify continuing the sanctions.[13]

Israel maintained a position of "nuclear ambiguity" until 1986, when a then-technician Mordechai Vanunu exposed photographs and details about Israel's nuclear weapon's program. Vanunu was sentenced to 18 years in high-security prison for treason. The extent of Israel's nuclear capability is still uncertain, but the country is believed to have more than 200 nuclear warheads and has violated scores of UN mandates, yet the US remains silent with regard to this violation of international law.[14]

Myth 4: The Iraqi government has weakened and undermined the UN weapons inspection program, in part by kicking out inspectors in December 1998, thus forcing the United States and United Kingdom to undertake "Operation Desert Fox."

The Iraqi government, knowing that the United States favors Saddam Hussein's ouster and will impose sanctions until a "regime change" occurs, has no incentive to cooperate with the United States or intrusive weapon's inspections. Top US administration officials have said publicly for more than a decade that sanctions will remain intact until Saddam Hussein is out of office, even though this is not stipulated under the UN resolutions enforcing the sanctions.[15]

Unscom director Richard Butler removed inspectors from Iraq prior to the December 1998 bombardment of the country, contrary to what is still commonly—and mistakenly—reported. The US government claims Iraq "threw out" inspectors. In fact, the opposite occurred. According to Butler's own records, his team of weapons inspectors made numerous unimpeded visits the week before the December bombing. On only a few intentionally provocative visits were inspectors prevented from inspecting a site.[16]

Butler himself confirmed that he was in constant communication with the US military the week before the bombing. He often took his cues from Washington. Furthermore, the US government admitted (after an embarrassing *Washington Post* story) that it had been using Unscom to spy on Iraq. Iraq had previously charged Unscom with spying—a claim that had been vehemently denied by the US government.[17] The irony is that Iraq pays for the entire UN operation in Iraq through oil revenues, thus financing UN workers to spy under United States cover.

In the past, efforts at negotiation with Iraq have produced cooperation and an opening for dialogue. Establishment of a clear timetable for ending inspections and recognizing progress made by the Iraqi government would provide clear incentives for future dialogue and compliance.

Myth 5: The Iraqi government is deliberately withholding and stockpiling food and medicine to exacerbate the human suffering for political sympathy and to draw attention to the need to lift sanctions.

The US State Department frequently alleges that Iraq appears to be warehousing and stockpiling medicines, with malicious intent.[18] Yet the United Nations, which heavily monitors the warehousing of medicines, contradicts this view. Tun Myat, the humanitarian coordinator and head of the UN's "oil-for-food" program in Baghdad from 2000–2002, praised Iraqi distribution of essential goods. He told the *New York Times,* "I think the Iraqi food-distribution system is probably second to none that you'll find anywhere in the world. It gets to everybody whom it's supposed to get to in the country."[19]

According to local UN administration and staff, the gaps in delivery that do exist are caused by logistical problems stemming from twelve years of sanctions and lingering Gulf War damage. Periodic UN reports on the humanitarian programs in Iraq list many technical issues that complicate providing medicine and other vital resources to a country of 22 million people. Obstacles to efficient distribution include the low wages of Iraqi warehouses workers, insufficient transport, and the poor condition of Iraqi warehouses in the provinces.

The United Nations conducts frequent inventories of the food and medicine stored in Iraq. Former humanitarian coordinator Hans von Sponeck (who resigned from the post in 2000 in protest against the sanctions) and his deputy, Farid Zarif, have repeatedly called for the "depoliticization" of distribution, arguing that stockpiling is the result of Iraq's damaged infrastructure, rather than malice on the part of the Iraqi government.[20]

In many cases, Iraq must purchase goods from foreign suppliers. Items come in pieces; for example, dental chairs arrive but compressors must be ordered from another company, or syringes arrive but needles take longer to be processed. Moreover, the UN sanctions committee takes longer to approve some orders than others, thus forcing Iraq to keep medicine in storage until the complements are approved.

Temperatures in Iraq during summer often reach 130 degrees Fahrenheit. Air-conditioned trucks are therefore essential for shipping perishable goods, including cancer medication, surgical gloves, and foodstuffs.[21] Yet air-conditioned trucks are practically nonexistent in Iraq, since the sanctions committee has barred them under "dual use" considerations.[22] While it is certainly true that air-conditioned trucks could be used for military purposes, they are also necessary to ship medication.

The infrastructure is so degraded throughout Iraq that medicine and even spare parts are "Band-Aids to a huge problem," according to von Sponeck.[23] "You can give all the food and medicine you want," Says Tun Myat, "but living standards would not improve unless housing, electricity, clean water and sanitation, and other essential services were restored."[24] Reconstructing Iraq's essential infrastructure could cost as much as an estimated $50 to $100 billion.[25]

After allocations are taken out of Iraq's oil revenues to finance Gulf War reparations, UN administrative costs, and other mandated expenses, the amount of money from the oil-for-food program that trickles down to the average person in Iraq is completely insufficient. Prior to May 2002, "[T]he total value of all food, medicines, education, sanitation, agricultural, and infrastructure supplies that have arrived in Iraq has amounted to $175 per person a year, or less than 49 cents a day," according to von Sponeck.[26]

Iraq cannot afford to rebuild its infrastructure under the oil-for-food program or under the new provisions of so-called smart sanctions. Water sanitation facilities, electrical grids, communication lines, and educational resources will remain permanently degraded until the sanctions are lifted.

Myth 6: The Iraqi leadership uses money intended for humanitarian purposes to build palaces and enrich itself.

In the years before the oil-for-food program began, it is important to recall that the Iraqi government was distributing food to its civilian population. The UN Food and Agriculture Organization (FAO) said in 1995 of the Iraqi rationing system that began in September 1990: "The food basket supplied through the rationing system is a life-saving nutritional benefit which also represents a very substantial income subsidy to Iraqi households."[27]

Iraq is pumping almost as much oil today as it did before the Gulf War, but is making less money because of the change in oil prices and the dramatic rise of inflation since 1990. When one considers that three Iraqi dinars could buy $1 in 1990 while today it takes more than 2,000 dinars the difference in purchasing power is significant. Although Iraq is permitted to sell as much oil as it can pump, these funds are not at the discretion of Saddam Hussein, but are kept in a UN escrow account with the Bank of Paris in New York City.

The sanctions, though intended to weaken Iraq's elite ruling class, only strengthen its political hegemony. With Iraq's population decimated by hunger, disease, and fear of US and UK bombs, the development of civil society is hampered, as are hopes for pluralism. Iraq's elite is empowered by a lucrative black market. With the continued devastation caused by sanctions, the Iraqi government can more readily rally popular support and bitterness against the US government.

Myth 7: The distribution in northern Iraq—where the United Nations is most heavily involved—is better than in the south, proving that the Iraqi government is failing to adequately distribute food and medicine to its people.

Sanctions are simply not the same in the north and south of Iraq. Differences in Iraqi mortality rates result from several factors: the Kurdish north has been receiving humanitarian assistance longer than other regions of Iraq; agriculture in the north is better; evading sanctions is easier in the north because its borders are far more porous; the north receives 22 percent more per capita from the oil-for-food program than the south-central region; and the north receives UN-controlled assistance in currency, while the rest of the country receives only commodities.[28] The south also suffered much more direct bombing, including attacks using depleted-uranium tipped bullets, during the Gulf War.

Myth 8: In May 2002, the UN Security Council voted unanimously to adopt "smart sanctions" on Iraq, demonstrating a determination to meet the needs of the Iraqi people.

Resolution 1409 (the "smart sanctions" resolution) is a hollow solution to an urgent humanitarian crisis. US and UK proponents of the resolution claim that by lifting restrictions on Iraq's ability to import civilian goods and focusing narrowly on preventing Iraq from importing or building weapons of mass destruction, the suffering in Iraq will be diminished.

But the change was mostly aimed at winning a public relations battle, not relieving ordinary Iraqis' suffering. "The resolution was intended to blunt any drive to end the sanctions altogether and to deflate criticism that the measures are hurting ordinary Iraqis more than their leader," Somini Sengupta reported in the *New York Times.* "It also seemed part of the diplomatic groundwork the Bush administration is seeking to lay as it presses its case that Mr. Hussein should be removed from power, perhaps by force."[29]

In the words of the *New York Times Magazine*, the UN sanctions were "creating a P.R. nightmare of hungry children," particularly for the US government, "but smart sanctions created the impression of doing something."[30]

Under the proposed smart sanctions, the United States will still be able to use its power in the UN to block essential goods by citing "dual use" concerns, blocking access to items that are badly needed in Iraq but which any modern society could also use in a chemical or biological weapons program.

At the time Resolution 1409 was adopted, $5 billion in contracts were "on hold," largely because of holds placed by the United States in the UN sanctions committee. Still, US and British officials place all of the blame on the Iraqi government. "Under the oil-for-food program it has always been possible to get humanitarian and civilian goods into Iraq, and I think the principal obstacle has been the refusal of the Iraqi regime to spend its own resources for the importation of those items," claims John D. Negroponte, the US permanent representative to the United Nations.[31]

UN workers on the ground in Iraq have a very different perspective, "The [oil-for-food] distribution network is second to none," Adnan Jarra, a UN spokesperson in Iraq, recently told the *Wall Street Journal*. "They [the Iraqis] are very efficient. We have not found anything that went anywhere it was not supposed to."[32]

The Security Council's own humanitarian panel reported in March 1999 that for Iraq to recover, "the oil for food system alone would not suffice and massive investment would be required in a number of key sectors, including oil, energy, agriculture, and sanitation."[33]

This will be impossible under "smart sanctions," which prohibit foreign investment into Iraq's war-damaged infrastructure, guaranteeing the prolonged collapse of the Iraqi economy.

As Hans von Sponeck notes, "Without massive investment to rebuild the war- and embargo-shattered infrastructure, most Iraqi families cannot earn income to purchase the civilian goods promised. Like all previous revisions, 'smart sanctions' leave the root cause of their troubles—strangulation of the civilian economy—unaddressed."[34]

Myth 9: The US and UK fighter planes patrolling the "no-fly" zones are protecting Iraqi minority groups. Since the end of the December 1998 bombing campaign, there has been no "collateral damage" in these regions.

Since the December 1998 bombing campaign against Iraq, US and UK fighter planes have flown thousands of sorties over the northern and southern "no-fly" zones, allegedly to protect northern Kurds and southern

Shiites. They patrol the Iraqi airspace, they say, so that Iraq cannot attack its own people, as it did during the 1980s. While UN resolutions do call for the protection of Iraqi minorities, there is no stipulation for military enforcement of the zones.[35]

According to the UN Office of the Humanitarian Coordinator for Iraq, US and UK planes have killed hundreds of innocent civilians and injured many more.[36] For example, on January 25, 1999, a guided missile killed more than ten people in Basra when it struck a civilian neighborhood. While the Pentagon denies any civilian casualties, eye-witness accounts describe encounters with scores of children and families wounded and killed when bombs missed their targets.[37]

While the US claims to be protecting northern Kurds from the Iraqi government, the US is silent when Turkey flies into Iraq, over the "no-fly" zone, to bomb Kurdish communities, because Turkey is a US ally.[38]

The bombing also complicates the humanitarian efforts of the United Nations. Aid workers have been forced to cancel trips into Kurdish and Shiite regions, and many civilians have been accidentally wounded, further burdening hospitals that are struggling to cope with daunting incidences of illness and preventable diseases.

Myth 10: There is no realistic alternative to the current policy.

The alternative to economic sanctions is termination. Termination combined with capital investment would enable the Iraqi government to rebuild the country's capacity for electric power that is essential for potable water, sanitation, and health care—all of which are required (as in any modern urbanized country) to keep children and adults alive and well. Likewise, capital is needed rebuild all the other sectors of the economy from transportation through agriculture, industry through education and technology.[39]

Any alternative policy would have to take into account the welfare of ordinary Iraqi people, who have suffered dramatically under a failed policy of depravation and violence, not simply the political interests of the United States and its allies.

The US, UK, and UN must offer incentives for Iraq to cooperate with its neighbors. A first step towards such a policy would be the beginning of a "confidence-building process, initially at a low level and behind closed doors, with all protagonists at the table."[40]

The isolation of Iraq, its people, and its economy must be ended to restore this international partner, once so cozy to the United States and other countries when they applauded and actively supported its bloody and tragic war against Iran.

Domestically, Iraq must improve its human rights record dramatically, and institute arrangements for the Kurds to be an integrated and prosperous part of the country's economy. The government must allow the people of Iraq to make their own choices and in due course—and with restoration of Iraqi's standard of living, as well as the elimination of the external focus for Iraqi's anger—opportunities for political change will increase.

The United States and other members of the Security Council must also take partial responsibility for the arming of Iraq in the decades leading up to the Gulf War, as well as the enormous suffering of the Iraqi people since the Gulf War in the name of Iraq's disarmament.

An alternative policy should also be concerned not only with Iraq's acquiring weapons of mass destruction, but with those countries and corporations who seek to arm Iraq—and its many neighbors in the region—for profit. Change in Iraq, to be effective, will need to be linked to broader regional changes.

Myth 11: US and UK plans to attack Iraq have nothing to do with oil interests.

Iraq possesses the world's second largest proven oil reserves, currently estimated at 112.5 billion barrels, about 11 percent of the world total, and its gas fields are immense as well. Many experts believe that Iraq has additional undiscovered oil reserves, which might double the total when serious prospecting resumes, putting Iraq nearly on a par with Saudi Arabia. Iraq's oil is of high quality and it is very inexpensive to produce, making it one of the world's most profitable oil sources. Oil companies hope to gain production rights over these rich fields of Iraqi oil, worth hundreds of billions of dollars. In the view of an industry source it is "a boom waiting to happen."[41]

As rising world demand depletes reserves in most world regions over the next 10 to 15 years, Iraq's oil will gain increasing importance in global energy supplies. According to one industry expert: "There is not an oil company in the world that doesn't have its eye on Iraq."[42]

Geopolitical rivalry among major nations throughout the past century has often turned on control of such key oil resources.[43] Five companies dominate the world oil industry, two US-based, two primarily UK-based, and one primarily based in France.[44] US-based Exxon Mobil looms largest among the world's oil companies and by some yardsticks measures as the world's biggest company. The United States consequently ranks first in the corporate oil sector, with the UK second and France trailing as a distant third.

Considering that the US and the UK act almost alone as sanctions advocates and enforcers, and that they are the headquarters of the world's four largest oil companies, we cannot ignore the possible relationship of sanctions policy with this powerful corporate interest.

US and UK companies long held a three-quarter share in Iraq's oil production, but they lost their position with the 1972 nationalization of the Iraq Petroleum Company.[45] The nationalization, following ten years of increasingly rancorous relations between the companies and the government, rocked the international oil industry, as Iraq sought to gain greater control of its oil resources. After the nationalization, Iraq turned to French companies and the Russian (Soviet) government for funds and partnerships.[46]

Today, the US and UK companies are very keen to regain their former position, which they see as critical to their future leading role in the world oil industry. The US and the UK governments also see control over Iraqi and Gulf oil as essential to their broader military, geostrategic, and economic interests. At the same time, though, other states and oil companies hope to gain a large or even dominant position in Iraq. As de-nationalization sweeps through the oil sector, international companies see Iraq as an extremely attractive potential field of expansion. France and Russia, the longstanding insiders, pose the biggest challenge to future Anglo-American domination, but serious competitors from China, Germany, and Japan also play in the Iraq sweepstakes.[47]

During the 1990s, Russia's Lukoil, China National Petroleum Corporation, and France's TotalFinaElf held contract talks with the government of Iraq over plans to develop Iraqi fields as soon as sanctions are lifted. Lukoil reached an agreement in 1997 to develop Iraq's West Qurna field, while China National signed an agreement for the North Rumailah field in the same year. France's Total at the same time held talks for future development of the fabulous Majnun field.

US and UK companies have been very concerned that their rivals might gain a major long-term advantage in the global oil business. "Iraq possesses huge reserves of oil and gas—reserves I'd love Chevron to have access to," enthused Chevron CEO Kenneth T. Derr in a 1998 speech at the Commonwealth Club of San Francisco, in which he pronounced his strong support for sanctions.[48] Sanctions have kept the rivals at bay, a clear advantage. US-UK companies hope that the regime will eventually collapse, giving them a strong edge over their competitors with a post-Saddam government. As the embargo weakens and Saddam holds on to power, however, stakes in the rivalry rise, since US-UK companies might eventually be shouldered aside. Direct military intervention by the US-UK offers a tempting but dangerous gamble that might put Exxon, Shell, BP, and Chevron in immediate control of the Iraqi oil boom, but at the risk of backlash from a regional political explosion.

In testimony to Congress in 1999, General Anthony C. Zinni, commander in chief of the US Central Command, testified that the Gulf region, with its huge oil reserves, is a "vital interest" of "long standing" for the United States and that the US "must have free access to the region's resources."[49] "Free access," it seems, means both military and economic control of these resources. This has been a major goal of US strategic doctrine ever since the end of World War II. Prior to 1971, Britain (the former colonial power) policed the region and its oil riches. Since then, the United States has deployed ever-larger military forces to assure "free access" through overwhelming armed might.[50]

A looming US war against Iraq is only comprehensible in this light. For all the talk about terrorism, weapons of mass destruction and human rights violations by Saddam Hussein, these are not the core issues driving US policy. Rather, it is "free access" to Iraqi oil and the ultimate control over that oil by US and UK companies that raises the stakes high enough to set US forces on the move and risk the stakes of global empire. As *Investor's Business Daily* notes, if the US were to occupy Iraq, it would not only "gain a central staging base for future [military] operations," but "It would take control of 11 percent of the world's oil reserves, too. That 11 percent would help pay for the occupation" and "could also be leverage against oil-dependent Arab nations—just as the US used cheap oil in the 1980s to bankrupt the USSR."[51]

Notes

1 See Unicef and Government of Iraq Ministry of Health, *Child and Maternal Mortality Survey 1999: Preliminary Report* (Baghdad: Unicef, 1999). Available online at http://www.unicef.org. See also WHO Resource Center, *Health Conditions of the Population in Iraq Since the Gulf Crisis* (Geneva: WHO, 1996). Available online at http://www.who.int.

2 See Unicef press release, "Iraq Survey Shows 'Humanitarian Emergency,'" August 12, 1999 (Cf/doc/pr/1999/29).

3 United Nations, "Report of the Second Panel Pursuant to the Note by the President of the Security Council of 30 January 1999 (S/1999/100), Concerning the Current Humanitarian Situation in Iraq," Annex II, S/1999/356, March 30, 1999, p. 6, article 20.

4 For a list of the holds, see UN Office of the Iraq Program website, http://www.un.org/Depts/oip/.

5 See Dr. Peter L. Pellett, "Sanctions, Food, Nutrition, and Health in Iraq" and Dr. Huda S. Ammash, "Toxic Pollution, the Gulf War, and Sanctions" in this volume for references to several of these studies.

6 The US spent more than $1 billion just to operate its bombing campaign against Iraq in 1999. See Steven Lee Myers, "In Intense But Little-Noticed Fight, Allies Have Bombed Iraq All Year," *New York Times*, August 13, 1999, p. A6. This number has declined only slightly in recent years. See Vernon Loeb, "'No-Fly' Patrols Praised: U.S. Says Effort Pressures Iraq, Yields Intelligence," *Washington Post*, July 26, 2002, p. A23.

7 See Marc Lynch, "Iraq: Why Not Do Nothing?" *Christian Science Monitor*, July 31, 2002, p. 9.

8 See Carola Hoyos, "Iraq Faces Hobson's Choice Over UN Arms Inspections," *Financial Times*, March 7, 2002, p. 20.

9 See Scott Ritter, "The Case for Iraq's Qualitative Disarmament," *Arms Control Today* 30: 5 (June 2000). Available online at http://www.armscontrol.org/act/2000_06/iraqjun.asp.

10 See Andrew Cockburn and Patrick Cockburn, *Out of the Ashes: The Resurrection of Saddam Hussein* (New York: Harper-Collins, 1999); Noam Chomsky, *Deterring Democracy, updated ed.* (New York: Hill and Wang, 1992), p. 152; Dilip Hiro, *The Longest War: The Iran-Iraq Conflict* (New York: Routledge, 1991); and Mark Phythian, *Arming Iraq: How the U.S. and Britain Secretly Built Saddam's War Machine* (Boston: Northeastern UP, 1996).

11 Late in 2002, the US government undermined attempts to establish international inspections of its own biological weapons facilities, worried that "intrusive inspections" and "outside inspectors might find that bioweapon-defense activities undertaken by the United States are in violation of the [biological weapons] treaty." See Editorial, "Germ War Treaty Redux," *Boston Globe*, November 6, 2001, p. A14.

12 In 2000 the US supplied Saudi Arabia with $1.97 billion in weapons, Turkey with $2.3 billion, and Israel with $2.9 billion. See Federation of American Scientists, http://www.fas.org. For more recent examples, see the excellent reports of the Arms Trade Resource Center, available online at http:// www.worldpolicy.org/projects/arms.

13 UN Security Council Resolution 687, paragraph 14. All UN resolutions cited are available online at http://www.un.org.

14 See Suzanne Goldenberg, "Our Son, the Rebel," *Guardian*, June 5, 2002, p. 6; see also Dan Ephron, "Lifting the Veil on How Israelis Got the A-Bomb," *Boston Globe*, November 11, 2001, p. A6. See also Seymour M. Hersh, *The Samson Option: Israel, America, and the Bomb* (Boston: Faber and Faber, 1993), pp. 198–99, and Avner Cohen, *Israel and the Bomb* (New York: Columbia UP, 1998).

15 See, for example, Tim Russert, interview with Madeleine Albright, NBC, *Meet the Press*, January 2, 2000. More recently, Secretary of Defense Donald Rumseld explained, "The United States government, for a number of years now, has believed that the solution in Iraq would be regime change." See Department of Defense, "Secretary [Donald] Rumsfeld's Media Availability at Kuwait City International Airport," June 10, 2002.

16 See Richard Butler, "Iraqi Bombshell," *Talk* 1:1 (September 1999): 240. See also Mark Huband, "Misery and Malnutrition Form Bedrock of Iraq's New National Character," *Financial Times*, March 21, 1998, p. 4, on Iraqi compliance with Unscom inspections.

17 Barton Gellman, "US Spied on Iraqi Military Via UN," *Washington Post*, March 2, 1999, p. A1.

18 See, for example, US Department of State, *Saddam Hussein's Iraq* (September 1999). Available online at http://www.usia.gov/regional/nea/nea.htm.

19 See Christopher S. Wren, "Iraq Poverty Said to Undermine Food Program," *New York Times*, October 20, 2000, p.16.

20 See Washington Physicians for Social Responsibility, interview with Hans von Sponeck, Baghdad, April 5, 1999 (http://www.wpsr.org), and Stephen Kinzer, "Smart Bombs, Dumb Sanctions," *New York Times*, January 3, 1999, p. 4: 4.

21 Washington Physicians for Social Responsibility, interview with Hans von Sponeck, Baghdad, April 5, 1999.

22 For a list of the holds, see UN Office of the Iraq Program website, http://www.un.org/Depts/oip/.

23 Washington Physicians for Social Responsibility, interview with Hans von Sponeck, Baghdad, April 5, 1999.

24 See Wren, "Iraq Poverty Said to Undermine Food Program," p.16.

25 See The Economist Intelligence Unit, "Iraq Country Outlook," *Country View*, July 13, 2000.

26 Hans von Sponeck, "Too Much Collateral Damage: 'Smart Sanctions' Hurt Innocent Iraqis," *Toronto Globe and Mail*, July 2, 2002.

27 UN Food and Agriculture Organization Technical Cooperation Program, *Evaluation of Food and Nutrition Situation in Iraq* (Rome: FAO, 1995), p. 8.

28 See Unicef press release, "Iraq Survey Shows 'Humanitarian Emergency,'" August 12, 1999 (Cf/doc/pr/1999/29). See also Pellett, "Sanctions, Food, Nutrition, and Health in Iraq."

29 Somini Sengupta, "U.N. Broadens List of Products Iraq Can Import," *New York Times*, May 15, 2002, p. A1.

30 Bill Keller, "Sunshine Warrior," *New York Times Magazine*, September 22, 2002, 6: 48ff.

31 John D. Negroponte, "UN Votes New Export Control Regime for Iraq," U.S. Department of State Press Release, May 14, 2002 (http://usinfo.state.gov/regional/nea/iraq/text/0514ngpt.htm). See also Reuters, "Russia Delays U.N. Vote on Iraq Penalties," *New York Times*, May 10, 2002, p. A14.

32 Hugh Pope, "Iraq's Economy Shows More Vitality," *Wall Street Journal*, May 2, 2002, p. A12.

33 See Campaign Against Sanctions on Iraq, "CASI Disappointed at 'Mirage' of Smart Sanctions," Press Release, May 15, 2002 (http://www.cam.ac.uk/societies/casi/briefing/prscr1409.html).

34 Hans von Sponeck, "Too Much Collateral Damage: 'Smart Sanctions' Hurt Innocent Iraqis," *Toronto Globe and Mail*, July 2, 2002.

35 See Steven Lee Myers, "US Jets Strike 2 Iraqi Missile Sites 30 Miles Outside Baghdad," *New York Times*, February 25, 1999, p. A7, for a rare admission that "In fact, no United Nations resolutions created the restricted zones."

36 UN Security Section/UN Office of the Humanitarian Coordinator for Iraq, Air Strikes in Iraq: 28 December 1998-31 May 1999 (Baghdad, UNOHCI, 1999), pp. 1-12. By the time von Sponeck had resigned in October 2000, his independent investigation had found 144 people killed and 446 people injured in less than one year.

37 Vijay Joshi, "Iraq Says American Attack Kills 11," Associated Press, January 26, 1999.

38 See Thomas E. Ricks, "Containing Iraq: A Forgotten War; As U.S. Tactics Are Softened, Questions About Mission Arise," *Washington Post*, October 25, 2000, p.A1; see also FAIR Action Alert, "*New York Times* on Iraq Airstrikes: Zero Dissent Allowed," February 23, 2001.

39 Washington Physicians for Social Responsibility, interview with Hans von Sponeck, Baghdad, April 5, 1999.

40 H.C. von Sponeck, "Iraq: International Sanctions and What Next?," *Middle East Policy Journal*, October 4, 2000.

41 Dan Morgan, David B. Ottaway, and Ken Bredemeier, "In Iraqi War Scenario, Oil Is Key Issue: U.S. Drillers Eye Huge Petroleum Pool," Washington Post, September 15, 2002, p. A1. See also, conversation on June 5, 2002, with the the authors of Global Policy Forum et al., *Iraq Sanctions: Humanitarian Implications and Options for the Future* (http://www.globalpolicy.org/security/sanction/iraq1/2002/paper.htm). This section of "Myths and Realities of Sanctions" was primarily based on James A. Paul, "Iraq: The Struggle for Oil," August 2002 (http://www.globalpolicy.org/security/oil/2002/08jim.htm), used with the kind permisssion of the author. Paul is the executive eirector of the Global Policy Forum (www.globalpolicy.org/).

42 See above.

43 See, for example, Daniel Yergin, *The Prize: The Epic Quest for Oil, Money, and Power* (New York: Touchstone Books, 1993).

44 In order of size these firms are: Exxon Mobil, Royal Dutch-Shell, British Petroleum-Amoco, Chevron-Texaco, and TotalFinaElf. Royal Dutch Shell is often described as a British-Dutch company, while TotalElfFina is sometimes described as a French-Italian company.

45 Major shareholders in IPC were: Shell, BP, Esso (later Exxon), Mobil, and CFP, the French national company.

46 For an account of this period, see Joe Stork, *Middle East Oil and the Energy Crisis* (New York: Monthly Review Press, 1975), pp. 188–94. Since 1918, France had considered Iraq to be its main source of international oil reserves and its main means to gain parity with the Anglo-American companies (see Yergin, *The Prize,* pp. 188–91).

47 See Michael Tanzer, "Oil and Military Power in the Middle East and the Crimean Sea Region," *The Black World Today*, February 28 and March 6, 2002 (athena.tbwt.com/content/article.asp?articleid=61 and athena.tbwt.com/content/article.asp?articleid=104).

48 Kenneth T. Derr, "Engagement - A Better Alternative," speech to the Commonwealth Club of California, San Francisco, California, November 5, 1998 (www.chevrontexaco.com/news/archive/chevron_speech/1998/98-11-05.asp). At the time, Condoleezza Rice, currently US national security adviser, was a board member of Chevron and one of the company's supertankers was named after her. Though it is tempting to insist on the many oil and energy industry connections of the Bush administration, including the President and Vice President Cheney, oil issues have consistently had a heavy influence on US foreign policy, regardless of party or personalities.

49 Testimony to the Senate Armed Services Committee, April 13, 1999.

50 See Michael T. Klare, *Resource Wars: The New Landscape of Global Conflict* (New York: Henry Holt, 2001), especially chapter 3, "Oil Conflict in the Persian Gulf," pp. 51–80.

51 Brian Mitchell, "U.S. Strategy In Middle East Goes Way Beyond Just Iraq," *Investor's Business Daily,* September 20, 2002, p.A16.

Chapter 6

The Media's Deadly Spin on Iraq

Ali Abunimah and Rania Masri

Twelve years after the beginning of the Gulf War and the imposition of UN sanctions, Iraq remains a major focus of US and world media. Media coverage of Iraq in the United States and United Kingdom still overwhelmingly ignores the devastating effect of United Nations sanctions and bombing on civilians; provides skewed reporting of major issues, such as weapons inspections; and focuses almost exclusively on the opinions of those aligned with US policy. Due to the overwhelming amount of reportage on Iraq since 1990, in this chapter, we focus on two recent periods of Iraq coverage to illustrate some of the more general phenomena we have observed: the first period is the week of December 15–22, 1998, during which the United States and Britain staged a major attack on Iraq, launching approximately 400 cruise missiles and 600 bombs; the second is the period from August 1, 1999, until October 1, 1999. The latter period covered both the August 12 publication of a major Unicef report on the effects of sanctions and the visit later that month of a delegation of congressional staffers to Iraq.[1]

For the purposes of this new edition of *Iraq Under Siege*, we have added examples from more recent coverage of Iraq. Unfortunately, these examples underscore our basic arguments here, with jingoistic and distorted coverage particularly in evidence as the US prepares for a possible ground invasion of Iraq.

The purpose of this chapter is not to quantify definitively coverage of Iraq, but rather to point out some major themes and tactics used by the media to distort the situation in Iraq and the US and UK governments' role in Iraq and the Middle East. Our main purpose is to equip the reader to become a more analytical "consumer" of news. We will note some positive trends that were in evidence in 1999—now on the wane in the aftermath of September 11 and the "war on terrorism"—and suggest strategies for activists to use in advocating for fair and truthful coverage of Iraq.

Although we could have adopted different strategies, we decided to focus our attention on the coverage of those issues that are of most concern to activists: the effect of sanctions and the fate of the Iraqi people. We also make some general observations about the coverage of military and political aspects of the situation.

Others have documented and analyzed the United States government's manipulation of the media, and the media's compliance with those efforts during the Gulf War, so we focus principally on more recent events.[2]

However, it is worth noting that portrayals of Iraq continue to reflect the US media's routine misrepresentation and denigration of Arab and Muslim culture. Popular culture routinely portrays Arabs as terrorists and purveyors of violence. These simplistic and distorted images both reinforce and are reinforced by images of Iraq.[3] Edward Said and others have explored the relationship between representations of Arabs and Muslims, government policy, and the media.[4]

Six deadly media sins

We categorized six major tendencies in the media coverage of Iraq that observers and activists should look out for, beyond the obvious problem of presenting false information and the general tendency of the media to neglect serious, in-depth analysis of events:

- Ignoring or downplaying the effects of UN sanctions on the Iraqi people
- Ignoring or discrediting reports of civilian victims from bombing
- Personifying Iraq as Saddam Hussein
- Speaking with the voice of the government
- Creating an artificial "balance" in coverage
- Using a narrow selection of "experts."

In the sections below, we discuss each of these in turn.

Our sources

Using the comprehensive Lexis-Nexis database, we searched for the key word "Iraq" in the two periods we examined. In the December period, we found more than 1,000 items in major newspapers. For the August period, we retrieved more than 800. Searching within these results for the keywords "civilian *or* civilians" yielded only seventy-eight articles in the December bombing period. Searching within the August to October period, the keywords "sanctions *and* Unicef" yielded only seventeen articles. We also reviewed transcripts of ABC, CBS, CNN, NBC, and National Public Radio (NPR) during the August period. These networks had a combined total of fifty-three reports that mentioned Iraq. Only NPR and CNN, however, had any reports about the effects of UN sanctions (one and two respectively). National Public Radio also featured Iraq in its *Talk of the Nation* program, with one of the authors, Rania Masri, as an on-air guest.[5] While we focused our attention on these two periods, we drew on examples from other periods to illustrate our observations.

Ignoring or downplaying the effects of UN sanctions on the Iraqi people

The tendency to discredit reports documenting the suffering caused by the sanctions continues to be a principal feature of American and British media coverage of Iraq. Most of the time, such reports are simply ignored. The large body of evidence from UN agencies and independent international human rights organizations since the start of the sanctions has been barely mentioned in the mainstream media. The release of the 1999 Unicef report—the first comprehensive, countrywide survey since 1991 of child and maternal mortality in Iraq—did little to affect this pattern.

In the two months following the publication of this report, 810 items in major newspapers included the word "Iraq," according to Lexis-Nexis, but only seventeen of them also mentioned "sanctions" and "Unicef."

The CBS and NBC television networks ignored the report completely. Perhaps more egregiously, on August 16, four days after the release of the Unicef survey, ABC's *World News Tonight* with Peter Jennings broadcast a report on life in Baghdad. The report completely ignored the Unicef findings, choosing instead to present a lighthearted account of the increased sale of wristwatches in Baghdad's street markets.[6] NPR's main news magazines did not report on the Unicef findings until September 22, more than a month after their publication.[7]

When the 1999 Unicef report was discussed, reporters generally cast doubt on its conclusion that sanctions were largely responsible for a doubling of childhood mortality by placing the blame on the Iraqi government instead of the sanctions policy. Statements, such as one in *The Independent* (London) that a "report by the UN Children's Fund (Unicef) said that in the south and centre of the country, *controlled by Saddam Hussein,* the death rate for children under five rose from 56 per 1,000 live births in the period 1984–89 to 131 per 1,000 in the last five years," implied that the deaths resulted from Hussein's control over the area.[8] The Unicef report, however, does not make this claim.[9]

One example of such manipulation of the Unicef study was the *Washington Post* editorial "The Suffering of Children," which stated:

> Saddam Hussein is not the first to use the suffering of children as an instrument of war, but he is surely distinctive in his manipulation of the suffering of his country's own children. His evident purpose in exploiting Iraq's most vulnerable citizens is to advance his campaign against the embargo imposed by the United Nations for his invasion of Kuwait nearly 10 years ago. In this way, he has sacrificed his nation's future in this grisly effort.[10]

The editorial then condemns Iraqi delays in ordering nutritional supplements for children, without mentioning the US and British delays in approving urgently needed humanitarian imports. While expressing outrage at the "suffering of children," the *Post* neglects to mention Unicef's most staggering estimate: 500,000 additional children would have lived had the declining child mortality rates in pre-sanctions Iraq continued.[11]

A *Los Angeles Times* article leaves one with the impression that the United States, not Iraq, is the principal victim of sanctions policy and politics. The article states that "the Clinton administration must decide over the next month whether to do battle with some of its own allies to keep alive a policy aimed at undoing the regime of Iraqi president Saddam Hussein—or compromise in ways that might help a leader who was once compared to Adolf Hitler stay in power."[12]

The Unicef survey is presented merely as one of the obstacles that Washington has to overcome to "sustain its policy and to contain Hussein." The condition and fate of the Iraqi people do not enter into the equation.

Omissions and half-truths are another method used to shift blame for the sanctions policy onto Iraqi shoulders. A *New York Times* article by Barbara Crossette on August 13, 1999, typifies this approach. The headline reads "Children's Death Rates Rising in Iraqi Lands, Unicef Reports," yet the article only briefly mentions the 1999 Unicef report. The rest of the article is filled with unsubstantiated allegations and deceitful statements. In one sentence alone, Crossette presents three demonstrably false statements: "From the beginning of sanctions, President Hussein has been permitted to import food and medicines free of restrictions, but with oil sales blocked, he chose to spend what money was available on lavish palaces and construction projects."[13]

First, stating "from the beginning of sanctions" falsely implies that the sanctions themselves do not in effect limit food and medicine imports. Second, the Iraqi government is not allowed to import food and medicines "free of restrictions." The UN Security Council sanctions committee in New York can arbitrarily reject submitted contracts, as it has done frequently.[14] (The new so-called smart sanctions resolution, UN Resolution 1409, has not changed the fact that essential goods are being kept out of Iraq because they have a potential military "dual use.")

Third, the Iraqi government does not have any "money available" from the oil-for-food deal; all the money is held in a UN-managed escrow account, and transactions are approved by the UN Security Council. Additionally, approximately 25 percent of the oil-for-food money is reserved to pay reparations.[15]

Crossette further states that "since [the oil-for-food deal was implemented], United Nations officials directing the program have said Iraq appears to be warehousing medicines and has not acted on recommendations that more nutritional goods be purchased for children under 5 and lactating mothers." However, leading UN humanitarian officials for Iraq, including former UN humanitarian coordinator Denis Halliday and his successors, Hans von Sponeck and Tun Myat, have substantively challenged this claim.[16] Crossette, paraphrasing then–State Department spokesperson James Rubin, writes that "Iraq is blocking aid available through the oil-for-food program, and ... there is nothing outsiders [can] do." Yet she does not interview von Sponeck, who three weeks earlier told Reuters that, while UN monitoring revealed a "not very satisfactory picture" of distribution in Iraq, "We have no evidence there is a conscious withholding of medicines ordered by the government."[17] (On July 13, 2001, Crossette again reported falsely that "Iraq is now free to spend the rest of the money [after it pays reparations and other UN deductions] on a wide range of imports," while adding, also erroneously, that the "new British-American ["smart sanctions"] plan would have removed remaining restrictions on civilian trade."[18]) Despite the evidence, such claims continue to be repeated. On May 8, 2002, the Associated Press reported, without any challenge, the view of State Department spokesman Richard Boucher that "the restriction and lack of distribution of civilian goods inside Iraq is not due to any outside controls, but rather to the behavior of the Iraqi regime."[19]

The US and UK governments exploited differences in the child mortality rates reported by Unicef, which were lower in the Kurdish-controlled north and higher in the Iraqi government–controlled south-central regions, as "evidence" that the Iraqi government was to blame for the plight of the people. Despite deep flaws in this argument, it generally went unchallenged in the media. Although the Unicef report found the disparity was connected to the more productive agriculture, higher per-capita aid, and significant cross-border trade with Turkey in the north, *The Independent* allowed British Foreign Office minister Geoff Hoon and James Rubin to present their questionable case unchallenged.[20]

Ignoring or discrediting reports of civilian victims from bombing

Of the more than 1,000 newspaper stories about Iraq in the week December 15–22, 1998, only 10 percent made any mention of "civilian casualties." While there are difficulties in determining an exact count of civilian victims, and while Iraq does place restrictions on journalists, few journalists tested the limits of their freedom to investigate the truth.

Because the December bombing was deeply unpopular in much of the world, British and American leaders were very concerned that large numbers of dead Iraqi civilians could tip the balance of opinion. Part of their war propaganda was to convince journalists to ignore or discredit reports of civilian victims. In the midst of the December bombing, British government ministers were reportedly "alarmed by the Iraqi tactic of allowing Western journalists access to hospitals in the city so they can beam emotive television pictures of suffering civilians to audiences at home," and called on British journalists "to exercise greater scepticism" over Iraqi claims about harm to civilians.[21]

Some American journalists required no such admonitions. The *Atlanta Journal Constitution* reported, without providing any countervailing perspective, the views of "defense experts" that "with shrewd use of the news media … the Iraqi president has tightly controlled the world's view of the nightly pounding by American and British missiles." The article continues, "Through such public relations offensives the Iraqi leader has placed blame for the suffering of the Iraqi people on Americans."[22]

On December 19, 1998, the *Los Angeles Times* stated that "the administration's extreme reluctance to risk civilian casualties is very evident."[23] While the government's efforts to suppress or discredit reports of such victims was evident, the *Times* did not offer any evidence for its claim, except assertions from the Pentagon.

Once the bombing stopped, many media outlets noted the difficulty of determining the numbers of civilian victims, but some simply dismissed Iraqi claims out of hand. An editorial in the *Cleveland Plain Dealer,* for example, announced that "a light civilian toll is ... cause for satisfaction."[24]

Few journalists sought out independent observers such as Hans von Sponeck, aid workers, academics, or peace activists who documented some of the effects of the bombing with photographs, firsthand accounts, and even shrapnel recovered from people's homes.

Largely ignored, too, was the disruption the bombing caused to the UN's distribution of food to Iraqi civilians. On December 22, 1998, NPR quoted US Assistant Secretary of State Thomas Pickering as saying that the bombing had caused no such disruption. NPR, like most other US news outlets, ignored statements carried a day earlier in the Associated Press from von Sponeck, who said the bombing had disrupted food distribution and destroyed a warehouse with 2,600 tons of rice.[25]

The US media consistently played up claims that civilians were at little risk because of the "precision" and "accuracy" of the bombing attacks. The *Washington Post,* for instance, noted that "this week, most of the strikes were with precision weapons, while the overwhelming majority made against the [Republican] guard in 1991 used conventional gravity bombs and many missed their targets."[26]

Once the bombing was over, few bothered to report, as the *Guardian* (London) did, that "US naval commanders conceded ... that more than a quarter of the laser-guided bombs dropped by planes from the American aircraft carrier the USS *Enterprise* missed their targets."[27] While much play was made of the Tomahawk cruise missiles' "85 percent accuracy standard," little time was spent on what might have been hit by the 15 percent—about sixty missiles—that may have gone astray, or what civilian targets were "accurately" hit.[28]

Personifying Iraq as Saddam Hussein

The tendency of the United States government and media to demonize foreign leaders has been widely noted. With Iraq, this is particularly insidious, because the habit of many in the media to use "Saddam" and "Iraq" as synonyms obscures the suffering—and even the existence—of more than 22 million Iraqis. While this tendency is common and unsurprising from the mouths of government officials whose purpose is to build public support for their policy, it is also noticeable in an ostensibly "objective" media. This conflation works to obscure the effects not only of sanctions, but of the devastating bombing attacks that have claimed so many civilian lives.

"Once again, the durable despot Saddam Hussein has emerged from the bomb rubble spitting defiance and claiming victory after surviving four days of US and British air strikes," the *San Francisco Chronicle* opened an editorial, taking this phenomenon to sinister extremes.[29] Such statements are particularly pervasive in the broadcast media. NBC's *Today Show* anchor Matt Lauer, for instance, asked a guest why US bombers continue to "target Saddam" in the "no-fly" zones.[30]

In the build up to an invasion and occupation of Iraq, military action has been presented as if it would impact only one person. "With an uncompromising message, Vice President Cheney put the world on notice, that if the administration opts to go to war against Saddam Hussein, it will attack with or without allied support," Campbell Brown reported on August 27, 2002, on *Today*.[31] Fox host Greta Van Susteren similarly asked one guest, retired army Lietenant Colonel Bob Maginnis, "[I]n terms of whether or not we should go to war against Saddam Hussein, what are the questions in your mind that must be answered?"[32]

Speaking with the voice of the government

While some in the media failed to distinguish between Iraq and Saddam Hussein, many also made no distinction between themselves as journalists and the US government. Interviewing a retired Air Force general, NBC's Lauer asked, "If he [Hussein] uses those air defenses against us, don't we automatically target them and take them out?"[33]

On another occasion, Lauer observed that "his anti-aircraft radar is targeting us," and asked, "Should we avoid that.... Should we just let them target us?" Lauer continued, "We initially began to—this whole problem began when he kicked our inspectors, the UN inspectors, out."[34] Contrary to repeated claims in the mainstream media, the Iraqi government did not kick out the Unscom inspectors; the inspectors left under the orders of Unscom's director, Richard Butler. (This line continues to be peddled, even though it has been refuted numerous times. On August 4, 2002, NPR's Linda Wertheimer stated, "It fell to the United Nations to disarm Iraq, but the government of Saddam Hussein never fully cooperated. A year and a half ago, Baghdad threw out the UN weapons inspectors."[35] On August 3, 2002, NPR's senior correspondent Daniel Schorr, said, "If

[Hussein] has secret weapons, he's had four years since he kicked out the inspectors to hide all of them."[36])

On December 16, 1998, the day the "Operation Desert Fox" or the Christmas/Ramadan bombing of Iraq began, NPR senior foreign editor Loren Jenkins used "we" and "the United States" interchangeably during his extensive comments. At one point, he observed, "We almost attacked Iraq last November [1997]." Asked if he thought the imminent attack could be prevented by Iraqi concessions, he said, "I don't think the Iraqis are going to reverse themselves, and I don't think we would believe them if they said they would."[37]

While failing to distinguish between Iraq and its leader obscures and misinforms the public about the situation in Iraq, the use of "we" by journalists in reference to the United States and British governments, and even the United Nations, imposes an artificial consensus that stifles the possibility of debate about alternatives, such as nonviolence, and gives the impression that there is one monolithic Anglo-American viewpoint. It also positions journalists as decision-makers, advocating strategies for punishing Iraq, including the possible occupation of the government, as some advocated as part of Bush's "war on terrorism."[38]

The use of "we" by journalists has been prominent in recent discussions of whether or not the United States government should invade Iraq. "[I]f all of our allies in the Middle East turn against us and don't continue to help us in the war on terrorism, because we decide to invade Iraq, at this particular time, wouldn't that be worse for the United States in the long run?" CNN anchor Carol Costello asked a guest on August 27, 2002.[39] In a remarkable twist on this convention, James Carville protested on *Crossfire,* August 19, 2002, "Are we just going to be doing *Crossfire* four years from now talking about whether or not we should invade Iraq? I mean, when is [President Bush] going to tell us what the hell we should do?"[40]

Creating an artificial "balance" in coverage

Sometimes even an ostensibly "balanced" news item, which reports more than one perspective on an issue, can be severely skewed. Three examples illustrate this clearly:

> Since the 1990–1991 Persian Gulf conflict, which was set off by Iraq's invasion of Kuwait, Baghdad has been the object of wide-ranging international

> sanctions. Iraq says the sanctions are causing vast civilian hardship, but the United States has accused the Government of starving its own people.[41]
>
> President Clinton said today the United States would support a partial suspension of the oil embargo against Iraq if Baghdad would provide detailed information on its weapons of mass destruction. The international oil embargo was imposed after Iraq's invasion of Kuwait in 1990. Baghdad claims the economic sanctions have had a devastating effect on civilians, especially children.[42]
>
> [T]he US and Iraq continue their cat-and-mouse game in the skies over the southern no-fly zone. Officials confirming today that American and British war jets did attack targets on the ground in Iraq earlier this week. Iraq claims that four people were injured in that attack, but one British official says there were no casualties whatsoever.[43]

In each of these examples, an issue of fact is presented as one of two equally credible competing "claims." Left out of the equation is any independent source or evidence on the topic that could support one and undermine the other of the claims. In this case, numerous independent reports and statements about the situation in Iraq are completely unmentioned by the *Times*, NPR, and Fox television in the pieces from which these quotes are taken. Thus, issues of fact about the devastation caused by sanctions are reduced to mere Iraqi "claims." The implication of this is that the reports are disputable or manufactured. This artificial balance allows a reporter to say: "I did my job. I reported both sides."

Artificial balance also appears in the time allotted to differing perspectives by the broadcast media. Again, NPR offers an example. Former UN humanitarian coordinator for Iraq Denis Halliday, for instance, a strong opponent of UN sanctions against Iraq, was invited to "debate" the policy of sanctions with a strong proponent of the policy, Patrick Clawson, from the Washington Institute for Near East Policy (an offshoot of the American Israeli Public Affairs Committee). The January 2, 1999, "debate" on NPR lasted all of six minutes. On January 9, Kenneth Pollack, a defender of sanctions and military intervention against Iraq from the National Defense University, was given a full six minutes all to himself to advance his views.[44] In the intervening period, as well as the following weeks, no critics of sanctions were given a similar opportunity.

While in its day-to-day reporting on Iraq, NPR's main news magazines, *All Things Considered* and *Morning Edition,* consistently ignored the sanctions and focused on military and diplomatic aspects of the conflict, its popular daily call-in show *Talk of the Nation* did occasionally feature Iraq and was generally comprehensive when it did so.[45]

Using a narrow selection of "experts"

During times of crisis, especially periods of intense bombing, such as in December 1998 or during the height of the bombing of Afghanistan in fall 2001, the media tend to rely for analysis on a narrow selection of "experts" composed primarily of retired military men and representatives of often conservative institutions such as the American Enterprise Institute, the pro-Israeli Washington Institute for Near East Policy, and the National Defense University. Opponents of bombing or sanctions, to the extent that they are ever interviewed, are most often portrayed as "outsiders," and generally are interviewed at protests or by telephone.

National Public Radio's coverage of the December 1998 bombing campaign against Iraq was characteristic of this phenomenon. From December 17 to December 22, NPR featured four segments about opposition to the war. One report featured a soundbite from Kathy Kelly of Voices in the Wilderness; another featured one of the present authors, among others; and the other two focused on Arab-American and Muslim-American opinions about the US attack.[46] While it did present an opposition perspective, this coverage amounted to a total of approximately sixteen minutes during a five-day period, presenting opposition to the war as an "outsider" viewpoint. In the same period, NPR ran extensive coverage on Iraq that featured numerous interviews by NPR hosts of "experts," most of whom had military or government backgrounds or were affiliated with conservative think tanks and institutions.[47]

In Tom Gjelten's report on President George W. Bush's first "foreign policy challenge" in Iraq, the selection of "experts" that Gjelten called on stayed safely within the framework of discussing the "options" open to Bush, which boiled down to—bomb or don't bomb Iraq. Gjelten's guests included Avigdor Haselkorn, whom Gjelten introduces only as a "Middle East analyst," without informing listeners that Haselkorn is a right-wing Israeli who has often called for aggressive action against both Iraq and Palestine. The other people quoted or featured in Gjelten's report, in order of appearance were: an unnamed US official; admiral Craig Quigley, a Pentagon spokesman; Charles Duelfer, a former chief UN weapons inspector; another unnamed US official; National Security Adviser Condoleezza Rice; and Daniel Byman of the Rand Corporation.[48]

An increase in positive coverage due to activism

Because so many of the important stories about Iraq are underreported or misreported, the media is a fertile target for activism. Activism by individuals and groups around the country has resulted in some meaningful coverage of Iraq where none would have occurred otherwise. During the December 1998 bombing, many local and regional newspapers carried reports about antiwar protests. Often, these reports were the only place where the views of activists were quoted. Similarly, the national speaking tour by Denis Halliday and Phyllis Bennis in spring 1999 produced a number of positive stories and provided an opportunity for several regional papers to carry op-ed pieces by Halliday and Bennis.[49] The dissenting views of Hans von Sponeck were largely ignored in the post–September 11 discussions of going to war against Iraq until activists campaigned to have his comments reported.[50]

These are examples where activities often organized and hosted by activist groups have increased coverage of Iraq. Direct activism targeting the media can also lead to improvements in coverage. A notable example is an eight-page color insert in the *Seattle Post-Intelligencer,* the result of years of anti-sanctions activists building a relationship with the newspaper's editors. The result has been among the most prominent and comprehensive reporting on the effects of sanctions and war on Iraq in the mainstream media.[51]

While it is possible to show a direct link to activism only anecdotally, we believe that anti-sanctions activism had begun to have an impact on the policy debate and on editorial policies around the United States in the period before the attacks on the Pentagon and World Trade Center—and can now play a critical role in helping turn the tide against the media's drive toward war on Iraq. In the latter half of 1999 alone, editorials or op-ed pieces calling for the lifting or serious reappraisal of economic sanctions appeared in the *San Jose Mercury News, Orange County Register, Los Angeles Times, Dallas Morning News,* and *Christian Science Monitor*.[52]

In an extraordinary editorial, the *Chicago Tribune* asked:

> Would the average American support killing innocent civilians to punish a despicable dictator?
>
> Hardly. Yet that, in starkest terms, has been probably the most notable result of nine years of economic sanctions against Iraq for its deadly invasion of Kuwait in 1990.[53]

Another example of prominent media coverage is the *Houston Chronicle*'s Sunday edition front-page coverage of Iraq on September 12, 1999, which included four extensive stories about daily life in Iraq.[54]

In the current environment, where Muslims are scapegoated as terrorists, Iraqis are demonized, and the media's spin on "smart sanctions" conveys the idea that most (or even all) restrictions on Iraq importing badly needed civilian goods have been lifted, such stories are urgently needed.

Strategies for activism

The experience of the authors of this chapter and other activists suggests that adopting the role of "educator" and "source" toward journalists often yields the most effective results. We have summarized this approach in a brief series of suggested steps to guide media activists.

Step 1: Become an "analyst"

For every report you hear or read, ask: "Whose voices are included, whose are excluded? What would it take to make this report better?" Don't make blanket statements that you can't support. If your local paper has ten bad articles on Iraq and one good one, don't tell them that all their coverage is bad. Rather, be prepared to praise the good piece, contrast it to the bad ones, and use it as a way to illustrate why more good reporting is needed.

Step 2: Learn the battlefield and choose your battles

None of us can read or listen to everything, but you can pick one or two sources and try to monitor them consistently. That way, you can become familiar with reporting patterns over time and even with the work of individual reporters, and build a much stronger case for your arguments. This knowledge will also provide you with a stronger basis to establish a dialogue with the people who you are trying to influence.

Step 3: Know your facts

Use Lexis-Nexis. This is a searchable, easy-to-use, full-text database of thousands of news sources, including major and regional newspapers, magazines, and transcripts of television and radio reportage. It is available free to many university students and faculty through their libraries and at some public libraries. Some universities now make it available over the web to authorized users.

Use wire services. These are "unedited" and contain a lot of information that doesn't make it into the newspapers or news shows.

Use the World Wide Web. The Internet offers ways of learning about and accessing alternative sources of information, though some web sites are more factually reliable and well-documented than others. (See the "Resources" listing.)

Read foreign media. Foreign media, such as the BBC, *Le Monde diplomatique*, the *Times of India*, and European newspapers, often have more accurate coverage of Iraq. Become familiar with them and use them to contrast with US and UK coverage. The work of reporters such as Robert Fisk of *The Independent* in London (see Chapter 7) and journalist and documentary filmmaker John Pilger (see Chapter 4) can regularly be read on the Internet.[55]

Do your research. Be accurate and precise. Don't say something is a fact unless you are sure. If you are not sure, check the source. Lexis-Nexis is an extremely valuable tool for fact-checking. You are always much more effective if you can show you command the facts.

Quote people accurately. Keep a pen and paper near the radio or television. Cite your sources. Remember, your credibility is a valuable asset.

Step 4: Communicate effectively

Before communicating with a journalist or media outlet, decide whether your purpose is to get a letter published or to educate the reporter or editor. If you represent a group, you can ask for a meeting with a newspaper's editorial board. Before going to such a meeting, carefully research the newspaper's editorial policy and reporting on Iraq and be equipped to point to both positive and negative elements.

When communicating with journalists or editors, remember that many reporters feel harried and under pressure. They hear from a lot of people and will easily dismiss you as just another crank unless you communicate effectively and professionally. When writing a letter, do not assume that the reader is as familiar with the subject as you are. Always include relevant information (date, name of reporter, subject), and briefly restate the subject of the report on which you are commenting. If you are writing a letter to the editor for publication, different rules apply: you must be concise and to the point. If the letter is supposed to educate a journalist, then you can afford to make it longer and include more information.

Never give in to frustration, even when you see a very hurtful or inaccurate report. Always address people as if they were colleagues. Often they will respect you and answer you, even if they still disagree with you. This will help to establish a dialogue between you and the editor or reporter.

Journalists are suspicious of "advocates." To avoid being dismissed as an advocate, you should be able to argue factually. You will not be taken seriously unless you can respond thoughtfully to other viewpoints. It is even better if you can anticipate and defuse opposing arguments.

Step 5: Become a source

In our experience, the vast majority of journalists are decent people. They may not be experts on the issue you are interested in, and they rely on the information their sources give them, so it pays to become a source of timely and reliable information and analysis. Provide information in moderate doses. If you bombard a journalist with lengthy emails of articles you find fascinating, he or she is unlikely to read them. Always inform reporters of local events that could educate them about Iraq.

Once you establish a record and some credibility, journalists will begin to turn to you to discuss ideas, or even ask for quotes and interviews. Now you have become a source.

Step 6: Develop networks

Share your letters with interested friends and fellow activists. This will encourage others to follow your example, and will help others to become more critical and astute consumers of news.

Step 7: Be persistent

Media advocacy can be frustrating and hard, but it works and it gets easier. The more expertise you develop and information you gather, the easier it is to respond and shape debate constructively.

Notes

1 See Los Angeles Times Wire Services, "US Congressional Staffers Pay Visit to Iraqi Hospital," *Los Angeles Times,* August 31, 1999, p. A9; and Unicef, *Child and Maternal Mortaliy Survey 1999: Preliminary Report* (Iraq: Unicef, 1999). Hereafter Unicef 1999. Available at http://www.unicef.org.

2 John MacArthur, *Second Front: Censorship and Propaganda in the Gulf War* (Berkeley: University of California Press, 1992); Douglas Kellner, *The Persian Gulf TV War* (Boulder: Westview Press, 1992); Hamid Mowlana, George Gerbner, and Herbert I. Schiller, eds., *Triumph of the Image: The*

Media's War in the Persian Gulf—A Global Perspective (Boulder: Westview Press, 1992).

3 Recent examples include the 1998 Hollywood film *The Siege,* which contained negative portrayals of Arab Americans as terrorists or suspected terrorists; a magazine advertising campaign for a video game called "Gulf War"; and a fall 1999 episode of the NBC drama "West Wing." The video game advertisement features a picture of a bathroom. On the toilet paper holder is the American flag. On the floor is an Arabic-language newspaper. The caption reads: "Hasn't Iraq made a mockery of us long enough?" The NBC program featured a story line in which Syria shoots down a US Air Force passenger jet, killing fifty people and prompting the United States to bomb Syria. The American-Arab Anti-Discrimination Committee protested in an October 7, 1999, letter to NBC that the program incited violence against Arabs, and portrayed an event—the shooting down of an airliner—that has only occurred three times: by the United States, by the Soviet Union, and by Israel (http://www.adc.org/action/1999/7oct99.htm).

4 Edward W. Said, *Covering Islam: How the Media and the Experts Determine How We See the Rest of the World,* revised ed. (New York: Vintage Books, 1997); Jack Shaheen, *The TV Arab* (Bowling Green: Bowling Green State UP, 1984) and *Arab and Muslim Stereotyping* (Washington: Georgetown UP, 1997); Hussein Ibish, "'They Are Absolutely Obsessed with Us': Anti-Arab Bias in American Discourse and Policy," in *Race in Twenty-First Century America*, ed. Curtis Stokes et al. (East Lansing: Michigan State University Press, 2001), pp. 119-42; and Jack G. Shaheen, *Reel Bad Arabs: How Hollywood Vilifies a People* (Northampton, MA: Interlink, 2001).

5 Ray Suarez, interview with Rania Masri and Patrick Clawson, NPR, *Talk of the Nation,* September 1, 1999.

6 "Making Time in Baghdad," ABC, *World News Tonight,* August 16, 1999.

7 Ted Clark, "UN Security Council Takes Up the Matter of Sanctions Imposed on Iraq," NPR, *All Things Considered,* September 22, 1999.

8 Rupert Cornwell and Clare Garner, "Children Pay Price for Blockade," *The Independent*, August 13, 1999, p. 11; emphasis added.

9 Unicef 1999.

10 Editorial, "The Suffering of Children," *Washington Post,* August 17, 1999, p. A14.

11 Unicef, *Child and Maternal Mortality Survey 1999* (Iraq: Unicef, 1999).

12 Robin Wright, "US Nearing Key Juncture in Iraq Policy," *Los Angeles Times*, August 29, 1999, p. A1.

13 Barbara Crossette, "Children's Death Rates Rising in Iraqi Lands, Unicef Reports," *New York Times*, August 13, 1999, p. A6.

14 See, for example, Stephen Kinzer, "Smart Bombs, Dumb Sanctions," *New York Times,* January 3, 1999, p. 4: 4.

15 In addition to the Gulf War reparations, for most of the period of the oil-for-food program, the UN diverted approximately 5 percent for its operations in Iraq; 2 percent to repair and maintain oil pipelines; and 15 percent for humanitarian supplies for 3 million Kurds in northern Iraq (UN Office of the Iraq Program "Oil-for-food—The Basic Facts." Available at http://www.un.org/Depts/oip/reports/basfact.html). The percentages were slightly revised in 2001, allowing a higher percentage to enter the escrow account.

16 See Denis Halliday and Jennifer Horan "A New Policy Needed for Iraq," *Boston Globe,* March 22, 1999, p. A19; and Michael Powell, "The Deaths He Cannot Sanction—Ex-UN Worker Details Harm to Iraqi Children," *Washington Post,* December 17, 1998, p. E1. Additional articles available at http://www.iraqaction.org/denis.html. "I think the Iraqi food-distribution system is probably second to none that you'll find anywhere in the world," Myat said. "It gets to everybody whom it's supposed to get to in the country." He also told the *Times* that (in their words) "living standards would not improve unless housing, electricity, clean water, and sanitation and other essential services were restored." Christopher S. Wren, "Iraq Poverty Said to Undermine Food Program," *New York Times,* October 20, 2000, p. A16.

17 Dominick Evans, "UN Sees British Concern on Iraq Embargo," Reuters, July 22, 1999.

18 Barbara Crossette, "Effort to Recast Iraq Oil Sanctions is Halted For Now," *New York Times,* July 3, 2001, p. A1.

19 Sonya Ross, "UN Security Council Agrees on Sanctions against Iraq, White House Says," Associated Press, May 7, 2002.

20 Rupert Cornwell and Clare Garner, "Children Pay Price for Blockade," *The Independent,* August 13, 1999, p. 11.

21 Jon Hibbs, "Reporters Warned of Lies Over Casualties," *Daily Telegraph,* December 19, 1998, p. 3.

22 Julia Malone, "In War of Words, Saddam May Be Winning," *Atlanta Journal Constitution,* December 20, 1998, p. 1.

23 Paul Richter, "Crisis in the Gulf," *Los Angeles Times,* December 19, 1998, p. A19.

24 Editorial, "Something Gained in Iraq," *Cleveland Plain Dealer,* December 22, 1998, p. 10B.

25 Neal Conan, interview with Thomas Pickering, NPR, *All Things Considered,* December 22, 1998. Leon Barkho, "Humanitarian Program Set Back, 2,600 Tons of Rice Destroyed," Associated Press, December 21, 1998.

26 Barton Gellman and Vernon Loeb, "US Strikes Iraq a Third Night," *Washington Post,* December 19, 1998, p. A1.

27 Richard Norton-Taylor, "Iraq: After the Missiles," *Guardian,* December 22, 1998, p. 4.

28 Dana Priest, "US Commander Unsure of How Long Iraq Will Need to Rebuild," *Washington Post,* December 22, 1998, p. A31.

29 Editorial, "Beyond the Bombing," *San Francisco Chronicle,* December 22, 1998, p. A24.

30 Matt Lauer, interview with Gideon Rose, NBC, *Today Show,* September 1, 1999.

31 Campbell Brown, NBC, *Today,* August 27, 2002.

32 Greta Van Susteren, Fox, *On the Record with Greta Van Susteren,* August 15, 2002.

33 Matt Lauer, interview with Perry Smith, NBC, *Today Show,* December 29, 1998.

34 Matt Lauer, interview with Gideon Rose, NBC, *Today Show,* September 1, 1999.

35 Linda Wertheimer, NPR, *All Things Considered,* August 4, 2000.

36 Daniel Schorr, NPR, *Weekend Edition Saturday,* August 3, 2002.

37 Loren Jenkins, NPR, *Talk of the Nation,* December 16, 1998.

38 See, for example, Richard Lowry, "End Iraq," *National Review* 53:20 (October 15, 2001).

39 Carol Costello, CNN, *CNN Daybreak,* August 27, 2002.

40 James Carville, CNN, *Crossfire,* August 19, 2002.

41 Alan Cowell, "Major Nations Report Progress on Pact to Ease Sanctions on Iraq," *New York Times,* September 16, 1999, p. A6.

42 Linda Wertheimer, NPR, *All Things Considered,* June 17, 1999.

43 Steve Centanni, Fox, *The Big Story with John Gibson,* August 15, 2002.

44 Scott Simon, interview with Kenneth Pollack, NPR, *Weekend Edition Saturday,* January 9, 1999; Daniel Zwerdling, interview with Patrick Clawson and Denis Halliday, NPR, *Weekend All Things Considered,* January 2, 1999.

45 For example, *Talk of the Nation* included Phyllis Bennis on December 17, 1998, and Rania Masri on September 1, 1999.

46 David Welna, "Peace Groups" and "Protests Against the US Air Strikes on Iraq Being Held Across the Country," NPR, *All Things Considered,* December 17, 1998; Andy Bowers, "Islamic Leaders on Iraq," NPR, *Morning Edition,* December 18, 1998; Don Gonyea, "How Arab-Americans Feel About Bombing of Iraq," NPR, *Weekend Edition Saturday,* December 19, 1998.

47 These interviewees included Richard Schultz, Pentagon consultant and Tufts University professor (*Morning Edition,* December 17, 1999); retired US Navy commander Tom Mariner (*Morning Edition,* December 17, 1999); retired US Army colonel Ralph Peters (*Morning Edition,* December 17, 1999); Dean of the Fletcher School of Law and Diplomacy John Galvin, a retired general (*Morning Edition,* December 18, 1999); Adeed Dawisha, professor of international relations at George Mason University (*Saturday Weekend Edition,* December 19, 1999); John Bolton of the American Enterprise Institute (*Weekend All Things Considered,* December 20, 1999); Georges Legelt, a disarmament specialist at the Eris Strategic Studies Institute (*Morning Edition,* December 22, 1999); and retired Air Force general Perry Smith (*All Things Considered,* December 22, 1999).

48 Tom Gjelten, NPR, *All Things Considered,* January 23, 2001.

49 See, for example, Denis Halliday and Phyllis Bennis, "End Iraqi Suffering and Focus on Mideast Arms Glut," *Houston Chroncile,* March 4, 1999, p. A29. See also Chapter 2.

50 See Hans von Sponeck and Denis Halliday, "The Hostage Nation," *The Guardian* (London), November 29, 2001, p. 21; and Tom Heinen, "Use U.N. to Resolve Conflict with Iraq," *Milwaukee Journal Sentinel,* August 1, 2002, p. 2A.

51 Larry Johnson, "Life and Death in Iraq," *Seattle Post-Intelligencer,* May 11, 1999. Available online at www.seattle-pi.com/iraq/. In 1995, Bert Sacks, a Seattle peace activist, decided to talk to news editors about what was happening in Iraq. Sacks, who is now facing a $10,000 government fine for violating the sanctions, had read reports in the *New England Journal of Medicine* and *Lancet* about the impact of the sanctions. Sacks was persistent in telephoning editors and visiting the offices of Seattle's two major newspapers, the *Seattle Times* and *Seattle Post-Intelligencer.* Eventually, a

few of the Seattle foreign desk editors began to pay attention to him. Sacks was probably the first person to tell them about the high mortality rates of children, and he demonstrated credibility for his careful research of the facts. When Sacks traveled with Randall Mullins to Baghdad the next year (Mullins has also been sent notice of a $10,000 fine for transporting material aid to Iraq), a wire service editor at the *Seattle Post-Intelligencer* encouraged the two to call collect from Baghdad to report on their trip. After the *Post-Intelligencer* hired a new foreign desk editor, Larry Johnson, they asked him if he would like to go to Iraq with a photographer and a local delegation led by Gerri Haynes of Physicians for Social Responsibility. Johnson agreed, bringing about the special *Post-Intelligencer* report. Both Seattle papers have covered the activities of local peace activists on Iraq and have published letters to the editor and op-ed pieces on Iraq fairly consistently. (Ruth Wilson contributed to this account.)

52 Editorial, "Silent Slaughter of Children," *San Jose Mercury News,* August 2, 1999, p. 6B; Editorial, "The Forgotten War," *Orange County Register,* August 16, 1999, p. B6; David Cortright and George A. Lopez, "End UN Sanctions Against Iraq," *Los Angeles Times,* August 20, 1999, p. B7; Robert Jensen, "Even a Child Sees Though Iraqi Policy," *Dallas Morning News,* August 27, 1999, p. A29; and Brett Wagner, "US Sanctions: Make Them More Precise, Less Ham-Handed," *Christian Science Monitor,* September 15, 1999, p. 21.

53 Editorial, "A Morally Unsustainable Iraq Policy," *Chicago Tribune,* September 17, 1999, p. 1: 18.

54 Deborah Horan,"Once-Prosperous Iraq Collapses Into Despair," *Houston Chronicle,* September 12, 1999, p. A1, and related articles by Horan on p. A24.

55 See http://www.johnpilger.com and http://www.independent.co.uk.

Chapter 7

The Hidden War

Robert Fisk

Across the sands of southern Iraq, the residue of Allied depleted uranium (DU) shells lies untreated in the soil. But in Britain, the government goes to enormous lengths to protect its people from the results of test-firing the very weapons suspected of causing an increase in cancers among Iraqi children.

A government document, published almost six months ago but virtually ignored, reveals that test-firing of DU shells in Britain is carried out into an open-sided concrete building called the "tunnel" and that radioactive residues are washed off, sealed in cement, and transported to Cumbria for disposal.

Iraqi doctors have long suspected that the children suffering from a fourfold increase in cancer in the south of the country—revealed in *The Independent* on March 4, 1998—contracted their sickness from the Allied use of depleted uranium shells in the 1991 war. Tens of thousands of these projectiles were fired at the Iraqis in February 1991 in the fields south of the city of Basra, the fertile lands from which millions of Iraqis acquire their food. Many of the children dying of leukemia and lymphoma cancer were not even born when the war took place.

There has been no attempt by the US or Britain to find out the cause of the cancer outbreaks in Iraq, though US veterans' groups suspect DU shells, made of hard alloys which are tougher than tungsten and which ignite inside armored vehicles, are responsible for thousands of cases of "Gulf War Syndrome" (including lymphoma cancers) among American soldiers who fought in the war. The US National Gulf War Resource Center says 40,000 US servicemen may have been exposed to depleted uranium dust on the battlefields.[1] Tony Flint, acting chairman of the British Gulf Veterans' and Families' Association says the same shells could be responsible for the death of thirty British veterans.

A review of the Ministry of Defense's radioactive waste management practices, published by the Department of the Environment in December

1997, however, shows government specialists here take the risk of contamination more seriously than imagined. According to the report by the Radioactive Waste Management Advisory Committee, depleted uranium shells tested at the range at Eskmeals, on the Cumbrian coast, are fired into a special tunnel fitted with a filtered extract system and pressure-washed with water to avoid contamination.

"The washings are transferred to collecting tanks for eventual disposal in cemented drums to Drigg," the report says. If the DU shell is fixed into armor plate, then the plate itself is sent to Drigg for disposal. So concerned are the British authorities about health hazards from DU shells that an on-site health physics laboratory exists to monitor the workforce on the Eskmeals firing range. The Department of the Environment report says firings involving uranium have been going on at the range since 1981, and "just over 90 per cent of the total weight of the shells has been recovered." On 1991 Gulf War battlefields, not a single attempt was made to recover contaminated residues.

The Eskmeals range possesses seven high-volume air samplers, and 1,000 samples are taken annually. A special sampler operates to check what the document calls "the critical group within the public [sic] ... identified as those living in Monk Moors." Depleted uranium shells are also test-fired at Kirkcudbright in Scotland where 1.5 tons of the projectiles are targeted every year into the Solway Firth. The shells, the report says alarmingly, "remain on the sea bed where they will corrode with time to form an insoluble sludge composed of hydrated uranium oxide.... Unsuccessful attempts were made in 1993 to recover some of these shells in order to assess their corrosion state." A small amount of depleted uranium waste also occurs at the Defense Evaluation and Research Agency's site at Fort Halstead in Kent, disposed of, like the contamination at Eskmeals, to Drigg in Cumbria.

According to another American Gulf veterans' association, Swords to Plowshares, when a depleted uranium shell strikes armor, up to 70 percent of the round burns, scattering radioactive and chemically toxic dust in and around the target.

A 1993 US General Accounting Office report stated that American soldiers of the 144th Supply Company of the National Guard were never told of radiation hazards when ordered to recover US military vehicles in the Gulf that were the victim of "friendly fire" attacks using depleted uranium projectiles.[2]

Western evidence is, thus, beginning to bear out the claim by Iraqi doctors that the residues of Allied DU shells may be a grave health hazard on the Gulf War battlefields. Almost all farm produce consumed by residents of Basra is grown in lands in which thousands of depleted uranium shells were fired. When *The Independent* visited the area in February 1998, local farmers complained of high levels of cancer in their families.

The effectiveness of armor-piercing ammunition principally depends on the density of the material from which is it manufactured, and the British government report says depleted uranium shows "significant performance advantages over other metals." Which is not much comfort to Iraqi cancer sufferers, or Gulf War veterans.

"The West's Poisonous Legacy," The Independent, *May 28, 1998, p. 13.*

We are now in the endgame, the final bankruptcy of Western policy toward Iraq, the very last throw of the dice. We fire 200 cruise missiles into Iraq and what do we expect? Is a chastened Saddam Hussein going to emerge from his bunker to explain to us how sorry he is? Will he tell us how much he wants those nice UN inspectors to return to Baghdad to find his "weapons of mass destruction"? Is that what we think? Is that what the Anglo-American bombardment is all about? And if so, what happens afterward? What happens when the missile attacks end—just before the Muslim holy month of Ramadan, because, of course, we really are very sensitive about Iraqi religious feelings—and Saddam Hussein tells us that the UN inspectors will never be allowed to return?

As the cruise missiles were launched, President Clinton announced that Saddam had "disarmed the [UN] inspectors," and Tony Blair—agonizing about the lives of the "British forces" involved (all fourteen pilots)—told us that "we act because we must."[3] In so infantile a manner did we go to war on Wednesday night. No policies. No perspective. Not the slightest hint as to what happens after the bombardment ends. With no UN inspectors back in Iraq, what are we going to do? Declare eternal war against Iraq?

We are "punishing" Saddam—or so Mr. Blair would have us believe. And all the old clichés are being trundled out. In 1985, just before he bombed them, Ronald Reagan told the Libyans that the United States had "no quarrel with the Libyan people." In 1991, just before he bombed them, George Bush told the Iraqis that he had "no quarrel with the Iraqi people." And now we have Tony Blair—as he bombs them—telling Iraqis that, yes, he has "no quarrel with the Iraqi people."[4]

Is there a computer that churns out this stuff? Is there a cliché department at Downing Street which also provides Robin Cook with the tired phrase of the American secretary of state, Madeleine Albright, about how Saddam used gas "against his own people"?

For little did we care when he did use that gas against the Kurds of Halabja—because, at the time, those Kurds were allied to Iran and we, the West, were supporting Saddam's invasion of Iran.

The lack of any sane long-term policy toward Iraq is the giveaway. Our patience—according to Clinton and Blair—is exhausted. Saddam cannot be trusted to keep his word (they've just realized). And so Saddam's ability to "threaten his neighbors"—neighbors who don't in fact want us to bomb Iraq—has to be "degraded." That word *degraded* is a military term, first used by General Schwarzkopf and his boys in the 1991 Gulf War, and it is now part of the vocabulary of the week. Saddam's weapons of mass destruction have to be "degraded." Our own dear Mr. Cook was at it again yesterday, informing us of the need to "degrade" Saddam's military capability.

How? The UN weapons inspectors—led for most of the time by Scott Ritter (the man who has admitted he kept flying to Israel to liaise with Israeli military intelligence)—could not find out where Saddam's nuclear, biological, and chemical weapons were hidden. They had been harassed by Iraq's intelligence thugs, and prevented from doing their work. Now we are bombing the weapons facilities which the inspectors could not find. Or are we? For there is a very serious question that is not being asked: if the inspectors couldn't find the weapons, how come we know where to fire the cruise missiles?

And all the while, we continue to impose genocidal sanctions on Iraq, sanctions that are killing innocent Iraqis and—by the admission of Mr. Cook and Mrs. Albright—not harming Saddam at all. Mrs. Albright rages at Saddam's ability to go on building palaces, and Mr. Cook is obsessed with a report of the regime's purchase of liposuction equipment, which, if true, merely proves that sanctions are a total failure.

Mr. Cook prattles on about how Iraq can sell more than $10 billion (£6 billion) of oil a year to pay for food, medicine, and other humanitarian goods. But since more than 30 percent of these oil revenues are diverted to the UN compensation fund and UN expenses in Iraq, his statement is totally untrue.[5]

Denis Halliday, the man who ran the UN oil-for-food program in Baghdad, until he realized that thousands of Iraqi children were dying every month because of sanctions, resigned his post with the declaration that "we are in the process of destroying an entire society. It is illegal and immoral." So either Mr. Halliday is a pathological liar—which I do not believe—or Mr. Cook has a serious problem with the truth—which I do believe.

Now we are bombing the people who are suffering under our sanctions. Not to mention the small matter of the explosion of child cancer in southern Iraq, most probably as a result of the Allied use of depleted uranium shells during the 1991 war. Gulf War veterans may be afflicted with the same sickness, although the British government refuses to contemplate the possibility. And what, in this latest strike, are some of our warheads made of? Depleted uranium, of course.

Maybe there really is a plan afoot for a coup d'état, though hopefully more ambitious than our call to the Iraqi people to rise up against their dictator in 1991, when they were abandoned by the Allies they thought would speed to their rescue. Mr. Clinton says he wants a democracy in Iraq—as fanciful a suggestion as any made recently. He is demanding an Iraqi government that "represents its people" and "respects" its citizens. Not a single Arab regime—especially not Washington's friends in Saudi Arabia—offers such luxuries to its people. We are supposed to believe, it seems, that Washington and London are terribly keen to favor the Iraqi people with a fully fledged democracy.

In reality, what we want in Iraq is another bullying dictator—but one who will do as he is told, invade the countries we wish to see invaded (Iran), and respect the integrity of those countries we do not wish to see invaded (Kuwait).

Yet no questions are being asked, no lies uncovered. Ritter, the Marine Corps inspector who worked with Israeli intelligence, claimed that Richard Butler—the man whose report triggered this week's new war—was aware of his visits to Israel. Is that true? Has anyone asked Mr. Butler? He may well have avoided such contacts—but it would be nice to have an answer.

So what to do with Saddam? Well, first, we could abandon the wicked sanctions regime against Iraq. We have taken enough innocent lives. We have killed enough children. Then we could back the real supporters of democracy in Iraq—not the ghouls and spooks who make up the so-called

Iraqi National Congress, but the genuine dissidents who gathered in Beirut in 1991 to demand freedom for their country, but were swiftly ignored by the Americans once it became clear that they didn't want a pro-Western strongman to lead them.

And we could stop believing in Washington. Vice President Al Gore told Americans yesterday that it was a time for "national resolve and unity."[6] You might have thought that the Japanese had just bombed Pearl Harbor, or that General MacArthur had just abandoned Bataan. When President Clinton faced the worst of the Monica Lewinsky scandal, he bombed Afghanistan and Sudan. Faced with impeachment, he now bombs Iraq. How far can a coincidence go?

This week, two Christian armies—America's and Britain's—went to war with a Muslim nation, Iraq. With no goals, but with an army of platitudes, they have abandoned the UN's weapons control system, closed the door on arms inspections, and opened the door to an unlimited military offensive against Iraq. And nobody has asked the obvious question: what happens next?

"Deadly Cost of a Degrading Act," The Independent, *December 18, 1998, p. 5.*

Phil Garner telephoned me this week to ask how he could make contact with the doctors treating Iraq's child cancer victims. He had been reading our series on the growing evidence of links between cancers in Iraq and the use of depleted uranium shells by American and British forces during the 1991 Gulf War.

During the conflict, Garner was in the Royal Army Medical Corps. He was not in the front lines, but he handled the uniforms of Britain's "friendly fire" casualties—men who were attacked by US aircraft using depleted uranium rounds. And now he suffers from asthma, incontinence, pain in the intestines and has a lump on the right side of his neck.

I know what those lumps on the neck look like. This month I've seen enough Iraqi children with tumors on their abdomen to feel horror as well as anger. When Hebba Mortaba's mother lifted her little girl's patterned blue dress in the Mansour hospital in Baghdad, her terribly swollen abdomen displayed numerous abscesses. Doctors had already surgically removed an earlier abdominal mass only to find, monster-like, that another grew in its place.

During the 1991 war, Hebba's suburb of Basra was bombed so heavily that her family fled to Baghdad. She is now just nine years old and, so her doctors told me gently, will not live to see her tenth birthday.

When I first reported from Iraq's child cancer wards in February and March 1998—and visited the fields and farms around Basra into which US and British tanks fired thousands of depleted uranium shells in the last days of the war—the British government went to great lengths to discredit what I wrote.

I still treasure a letter from Lord Gilbert, Minister of State for Defense Procurement, who told *Independent* readers that my account of a possible link between DU ammunition and increased Iraqi child cancer cases would, "[c]oming from anyone other than Robert Fisk ... be regarded as a wilful perversion of reality." According to his Lordship, particles from the DU-hardened warheads—used against tank armor—"are extremely small and are rapidly diluted and dispersed by the weather" and "become difficult to detect, even with the most sophisticated monitoring equipment."[7] Over the past few months I've been sent enough evidence to suggest that, had this letter come from anyone other than his Lordship, its implications would be mendacious as well as misleading.

Let us start with an equally eloquent but far more accurate letter sent to the Royal Ordnance in London on April 21, 1991, by Paddy Bartholomew, business development manager of AEA Technology, the trading name for the UK Atomic Energy Authority.

Mr. Bartholomew's letter—of which I have obtained a copy—refers to a telephone conversation with a Royal Ordnance official on the dangers of the possible contamination of Kuwait by depleted uranium ammunition. In an accompanying "threat paper" by Mr. Bartholomew, he notes that while the hazards caused by the spread of radioactivity and toxic contamination from these weapons "are small when compared to those during a war," they nonetheless "can become a long-term problem if not dealt with in peacetime and are a risk to both military and civilian population."

The document, marked "UK Restricted," goes on to say that

> US tanks fired 5,000 DU rounds, US aircraft many tens of thousands and UK tanks a small number of DU rounds. The tank ammunition alone will amount to greater than 50,000lb of DU ... [I]f the tank inventory of DU was inhaled, the latest International Committee of Radiological Protection risk factor ... calculates 500,000 potential deaths.
>
> The DU will spread around the battlefield and target vehicles in various sizes and quantities ... [I]t would be unwise for people to stay close to large

> quantities of DU for long periods and this would obviously be of concern to the local population if they collect this heavy metal and keep it.

Mr. Bartholomew's covering letter says that the contamination of Kuwait is "emotive and thus must be dealt with in a sensitive manner."

Needless to say, no one has bothered even to suggest a cleanup in southern Iraq where Hebba Mortaba and other child victims are dying. Why not? And why doesn't the government come clean and tell us what really happened?

Here is a clue. It comes in a letter dated March 1, 1991, from a US lieutenant colonel at the Los Alamos National Laboratory to a Major Larson at the organization's Studies and Analysis Branch and states that:

> There has been and continues to be a concern [sic] regarding the impact of DU on the environment. Therefore, if no one makes a case for the effectiveness of DU on the battlefield, DU rounds may become politically unacceptable and thus be deleted from the arsenal. If DU penetrators proved their worth during our recent combat activities, then we should assure their future existence (until something better is developed).

So there it is. Shorn of the colonel's execrable English, the message is simple: the health risks of DU ammunition are acceptable until we—the West—invent something even more lethal to take its place.

So with tens of thousands of 1991 Gulf War veterans suffering unexplained and potentially terminal illnesses and with thousands of Iraqi civilians, including children unborn when the war ended, now suffering from unexplained cancers, I can only repeat what I wrote last March: that something terrible happened at the end of the Gulf War about which we have still not been told the truth.[8]

As former acting Sergeant Tony Duff of the Gulf War Veterans put it to me yesterday, "A lot of things we are now calling victories about the Gulf War will be seen one day as atrocities—I wonder whether this is why the powers that be don't want this DU thing to come out?"

And what exactly is this awful secret which we are not allowed to know? Is it, as Professor Malcolm Hooper, professor of medicinal chemistry at Sunderland University, remarks, the result of the US-British bombing of Saddam Hussein's Sarin and Tabun poison gas factories (around 900 facilities were bombed, it now turns out)? Or is it the secret DU factor?

I don't know whether this can be classed as a war crime. But anyone who thinks there's no connection between our use of depleted uranium ammunition in the 1991 Gulf War and the tide of sickness that has followed in its wake must also believe in Father Christmas.

Does Lord Gilbert believe in Father Christmas, I wonder?

"The Evidence Is There—We Caused Cancer in the Gulf,"
The Independent, *October 16, 1998, p. 4.*

Something terrible happened toward the end of the 1991 Gulf War. While we were congratulating ourselves that the Iraqi army had been driven out of Kuwait and Saddam Hussein had been (supposedly) "defanged," an unknown chemical plague spread across southern Mesopotamia. It was to cripple British and American soldiers, along with untold thousands of Iraqis, some of them children as yet unborn. In the years to come—when it began to afflict our own veterans—we called it "Gulf War Syndrome."

So did the Americans. As for the Iraqis, they remained silent for years—even as their own people began to fall victim to unexplained cancers around the former battlefields. Even now, Saddam Hussein's regime has not made a single statement about the epidemic of cancers afflicting the largely Shiite Muslim population. Here, then, is something which President Clinton, Prime Minister Blair, and Saddam Hussein have in common: a total failure to explain the calamity affecting thousands of their people after the 1991 conflict.

Nor can there be any doubt that Americans, British, and Iraqis are suffering from the same affliction. As I was touring cancer wards of Basra and Baghdad last week, looking at the men and women and especially children who are dying of lymphatic cancers—the cause of which, Iraqi doctors said, was use by the Allies of depleted uranium shells—Tony Flint, the acting chairman of the British Gulf Veterans' and Families' Association, was warning that the very same shells could be responsible for cancers that have killed at least thirty British veterans. Just one day later, the American National Gulf War Resource Center, representing a coalition of US veterans, announced that as many as 40,000 American servicemen may have been exposed to depleted uranium dust on the 1991 battlefields.

The kidney problems, respiratory failures, and cancers now being diagnosed among Allied veterans appear to be identical to those afflicting Iraqis. In most cases, the Iraqi victims were diagnosed only years later—just as Gulf War Syndrome was only grudgingly acknowledged in London and Washington, long after Allied troops had returned home. I first heard of these symptoms among Iraqis in 1997, when an Iraqi opposition leader in Damascus—a Shiite cleric who knew former Iraqi troops seeking refuge in southern Iran following the 1991 war—told me that many of these ex-soldiers had fallen ill. Most had fought in tank battles southwest of Basra; their armor was being bombarded with depleted uranium shells by the US First Infantry Division. American troops were exposed to the same dust when they moved forward after the battles and helped destroy the contaminated wreckage of the Iraqi armored units.

In southern Iraq, the battlefields west of Basra include some of the city's best farmland; its inhabitants continue to eat tomatoes, onions, potatoes, and meat from fields that were certainly drenched in uranium dust. The same toxic residues must have drained into the rivers and sewers of Basra, polluting even further the city's water supplies. This, at least, is the opinion of Basra's cancer surgeons. The implication is terrifying: for the first time since the bombing of Hiroshima, cancer has been linked to warfare.

No wonder, then, that no one really wants to find out the cause of this sickness. American veterans' groups have accused the US Defense Department of "a deliberate attempt to avoid responsibility for consciously allowing widespread exposure of hundreds of thousands of servicemen and women." The Ministry of Defense in London, investigating depleted uranium as part of a Gulf War Syndrome inquiry, still claims there is no evidence of the metal being responsible for any abnormal diseases.

Western aid agencies inside Iraq are equally cavalier. Unicef has sought no details of child cancer deaths related to the war—though it admits to hearing of the reports. Even more shameful is our own failure—that of the UN and all those involved in the sanctions imposition—to provide enough of the medicine that could cure Iraqi child leukemia victims who are otherwise going to die. To deny the existence of Gulf War Syndrome is maybe sin enough. To deny medicine to its Iraqi civilian victims is shameful.

There is an obvious response to this. Why should we—the British, the Americans, the West—do anything when we do not know for sure what is blighting the people of southern Iraq, as well as our own military veterans? Saddam is to blame—write that out 100 times. But there is an equally obvious retort: open a UN investigation into the pestilence that is sweeping through those who fought in 1991 and those who live there now but who were unborn at the time. UN inspectors inside Iraq can paw through the palaces and offices of the highest Iraqi officials in their hunt for evidence of biochemical warfare. So why cannot the UN carry out an equally intrusive—equally humanitarian—inquiry into the cancers, kidney failures, and deaths that accompanied the creation of the New World Order?

"The Catastrophe Blair, Clinton, and Saddam Have in Common,"
The Independent, *March 9, 1998, p. 17.*[9]

Notes

1 See http://www.gulfweb.org.
2 US General Accounting Office, *Operation Desert Storm: Army Not Adequately Prepared to Deal with Depleted Uranium Contamination,* GAO/NSIAD-93-90 (Washington, DC: GAO, 1993).
3 See Bill Clinton, "'A Clear and Present Danger," *Financial Times,* December 17, 1998, p. 12, and Tony Blair, "Why We Had to Act Now," *Daily Mail,* December 17, 1998, p. 3.
4 See Sarah Schaefer, "Commons Debate—Blair Vows to Weaken Dictator," *The Independent,* December 18, 1998, p. 7.
5 See UN Office of the Iraq Program "Oil-for-food—The Basic Facts." Available at http://www.un.org/Depts/oip/reports/basfact.html.
6 Larry King, interview with Al Gore, CNN, *Larry King Live,* December 16, 1998.
7 Lord Gilbert, Letter to the Editor, "'Poisonous' Gulf Shells," *The Independent,* May 30, 1998, p. 22.
8 See "The Catastrophe Blair, Clinton, and Saddam Have in Common," *The Independent,* March 9, 1998, p. 17 (printed below).
9 See also Robert Fisk, "Allies Blamed for Iraq Cancer Torment," *The Independent,* March 4, 1998, p. 1, and "Dusty Farm Ditches and Disused Trenches—The Tomato Plantations Are Still Killing Fields," *The Independent,* March 4, 1998, p. 13.

Chapter 8

One Iraqi's Story

Howard Zinn

As Bill Clinton and Tony Blair were bombing Iraq on December 20, 1998, I received an e-mail message from England:

> Dear Professor Zinn,
>
> I am an Iraqi citizen who sought refuge here in the UK because of the brutality of Saddam's regime, which, within two years, killed my innocent old father and my youngest brother, who left a wife and three children....
>
> I am writing to you to let you know that during the second day of bombarding Iraq, a cruise missile hit my parents' house in a suburb of Baghdad. My mother, my sister-in-law (wife of my deceased brother), and her three children were all killed instantly.
>
> Such a tragedy shocked me to such an extent I lost my tears. I am crying without tears. I wish I could show my eyes and express my severe and painful suffering to every American and British [citizen]. I wish I could tell my story to those sitting in the American Administration, the UN, and at Number 10 Downing Street. For the sake of Monica and Clinton, my family has to pay this expensive and invaluable cost. I am wondering, who will compensate me for my loss? I wish I could go to Iraq to drop some tears on my mother's grave, who always wanted to see me before her death....
>
> Please convey my story to all those whom you think can still see the truth in their eyes and can hear this tragic story with their ears.
>
> Sincerely yours,
>
> Dr. Mohammed Al-Obaidi

It seems to me this conveys with terrible clarity that Saddam Hussein and the leaders of our government have much in common. They are both visiting death and suffering on the people of Iraq.

In response to the possibility that Saddam Hussein may have "weapons of mass destruction" and the additional possibility that he may use them in the future, the United States, in the present, shows no compunction about using weapons of mass destruction, cruise missiles, B-52 bombers, and, most of all, economic sanctions, which have resulted in the deaths of hundreds of thousands of Iraqi children.

In the December bombings, Bill Clinton was perfectly willing to kill a number (how many we do not know) of Iraqis, including five members of Dr. Mohammed Al-Obaidi's family. Why? "To send a message," his administration said.[1]

Would the United States be willing to take the lives of a similar number of Americans "to send a message"? Are Iraqis less worthy of life than we are? Are their children less innocent than ours?

President Clinton said that Saddam Hussein poses a "clear and present danger" to the peace of the world.[2] Whatever danger Saddam Hussein may pose in the future, he is not a clear and present danger to the peace of the world. We are. Notice the president's use of this much-abused phrase. The Supreme Court of the United States invoked it to justify the imprisonment of people distributing leaflets protesting the US entrance into World War I. Cold Warriors used it to justify McCarthyism and the nuclear arms race.[3] Now President Clinton has pulled it off the shelf for equally disreputable purposes.

President Clinton also said that other nations besides Iraq have weapons of mass destruction, but Iraq alone has used them.[4] He could say this only to a population deprived of history. No nation in the world possesses greater weapons of mass destruction than we do, and none has used them more often, or with greater loss of civilian life. In Hiroshima and Nagasaki, more than 100,000 civilians died after the United States dropped atom bombs on them. In Korea and Vietnam, millions died after the United States dropped "conventional" weapons on them. So who are we to brag about our restraint in using weapons of mass destruction?

The US penchant for bombing blots out the government's ability to focus on humanitarian crises—and not just in Iraq. When Hurricane Mitch devastated Central America, leaving tens of thousands dead and more than a million people homeless, there was a desperate need for helicopters to transport people to safety and deliver food and medicine. Mexico supplied sixteen helicopters to Honduras. The United States supplied twelve. At the same time, the Pentagon dispatched a huge armada—helicopters, transport planes, B-52s—to the Middle East.[5]

Every cruise missile used to bomb Iraq cost about $1 million, and the Pentagon used more than 300 of them.[6]

At the same time, the Knight Ridder news service reported that the Department of Defense had stopped the distribution of blankets to homeless programs around the country. The Senate Armed Services Committee had not approved the appropriation. According to the news dispatch,

"The committee said the $3.5 million annual cost [of the blanket program] diverted money from weapons."[7]

Thus, our weapons kill people abroad, while in this country homeless people freeze.

Are not our government's moral priorities absurdly distorted?

When I received the message from Dr. Al-Obaidi, I tried to meet his request by reading from his letter on a number of radio interviews in various parts of the country. I have written to him to tell him that. Nothing, of course, can restore his family. All we can do is try to convey to the American public the human consequences of our government's repeated use of violence for political and economic gain. When enough of them see and feel what is happening to people just like us—to families, to children—we may see the beginning of a new movement in this country against militarism and war.

Notes

1 See Lawrence F. Kaplan, "How to Send a 'Message': Use AT&T, Not USAF," *Wall Street Journal,* December 23, 1998, p. A14.

2 Bill Clinton, "Now is the Time to Strike," *Boston Globe,* December 17, 1998, p. A53.

3 See Ellen Schrecker, *Many Are the Crimes: McCarthyism in America* (Princeton: Princeton UP, 1998), pp. 60–61 and 199.

4 Bill Clinton, "Now is the Time to Strike," *Boston Globe,* December 17, 1998, p. A53.

5 Michelle Ray Ortiz, Associated Press, "Many Remote Villages Hit by Mitch Still Lost," *Boston Globe,* November 14, 1998, p. A2, and Steven Lee Myers, "Air Force Scrambles to Send More Warplanes to the Gulf," *New York Times,* November 14, 1998, p. A6.

6 Dana Priest, "US Commander Unsure of How Long Iraq Will Need to Rebuild," *Washingon Post,* December 22, 1998, p. A31, and Steven Lee Myers, "US Says 85% of Iraqi Targets Were Hit," *New York Times,* December 22, 1998, p. A18.

7 Mary Otto, Knight Ridder, "Blanket Policy Covers Homeless," December 25, 1998.

The entrance to the ancient Al Ashari mosque in the town of Samarra, on the road between Baghdad and Mosul. Iraqi people put up banners like these when someone dies. Today they are a frequent sight in the streets of Iraq. Anti-Western feeling is growing as the sanctions continue to bite, although signs in English like this one ("Down U.S.A.") are rare. Photo by Nikki van der Gaag (May 26, 1999).

Central Baghdad. Photo by Alan Pogue (July 1998).

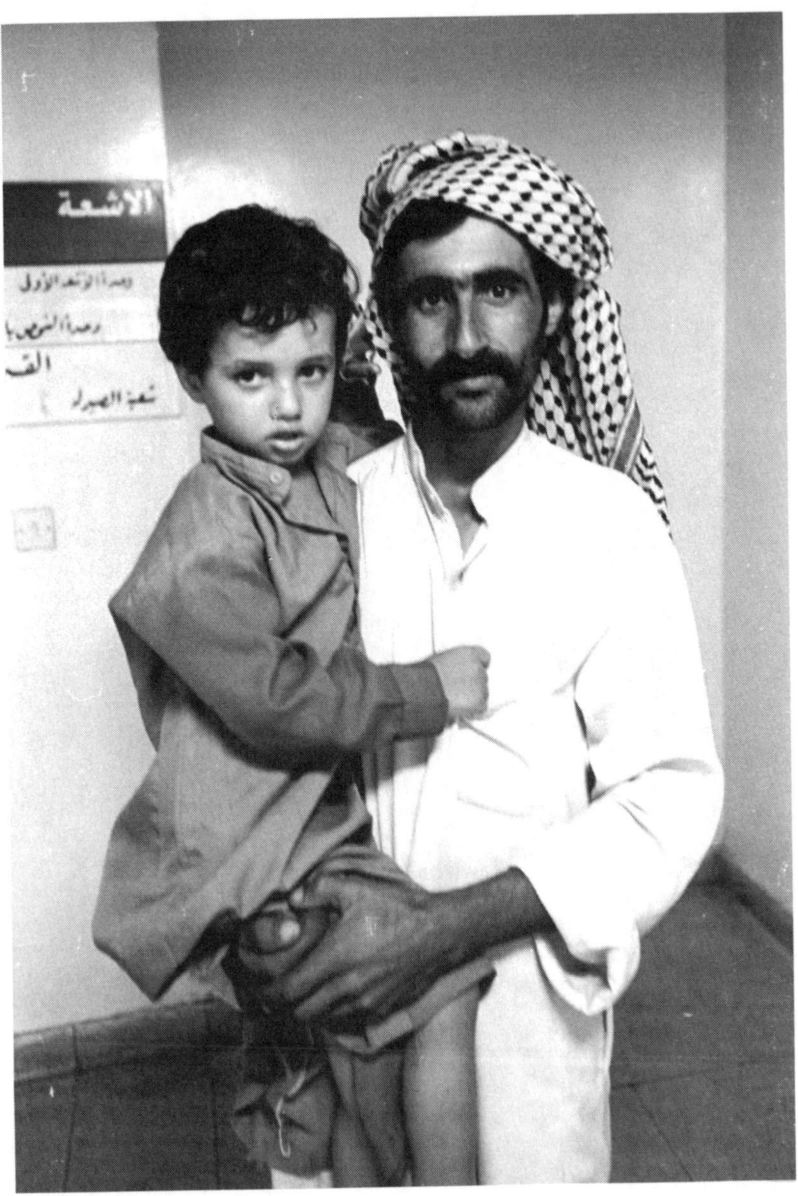

Man with son at the Al Monsour Hospital in Baghdad. The leukemia rate for children has quadrupled but hospitals lack even the simplest medicines. The hospital administrator makes the equivalent of $30 per month. Photo by Alan Pogue (July 1998).

Damage caused by US bombing of the Amariyah shelter (see pp. 115–16). Photo by Alan Pogue (July 1998).

Man selling cigarettes at the Friday market in downtown Baghdad. The market is mainly for selling animals, but people now come to sell whatever they can to make a little money. Photo by Nikki van der Gaag (May 21, 1999).

Mohamed Ghani in his studio in Baghdad. The glass was broken when a bomb fell in 1991, and materials are increasingly hard to get, but this famous Iraqi sculptor, who has exhibited all over the world, refuses to leave his country (see pp. 59–60). Photo by Nikki van der Gaag (May 21, 1999).

Part 3

Life Under Sanctions

Children in Basra. Photo by Alan Pogue (July 1998).

Chapter 9

Raising Voices

The Children of Iraq, 1990–1999

Kathy Kelly

It is January 8, 1997. I am in a car driving from Baltimore to Washington, DC, at 6:15 a.m. With me are Simon Harak, a Jesuit priest and theology professor, and Ardeth Platte and Carol Gilbert, Dominican sisters from Baltimore. We will later meet Art Laffin, a Catholic lay worker, at the Senate Hart Office Building. Our plan is to enter the Senate confirmation hearings of Madeleine Albright for secretary of state.

Leslie Stahl went to Iraq for *60 Minutes*. On the program that aired May 12, 1996, she asked Albright, who was then the US ambassador to the United Nations, to explain US policy in the context of the devastation she had seen among the children of Iraq. Albright responded: "I think this is a very hard choice, but the price, we think the price is worth it."[1]

We arrive two hours before the hearing. Already thirty people are in line. Tucked inside our coats are folded enlargements of pictures of Iraqi children I visited in August 1996, children whose sunken eyes plead for relief from starvation and disease.

The hearings begin and we hear mutterings that there is no room inside for members of the public. I feel disappointed and a bit silly, having raced from Chicago to Washington on a moment's notice, apparently for naught. Much to our relief, after then–Secretary of State Warren Christopher is escorted out, the security guards allow the people in line to enter in groups of ten as the hearings proceed.

We are among the first forty admitted. We have agreed beforehand that immediately after Albright concludes her remarks, we'll stand, one by one, to raise our pictures of the children and express our urgent concerns.

Albright stresses her commitment to universal human rights, but as regards Iraq she only affirms readiness to maintain a tough policy. As the applause subsides, I stand up.

"Ms. Albright," I call out, "over half a million Iraqi children have died because of US/UN sanctions. In May 1996, you told *60 Minutes* that this was an acceptable price to pay in order to maintain US interests in the region. Are you prepared to withdraw that statement?"

A security guard, Officer Goodine, is at my elbow. Senator Jesse Helms motions to him to remove me, but the young officer raises his hand politely as if to indicate "just a moment, let her finish," and he gently taps my arm.

"These children are helpless victims," I call out again, moving into the aisle. "Ms. Albright, please, you could do so much good."

The officer leads me out as though he were ushering at the opera. Simon Harak is already on his feet, asking Albright if she would impose the same punishment on every other country that fails to comply with US demands.

Ardeth, Carole, and Art rise, in turn, to speak. After we are all escorted out, Albright addresses the committee:

> I am as concerned about the children of Iraq as any person in this room.... Saddam Hussein is the one who has the fate of his country in his hands.... He is the one responsible for starving children, not the United States of America.[2]

On January 10, 1997, Voices in the Wilderness, a campaign to end sanctions on Iraq, sent out a statement of our response, saying in part:

> Iraqi children are totally innocent of oil power politics. All those who prevent the lifting of sanctions, including Madeleine Albright, are not. One line disclaimers of responsibility may appear suavely diplomatic, but the children are dead and we have seen them dying. According to the UN itself, they died as a direct result of the embargo on commerce with Iraq. Many United Nations members favored significantly easing these sanctions. The US government and Madeleine Albright as its spokesperson prevented that from happening.
>
> This economic embargo continues warfare against Iraq, a silent war in which only the weakest, most vulnerable and innocent non-combatant civilians—women, children and families—continue to suffer.[3]

One year earlier, in a modest act of nonviolence, we wrote to US Attorney General Janet Reno declaring our intent to deliberately violate the UN and US sanctions against the people of Iraq. We said we realized the possible penalties we faced, but that we hoped she would join us in demanding that the US government lift the embargo against Iraq.

Four Voices delegations traveled to Iraq in 1996 and thirty more have gone as of the end of 1999. Each group openly defies the sanctions by taking medical relief supplies directly to Iraqi children and families. Our trips create a drama that we hope will gain attention for the plight of the Iraqi people, especially the children. Upon return, we "hit the ground running," with presentations in classrooms and to community groups. We contact our legislators, send out mailings, and try very hard to push the issue into the mainstream media.

In the meantime, 150 Iraqi children die every day.

The "silent" war

It is January 16, 1997. I arrive breathless but on time for a religious studies class at De Paul University, where my Kenyan friend, Dr. Teresia Hinga, teaches a class on conscience and moral decision-making.

Teresia warmly welcomes me as a woman who went to Iraq during the Gulf War and helped establish a peace camp on the border between Saudi Arabia and Iraq. She tells them that I have returned to Iraq several times since then, at great personal risk, and she urges them to listen to what I have to say.

By now, I've spotted Dr. Adnan Almaney in the back of the classroom. I thank Teresia and then say how glad I am that someone who is actually from Iraq can be with us as well. Dr. Almaney teaches business management at De Paul. His kindly nod reassures me.

I tell the students a bit of personal background, hoping they can identify with me on some levels. A few heads nod, with wry smiles, when I describe the Chicago neighborhood where I grew up—a blue-collar, not-quite-middle-class area on the southwest side. I tell them about a key moment in my teen years when an English teacher showed us *Night and Fog,* a haunting documentary film about the Nazi holocaust. I confess to the students that it would be another decade before I would involve myself in public activism and resistance movements. Yet somehow, at a deep emotional level, I realized then that I wanted to confront injustice rather than pretend to be an innocent, powerless bystander. I began, in those days, to read more about people I admired intensely for having taken risks for love and justice, people like Mahatma Gandhi, Dorothy Day, and Martin Luther King, Jr.

A glance at the clock prompts me to fast-forward. I mention that I majored in theology, taught high school religion for two years, and then earned a master's degree in theology—which thoroughly equips me to be a waitress.

I tell them that finally, in my last year of graduate theology studies, I felt uneasy about my remoteness from the cares and concerns of the poor. I lived and studied in an academic ghetto where I seldom saw anyone who struggled with oppression.

My decision to break out of this isolation has led me to prison and to several war zones. I was in Iraq during the first sixteen days of the Gulf War, one of seventy-three people who volunteered from eighteen countries to form the Gulf Peace Team. We intended to sit in the middle of a likely battlefield and call for an end to hostilities. I feel a glimmer of pride recalling that we succeeded in setting up an encampment in the desert almost exactly on the border between Iraq and Saudi Arabia near a US military camp.

The night the war broke out, our team members took turns clustering around a tiny short-wave radio, anxious to know whether there would be a last-minute resolution to prevent the war. Military experts had predicted that the bombing would begin on a moonless night. That night, there was no moon. At about 2 a.m., word spread through the camp that the bombing had started.

"Weren't you scared?" blurts a woman sitting in front of me. I shake my head. "No, honestly, what I felt was the deepest dismay I've ever known. I remember that every dog in the region began barking when the US and allied war planes appeared overhead. Those dogs barked themselves hoarse. I felt that was the most appropriate response to the war. Bombers flew overhead every night, sometimes at five-minute intervals. And each one carried a devastating payload of bombs. I imagined there would be nothing left of Iraq."

On January 27, 1991, as the ground war loomed, the Iraqi government decided to evacuate us. They sent in a team of civilians to persuade us to pack quickly and accompany them to Baghdad. We were divided about whether to stay or to go. A hard argument ensued, followed by a brief but moving demonstration by those who chose to stay but were, after a tense hour, hoisted onto buses by somewhat bewildered Iraqis.

By late afternoon, our buses were traveling a road that was under constant bombardment. The drivers swerved around huge bomb craters and we saw the charred, smoking remains of not only oil tankers, but also an ambulance, a passenger bus, and several civilian cars.

In Baghdad, we stayed at the plush Al-Rashid Hotel, which could offer no running water and was pitch dark because all electrical power had been knocked out. When a bomb exploded in a nearby parking lot, the Iraqi authorities, once again concerned about our safety, hurried the whole Gulf Peace Team onto buses and moved us to Amman, Jordan.

In Amman, a large press conference had been arranged for us. I was to speak for the US Gulf Peace Team participants, but I felt at a loss for words. "How can I begin?" I asked George Rumens, a British journalist and a member of our team. "Tell them," he said, "that when the war fever and hysteria subside, we believe the lasting and more appropriate responses to this war will be felt throughout the world: deepest remorse and regret for the suffering we've caused."

During the remainder of the war, we joined medical relief convoys that traveled the road from Amman to Baghdad. In accompanying the convoys, we hoped that the US and British forces would refrain from targeting them out of reluctance to bomb citizens of their own countries.

After the war, Iraq agreed to let us enter the country with study teams to document the combined effects of the war and economic sanctions. I stayed in the region for the next six months helping to organize medical relief teams.

US aircraft alone had dropped 88,000 tons of explosives on Iraq, the equivalent of nearly five Hiroshima nuclear blasts.[4] Seventy percent of the so-called smart bombs missed their intended targets, falling sometimes on civilian dwellings, schools, churches, mosques, or empty fields.[5] But the 30 percent that blasted on target wiped out Iraq's electrical generating plants and sewage treatment networks. Iraq's infrastructure—bridges, roads, highways, canals, and communication centers—was systematically destroyed.[6]

On February 12, 1991, the Allied assault on Iraq was at full throttle. As Christians throughout the world observed Ash Wednesday, Muslims marked the special Id al-Fitr feast. Families in a prosperous Baghdad neighborhood had decided to celebrate the Id despite the relentless bombing. They were to make use of the Amariyah bomb shelter, the best in Baghdad after the shelter near the Al-Rashid Hotel.

As evening fell, the whole neighborhood gathered for a common meal. After eating, the men left to make room in the shelter for as many women and children as possible, including refugees from other areas. Mothers, grandmothers, infants, children, and teenagers hoped to sleep in safety during the blistering explosions.

That night, two US "smart bombs" found the ventilation shafts of the Amariyah shelter. The exit doors were sealed and the temperature rose to 900 degrees Fahrenheit. More than 400 Iraqis perished.[7]

In March 1991, a Red Crescent vehicle delivered four of us study team members to the Amariyah neighborhood. Single-family homes surrounded the cavernous remains of the shelter. Stretched across the brick facade of each house was a black banner bearing in graceful, white Arabic letters the names of the family members from the home who had died in the massacre.

Staring at the scene, I began to cry. Then I felt a tiny arm encircling my waist. A beautiful Iraqi child smiled up at me. "Welcome," she said.

Then I saw two women dressed in black cross the street. I thought surely they were coming to withdraw the children who now surrounded us. As they drew closer, I spoke the few Arabic words I knew: *"Ana Amrikyyah, wa ana aasifa"*—I'm American and I'm sorry.

But they said, *"La, la, la"*—No, no, no. And they explained. "We know that you are not your government and that your people would never do this to us." Both the women had lost family members to the American bombs.

Never again do I expect to experience such understanding.

In retrospect, I wonder if they weren't better off without electricity. Wasn't it better for them never to hear on television or radio what was being said, just then, in the United States? When asked about the number of Iraqis who died in the war, General Colin Powell replied: "It's really not a number I'm terribly interested in."[8]

Then I tell the students about my visit to Amariyah. A journalist asked survivors if they thought such massacres could happen again. Incredulous, they nodded their heads and said in unison, "Of course!" One added, "Worse than this happens every day with the sanctions."

I hold up a poster bearing the photos from my visit to the Amariyah neighborhood and point to the little girl who welcomed me. I wonder, is she a teenager now? Did she survive the ongoing war? Is she lucky enough to get clean water and adequate food, despite the merciless embargo that has created a veritable state of siege in Iraq?

My poster shows other Iraqi children, giggling and smiling. The headline says "Faces of War: The 'Enemy' in Baghdad."

I don't want the students to think that the Gulf War was a series of "surgical" strikes that, as modern wars go, were not too destructive. I want them to understand that when you destroy a nation's infrastructure and then cripple it further with punishing sanctions, the victims are always the society's most vulnerable people—the poor, the elderly, the sick, and, most of all, the children.

I show the class a poster made from photos our delegation took in August 1996—haunting pictures of emaciated children, infants who look like old men, hairless and skeletal. I remember cradling the fragile body of one of the children and wondering if I were interrupting the final hours together for the mother and her child.

A student poses a thoughtful question: "What can you tell us about what Iraqi people think?" Teresia's eyes light up as she nods toward our guest, Dr. Almaney. The young man continues: "I mean, they must want things to change. Why aren't they taking steps?"

Dr. Almaney asks students to understand that while Iraqis are very unhappy about their present conditions, it is not so easy for them to make a change. Freedom of speech is not as readily enjoyed in Iraq as it is in other countries. When families are worried about where their next meal will come from, they are not so likely to involve themselves in organizing political movements. What's more, because of sanctions, almost every family in Iraq directly depends on government rationing to get whatever meager food supplies they have.

Dr. Almaney said many Iraqis have good reason to fear that if Saddam Hussein's regime were to lose power, the country would sink into a bloody civil war, one that could be exacerbated by hostile neighbors.

The class is nearly over. I wonder if I've been convincing. It is not necessary to condemn all war, as I do, to critically examine the "bombing" and "silent" wars against Iraq. The evidence is in, much of it, like the number of children's deaths, statistically certified by the United Nations itself, and much of it emerging in a growing body of eyewitness testimony like my own.

My audience files out, some offering help if it's needed, most murmuring a word of appreciation. These students—indeed, everyone—can make a reasoned judgment by looking at the record. *Have the ends justified the means? Should sanctions continue?*

"We don't want handouts"

It's August 10, 1996, a sweltering day in southern Iraq during one of the hottest summers on record. I sink into my bed at the Basra Towers Hotel, grateful for the fan overhead and the promise of slightly less intense heat as evening falls. I don't feel particularly tired, but my companions insisted I take a break because I fainted after visiting the Basra Pediatrics and Gynecology Hospital.

Dr. Tarik Hasim Habeh, the young director of residents, had taken us through several children's wards. Infant after infant lay wasting and skeletal in squalid conditions. We saw children suffering severe malnutrition, respiratory diseases, leukemia, and kidney disease. In one room, fourteen incubators were stacked against a wall, useless because of the lack of repair parts. The blood bank consisted of one miniature refrigerator and an ancient centrifuge.

Dr. Habeh explains that the hospital is chronically short-staffed. Doctors can't earn enough to feed their families, sometimes making no more than $3 per month, so some work instead as taxi drivers, street vendors, or waiters. Many nurses also find it impossible to continue the work for which they were trained.

Absent hospital staff to minister to their children, families are at their bedsides around the clock, arranging as best they can for the care of other children left at home. Dr. Habeh spoke about how demoralizing it is, salaries notwithstanding, to practice medicine without the proper tools and lacking medication.

"The only difference between me and the patient is the white coat," he said with a sad shrug as he left the bedside of a child likely to die of a respiratory infection that antibiotics could cure.

The temperature in Basra today is 140 degrees. Under these conditions, one should drink at least a gallon of water a day. Because sanctions bar chlorine used for water purification, even most bottled water, for the few who can afford it, is contaminated. At the water ministry, officials showed us rusted pipe sections with large holes that allow contaminants to leak into Basra's drinking water.

I reach for the bottled water that Archbishop Dijbraeel Kassab gave us. "Drink this," he said, "and mark your bottles. We call this sweet water, water from Baghdad. I can tell you that if you drink the other bottled water here, it will make you very sick." I think of the desperately ill children

I met earlier today, and put the bottle aside. My thoughts return to Archbishop Kassab.

I first encountered him at Sacred Heart Parish in Baghdad. Iraqi friends in Chicago had given me his number. When I called him in March 1996, on my first day in Baghdad, he invited me to visit that same day. He was sweeping the courtyard when I arrived. He and a few helpers were preparing for a weekly distribution of lentils, rice, sugar, and tea, which his parish gave to the nearby needy.

Later, in his office, he read descriptions of our campaign. "That's good," he stated. "Keep doing just what you are doing. You challenge this embargo. But we are a proud people and we don't want handouts—we just want to be able to work again and can take care of ourselves."

In August 1996, I returned to Baghdad with a second Voices in the Wilderness delegation. Archbishop Kassab was no longer in Baghdad, having been appointed Archbishop of the Chaldean Catholic Church in Basra and Nasiriyah, located in southern Iraq. This was good news because we hoped to visit Basra and needed a contact.

Two days later, we sat with him in his modest office. I introduced my friends. Then I told him I felt relieved that he had encouraged us to simply work toward ending the embargo since we really had only a pittance of medical supplies to offer.

"No, I have completely changed my mind." Archbishop Kassab was characteristically emphatic. "Now, after three months here, I must say 'yes' to handouts. We'll take anything we can get. That's how critical the reality is."

Basra is Iraq's third-largest city. Before the long years of the Iran-Iraq War, the Gulf War, and the sanctions, it was a thriving oil port. Now, of 300 families interviewed by Archbishop Kassab, only forty-five had at least one working family member. Unwillingly idle, frustrated, and humiliated, Basrans trudge through streets fouled with piles of human waste. The piles, five to six feet tall, spaced every thirty feet, are left to dry. Adults negotiate residential sidewalks with care, stepping over human feces, and wastewater spills from the streets into nearby homes.

Defying sanctions

I sit in my living room surrounded by some of the finest people in the world. It is January 18, 1997, six years since the Gulf War began and one year since a handful of us initiated the Voices campaign.

Four of our delegates have gone to Iraq carrying nearly $60,000 worth of medical supplies. We are on notice from the US Treasury Department that we risk twelve years in jail and $1 million in fines for failing to receive explicit authorization for our travel and humanitarian cargo.

On January 22, 1996, the US Department of the Treasury's Office of Foreign Assets faxed a letter notifying us:

> This Office has learned that you and other members of Voices in the Wilderness recently announced your intention to collect medical relief supplies for the people of Iraq at various locations in the United States and to personally transport the supplies to Iraq.
>
> Section 575.205 of the Regulations prohibits the exportation or reexportation of goods, technology, or services to Iraq, except as specifically provided in the Regulations.[9]

On moral grounds, we won't acknowledge veto power over our taking medical supplies, medicine, and solace to fellow human beings in dire need. On practical grounds, we cannot accept months of bureaucratic delay for a superfluous stamp of approval.

I again recall George Rumens' assurance that the lasting response to the war would be deepest regret and remorse. In many places, his words have been borne out. We find ourselves heard in classrooms and community centers. Our views find expression in small-town papers and radio stations. Consistently, a more sober response grows. "We didn't know. We didn't realize."

Now we want to harvest the results of our first year of campaign work and carefully strategize our next steps. We've spent most of the day together, informally evaluating, brainstorming, and reminiscing. We go over our pictures.

Pictures are crucial for our outreach and education. Most of the photos come from the main hospital in Basra and the Qadissiya Hospital on the outskirts of Baghdad. During an August 1996 visit to the Qadissiya Hospital, I was determined to identify some of the women and children we met, and to record details about their plight. What a grim necessity. Rick McDowell, a carpenter from Akron, Ohio, and I teamed up to photograph mothers and children and then, with a translator, question the weary mothers. How old are you? And your child? From what does your child suffer? For how long has your child been ill? Do you have other children? Who cares for them now?

And so the stories emerge. Ana Anba is twenty-seven years old. She is glassy-eyed, exhausted, on the verge of tears. For eleven days she has been at the bedside of her nine-year-old son, Ali. He is listless, barely conscious. Ana has purchased thousands of dinars of medicine since he became ill months ago with a respiratory infection. There's been no improvement. She wonders now if the medicine she bought on the black market was outdated. Or perhaps it was not what he really needed.

We tell her that we hope her story will help awaken parents and families in the United States. "When?" she asks with sharp insistence. The interpreter tries to gloss over her obvious anger. "She is frustrated and tired from six years of sanctions."

Ana interrupts sharply. "In America, would women want this for their children?" Then she turns to Ali and whispers softly, "It is for the children that we ask an end to the suffering, not for us."

Along with notes and photos, we also pool the personal requests we received—notes slipped into our hands begging for particular medicines. Even government workers in cabinet-level offices asked us for aspirin, eye drops, children's vitamins, and other over-the-counter items easily acquired in this country.

Our agenda is long and the tasks ahead seem daunting. Primarily, we need to find ways to dramatize our confrontations with the sanctions. The best way forward seems to be that of continuing our present effort to bring medical relief supplies to people in Iraq, in open and public violation of the sanctions.

Bob Bossie, a Catholic priest from Chicago, who traveled to Iraq twice in 1996 and was part of the Gulf Peace Team, speaks somberly. "The oil-for-food deal passed under [UN] Resolution 986 gives the impression to many people, even some of our supporters, that it will eliminate human suffering in Iraq. Really it's just a slower form of death."

Would it help, we wonder, to involve Gulf War veterans in our delegations? In July 1996, the Presidential Advisory Committee on Gulf War Veterans' Illnesses held a public hearing in Chicago.[10] I applied to speak to them on behalf of Iraqi children and was quite surprised to learn that I was allotted ten minutes, the same time given to veterans who had served in the Gulf.

All the veterans who spoke to the commission became so overcome with emotion that at some point they wept or halted their testimony to regain composure. They were painfully burdened physically, psychologically, or both, and some suspected their wartime service had led to family members' health problems. Clearly something happened to these men and women while they were in the Persian Gulf, and the government responsible for placing them there has been largely unresponsive.

One of the veterans testified to having been near a chemical weapons depot blown up by the US military. He described having undergone other traumas while serving in the Gulf War and following his return to the United States. A physician responded, "You seem to have been in the wrong place at the wrong time"—words of little comfort to the distraught soldier. Later, during my testimony, I had the doctor's comment in mind: "Surely we can't conclude that hundreds of thousands of Iraqi children were simply in the wrong place at the wrong time."

One cause of widespread anxiety is depleted uranium (DU), a subject that has stirred public debate and generated official military studies because of DU's toxic and radioactive effects on humans.

In metal form, DU is one of the densest materials known to science. As a by-product of the process to produce enriched uranium for nuclear reactors around the world, DU accumulates in huge stockpiles with few recycling opportunities to diminish the disposal problem. To the US military, DU has the double appeal of "improving" weaponry while eating into the DU stockpile.

But DU-tipped munitions had never been used in warfare before US and British forces employed them in Iraq. Particles and fragments of DU, more than 300 tons of such debris by the most conservative military estimates, remain scattered across Gulf War battlefields.[11] The consequences of ingesting DU particulate from the air or contaminated water supplies can be compared to the serious health hazards associated with lead, which is—like uranium—a toxic heavy metal.[12]

Actions commensurate with the crime

On a sweltering day, a camera crew positions itself in front of the Children's Hospital of the Saddam Medical Center. The crew is stringing for a London television company that wants to film me breaking a US law. When the cameraman signals, I grab my briefcase and clamber out of a parked car, then walk to the hospital entrance. Curious onlookers, some with sick children in their arms, read a handout I'd already passed out that briefly describes Voices in the Wilderness. I feel a bit awkward but, as planned, position myself in front of the hospital entrance. Squinting in the sunlight and clutching my briefcase, I announce:

> Inside this hospital is a little boy named Bishar. He suffers from leukemia and arrived here yesterday because he's gone out of remission. I believe I'm carrying, in my briefcase, medicines that could save his life, a cytotoxin called vincristin and a third-generation antibiotic. My government says that if I give Bishar these medicines, I'm committing a crime. I can tell you that I don't believe what I'm about to do is wrongful. Rather, the economic sanctions themselves are criminal, constituting one of the most egregious instances of child abuse in the entire world.

We then enter the hospital and go to Bishar's bedside, where I deliver the medicines to the hospital director.

The British television company was astonished to learn that we are threatened with twelve years in prison, a $1 million fine, and a $250,000 administrative penalty for the "crime" of bringing medicines and medical relief supplies to Iraqi children and families. In late 1998, we received another letter from the Treasury Department, a pre-penalty notice of a $160,000 fine. The Office of Foreign Assets Control mailed us a letter dated December 3, 1998, stating:

> The violations of the regulations and underlying statutes and Executive Orders for which this Notice is issued concern your and VW's exportation of donated goods, including medical supplies and toys, to Iraq absent specific prior authorization by OFAC and transactions relating to travel to Iraq and activities in Iraq.[13]

We had thirty days in which to respond, during which time our group jointly authored a letter thanking the Treasury Department for the clarity of its warning and assuring them that we had done what they accused us of, that we would continue to do so, and that we invited them to join us.

With respect to the enforcement of this embargo, we are conscientious objectors. We will not allow a government to dictate to our conscience. We will not allow the US government, in the name of democracy or national security, to order us to cooperate with a strategy designed to starve the people of Iraq, to deprive them of medicine and medical supplies, spare parts for infrastructure, pencils for schoolchildren, chlorine for water and sewage treatment, toys, employment, or any of the essentials necessary to sustain daily life.

However, we said we would not be paying any penalties, since money entrusted to us had been designated to assist with organizing our campaign and sending more delegations with medicines to Iraq: "Our funds have been contributed by citizens across this country for the expressed purpose of purchasing medicine and continuing the work of ending the embargo. In conscience, we cannot deviate from our stated mission."[14]

By creating a drama of confrontation with a law we believe to be wrongful, we continue hoping to build a means to reach out to and educate people. We think the sanctions wouldn't withstand the light of day if people really knew the terrible impact they have on innocent people. We try to convey, through eyewitness reports, the suffering and agony Iraqi families experience. Then we hope to contribute toward legislative efforts, media outreach, teach-ins, vigils, demonstrations, and written reports that are all essential components of campaigns to end the economic sanctions against Iraq.

Over the past few years, we've come to believe that the sanctions have strengthened President Hussein's regime. Because only the government can negotiate imports, people have to depend on it for rations. Fearing the loss of these basic necessities, as well as potential civil war were the government to weaken, many Iraqis reluctantly support the current regime. Iraqis have been cut off from communication with the outside world and are generally beleaguered; the middle class has been decimated; there has been a staggering "brain drain"; and most face mounting pressures just to survive. The generation coming of age in Iraq has experienced chronic malnutrition, its growth is stunted, and it is more vulnerable to illnesses. The death toll continues to rise as the medical infrastructure collapses.

Voices in the Wilderness will continue to work to ensure that the Iraqi people do not have to pay such a price. We must find actions that are commensurate with the crimes being committed.

Notes

1 Leslie Stahl, "Punishing Saddam," produced by Catherine Olian, CBS, *60 Minutes,* May 12, 1996.

2 See Lee Michael Katz, "Protest Doesn't Spoil Lovefest for Albright," *USA Today,* January 9, 1997, p. 10A.

3 Voices in the Wilderness Update, January 10, 1997. See the Voices web site for this and other letters (http://www.nonviolence.org/ vitw).

4 Eric Schmitt, "US Weighs the Value of Bombing to Coerce Iraq," *New York Times,* November 16, 1997, p. 1: 3, and Scott Shepard and Joseph Albright, "Allied Air Strikes Reportedly Shatter Iraq's War Machine," *Atlanta Journal and Constitution,* January 17, 1991, p. A1.

5 Barton Gellman, "US Bombs Missed 70% of Time," *Washington Post,* March 16, 1991, p. A1.

6 See Barton Gellman, "Allied Air War Struck Broadly in Iraq," *Washington Post,* June 23, 1991, p. A1.

7 See Maggie O'Kane, "Under the Shadow of the Bomb," *Manchester Guardian Weekly,* February 22, 1998, p. 1.

8 Fred Kaplan, "Powell: US to Be in Iraq for 'Months,'" *Boston Globe,* March 23, 1991, p. 1, and Patrick E. Tyler, "After the War," *New York Times,* March 23, 1991, p. 1.

9 David H. Harmon, Acting Supervisor, Enforcement Division, Office of Foreign Assets Control, January 22, 1996 (http://www.nonviolence.org/vitw/documents2.html).

10 See Olivia Wu, "Gulf Veteran Testifies on Illness," *Chicago Sun-Times,* July 9, 1996, p. 20.

11 Cherry Norton, "Danger That Divides Medical Opinion," *The Independent,* October 4, 1999, p. 3, and Paul Lashmar, "Why the Military Use 'Heavy Metal Poision' to Target Tanks," *The Independent,* October 4, 1999, p. 3. See also Huda Ammash, Chapter 13.

12 See Richard Norton-Taylor, "Doctor Blames West for Deformities," *Guardian,* July 30, 1999, p. 13, and Gary Finn, "Uranium 'Risk to 90,000 UK Troops,'" *The Independent,* November 22, 1998, p. 12.

13 R. Richard Newcomb, Director, Office of Foreign Assets Control, "Prepenalty Notice," OFAC Nos. IQ-162016 and IQ-162433, December 3, 1998 (http://www.nonviolence.org/vitw/htv2.html).

14 Kathy Kelly, for Voices in the Wilderness, letter to R. Richard Newcomb, December 30, 1998 (http://www.nonviolence.org/vitw/htv6.html).

Chapter 10

Targets—Not Victims

Barbara Nimri Aziz

Their father is gone. A heart attack. Sudden, uncomplicated, painless.

"Mustafa had a medical checkup only weeks before; our doctor said he was in good shape. Mustafa felt excellent. He was at work." His wife, Nasra Al-Sa'adoon, remembered that he was finishing up an article on the inconsistencies in United Nations sanctions regulations against Iraq. "It was a brilliant piece; he had been thinking about it and examining the documents for months. Finally, he understood and he was preparing it for publication. We talked about it that morning."

Mustafa just collapsed at his desk, they said. They phoned her at her office; by the time Nasra reached the hospital, he was gone. "I went back to his office that very day to collect his papers. I found the essay. He had essentially completed it, and I felt so good for him. I will see that it is published."

Nasra spoke about her husband's mission and his unfinished work, rather than her own personal grief. For an intellectual like her, perhaps it was a way to deal with her terrible sadness, at least publicly.

As far as I could tell, the fifty-three-year-old husband, father of two, and uncle of many showed no obvious strain as difficulties created by the sanctions mounted year after year. As the hardships affected more and more of those he loved, he felt more responsibility to them. If he could do little materially, he at least gave them hope. Many people across Iraq had grown confused and angry about the sanctions—quite naturally and justifiably. Mustafa, too, was perplexed, although he showed no bitterness.

Mustafa Al-Mukhtar saw potential in everything around him, from the fragrances in his garden to the books in his library, from the curious visitors at his door to a careless media report that needed correcting. I never witnessed any rancor in him, and I believe he truly felt none. I never heard him scorn Washington, London, or the United Nations during our many political discussions. He was a critical man—intellectually, not personally. Thus, he pointed to a specific falsehood, an inconsistency, an essential historical precursor to the big powers' present military and economic policies or to his own government's position.

It is possible that, as pressure on Iraq continued, and the government seemed to make no progress toward an easing of the embargo, Mustafa privately questioned its strategies. He may have criticized a particular decision by the leadership or proposed how a policy could be refined and improved; but, in general, he remained solidly in support of his people and his government. I mention this because I know it is hard for foreigners who hear only about the oppression in Iraq to imagine this, although British and American intelligence doubtless know Iraq has abundant dedicated and capable people like him. Moreover, despite their government's blunders and the mounting hardships, thousands of critical Iraqis like Mustafa won't give up. They continued to work long days during the embargo, even when facilities broke down. Both Mustafa and Nasra worked at home, too, where they had a library that is surely unique in the country. Most walls in their bungalow are lined with brimming bookshelves, and whatever wall space is free is dense with paintings by the best modern Iraqi artists and photographs of themselves, their ancestors, and their children.

Nasra and her husband seemed always available to talk to any visitor. The discussions that invariably flowed during these visits became part of an evening of stories, food, more friends. Both Mustafa and Nasra read profusely, reviewing literature in Arabic, English, and French. Both relished intellectual combat, testing their assessment of issues against anyone. This in itself did not distinguish them, since Baghdad was home to a robust community of thinkers, performers, and artists; but this family was unusual in its decision to remain on the margin of Baghdad's intellectual circle. They found it sometimes a little pretentious and more social than scholarly, said Mustafa. So, when the sanctions gradually decimated that group—because most painters, archaeologists, musicians, and professors either died, moved away, or became too depressed or impoverished to continue—this couple was less affected. Their vigor seemed unabated.

Mustafa and Nasra had their own projects, she in economic theory, and he in Iraqi political economy and nationalization policy. Still, they collaborated and shared ideas as a team. Nasra told me how, when they met a journalist or author, saw a film, or read a book or article, they came together afterward to compare notes. I am certain they did not always agree with one another. Yet, on the surface, they had a fine-tuned partnership.

Being such an easygoing, engaging family, they attracted some foreign visitors, first following the war, then through the regime of the sanctions;

and this seemed to offer even more nourishment for them. As the siege persisted, though, they became more selective of whom they spent their time with. Initially, a number of journalists came to the house to interview Nasra. Nasra Al-Sa'adoon is a powerful a critic of US policy and a tireless champion for Iraq. Dealing with the media, she is as sharp and articulate as the Palestinian spokesperson Hanan Ashrawi. Nasra could challenge and set straight any journalist or scholar.

One frequently found Japanese, Italian, Spanish, or French television crews at the house. Mustafa was usually present, letting Nasra take the spotlight. It was his style to quietly engage one or more producers on the other side of a room while the cameras were on Nasra.

The hardships of the embargo intensified as the decade wore on. One could not ignore the growing sense of despair. Whoever managed to survive paid a price, and many seemed to drag themselves through the day. Yet this couple became more determined to resist. Perhaps they realized how really important their skills and resources were. Like the few foreigners involved in the anti-sanctions campaign, Nasra and Mustafa were driven by the conviction that the United States and Britain were leading a venal campaign against Iraq and that this hypocrisy had to be exposed.

I have never been convinced that oil was the only concern for American and British ambitions in the region. Rather, I suspect that Iraq's resistance to the US government–led privatization program for the world was equally troubling to Washington. Iraq furthermore held steadfastly to its Baathist philosophy and showed no readiness to abandon its particular variety of Arab nationalism. Indeed, Iraq saw itself as the leading champion of Arab nationalism and, as such, it sought greater regional influence.

In 1988, as soon as Iraq signed its cease-fire with Iran and the two country's attacks on one another ended, Iraq swiftly turned its attention to helping define a new economic shape for the region. At home, it had already begun to permit some degree of private enterprise, and it encouraged what Mustafa described as cooperative government-private industries. During the 1980s, the government had begun to permit the sale of limited shares of some secondary industries. Aspects of transport and tourism, agriculture, fisheries, and even some sectors of the oil industry, such as gasoline stations and oil transport, could be partially held by private companies. But the Baathist government would never relinquish ultimate control over oil production and other major industries. (This is a position virtually all Iraqis share.)

No longer at war, Iraq also stepped up its activity in international affairs after 1988. It was a major financial and political supporter of the Palestinian intifada, which broke out in late 1987. Iraq was a leading member of the non-aligned movement and, within a year of the end of the war with Iran, moved to strengthen Arab solidarity with the establishment of regional co-operative economic councils. It sought to reestablish its status among other Arab states by hosting a summit of twenty-one Arab countries in June 1990. Baghdad also led the Arab states in rehabilitating Egypt, ostracized after its 1979 treaty with Israel, and engineered the shift of the office of the Arab League from Tunis to Cairo that year.

Although it had lost many young men in battle and was badly in debt, Iraq was moving rapidly ahead with economic development and with diplomacy, with the aim of defining itself once again as a leader. It made no reforms of oppressive civil policies at home, but on other fronts Iraqis were set to move forward. I visited Iraq three times between 1989 and 1990 and found the level of energy quite phenomenal. Reconstruction went on at a fierce pace. Travel restrictions were eased.

When Iraq invaded Kuwait in 1990, the country was suddenly presented as a threat to the world and "the American way of life." Western ideological strategists went to work. To convince the public of this danger, its media and political machinery served up an image of Iraq that was truly formidable. Fed by exaggerated reports about Iraq's biological and chemical weapons potential, world opinion continues to hold extreme fears of Iraq. Like Islamic fundamentalism, Iraq was "out of control" and had to be thwarted.

In his preface to his updated edition of *Fateful Triangle,* critic Noam Chomsky reviews the ubiquitous US interest in the Middle East. He notes, "In reality, the 'threats to [US] interests' in the Middle East, as elsewhere, had always been indigenous nationalism, a fact stressed in internal documents and sometimes publicly."[1] Here, Chomsky is concerned with Palestinian-Israeli relations, so he discusses the particular "indigenous nationalism" of Islamic fundamentalism manifested in the resistance movements of Hamas and Hezbollah. How far the US media and certain experts go to demonize Islam is well known. Washington has engaged in numerous campaigns to ostracize and destabilize nationalism—except, of course, where it can be used to garner opposition to another nationalism, as in the case of Afghanistan. Chomsky points out that an "indigenous nationalism" is only labeled as "ultranationalism," or "radical nationalism"—an enemy—when it is out of sync with US policy.[2]

For eight years, in its fight against Iran's new Islamic government, Washington wholeheartedly supported Iraq against Iran. When that war ended, Iraq, instead of being exhausted and impoverished, emerged ready to press ahead with its own ambitions. It also possessed a considerable arsenal—thanks to the assistance of its Western patrons during its war with Iran—though Iraq's supplies were small and low-tech compared with US and European weaponry.

In 1991, Iraq was easily driven from Kuwait and defeated militarily. But the assault led by the US and British governments would not halt with a military victory. Despite Iraq's handy defeat and the destruction of much of the country, they insist that Iraq is still uncontrollable. So, the sanctions remain, creating civil chaos, destroying the young, decimating the education system, crushing people's dignity, and driving out much of its professional class.

As the years have worn on, Iraq has become more isolated internationally. Culturally, the Iraqis had relied heavily on interaction with the West, which they so admired, and with Arab sister states. But that interaction has ground to a halt. Intellectually, Iraq has been cut off; it cannot import books or obtain paper to manufacture its own. Iraqis are hardly ever invited to professional conferences abroad. This has been particularly debilitating for a culture whose modernity was dependent on a keen communication with the US, Europe, and the Middle East. I recall a senior professor asking me to bring him a textbook in political science, his specialty. When I asked which title, he replied, "Anything, anything." He was gasping, as if on his death bed, and desperate from lack of contact.

Somehow, Mustafa was able to avoid this alienation. He managed to locate news of recent publications, though Iraq lacked (and still lacks) Internet access. He noted titles of general books I had not yet heard of, as well as specialist publications. He had a librarian's passion for compiling sources and was undeterred by the probability that barely 1 percent of what he might list would be attainable under sanctions. He took on a project to expand the bibliography of the Academy of Science newsletter, listing titles of whatever new books he could identify. Even if Iraq's scientists, diplomats, and researchers could not obtain these books, they would at least have some sense of the directions others were moving intellectually.

As economists and social critics, both Mustafa and Nasra were admirers and followers of Noam Chomsky. Mustafa heard about his book *Year 501: The Conquest Continues* within months of its appearance.[3]

Mustafa knew the US-led global economic campaign could weaken countries like Iraq. Like many in his generation, he remained a convinced Arab nationalist. He believed the oil wealth that Arab states like Iraq had been endowed with should never return to private or foreign control. He maintained that Iraq's economy was flexible and had become more pluralistic to work with private business and investment. Both Mustafa and Nasra were born into rich, landowning families, a class whose privileges and wealth ended with the monarchy and colonial rule over Iraq. That was a past era, and they held no nostalgia for it. They fully embraced the policies of land reform and the benefits of nationalization when Iraq became independent. Although many economic schemes had failed and improvements were needed, they believed postcolonial Iraq had managed to redistribute wealth fairly widely and to provide top facilities in education, research, and health.

This prosperity nourished Iraqi national pride across the country, but it could not be sustained under the sanctions. To hell with national pride when you can't find even a used tire for your wretched Toyota. To hell with my son becoming a civil engineer like his father; let him try to get a visa for New Zealand. To hell with guarding the national museum when I can't find some simple antibiotic to save my mother. Desperation swept aside work and civic ethics. People killed to steal a car tire; civil servants abandoned any notion of service. Coming out of the mosque, worshipers would find their shoes stolen. Women stopped going to the office because they could not dress properly and still provide the few supplies their children needed for school.

Mustafa Al-Mukhtar has been gone almost a year now, since January 1999. That leaves Nasra, his wife and partner of twenty-nine years, his daughter, Du'aa, born in France, and a graduate in French and English literature, and his son, Dhirar, about to enter college and studying for his high school finals even during the forlorn days following his father's death. I often thought when I met these youngsters over the years, "What a wonderful environment for a boy and girl to grow up in." In the extended family alone, they had a host of experts, a rainbow of opinions, and abundant love. Du'aa is so close to her father's sister, whose house is next door, that she almost lives with her. In recent years, Du'aa and her brother have joined their aunt in fasting together during Ramadan. Was this a sign of their maturity, or was it an outcome of the calamities created by the sanctions? I do not know.

No one escapes the sanctions. Even when they are not driven into poverty, everyone's dreams are somehow thwarted. Du'aa, who has the alert, watchful eyes of her mother, and relaxed composure of Mustafa, decided not to attend graduate school abroad. Nasra closed the bookstore she had opened just two years earlier and took up government service. Mustafa abandoned his business plans for a publishing company and concentrated on research and writing. The family ceased traveling, and the car was a wreck, although somehow, most of the time, they kept it running. When they stopped eating meat, Mustafa took it as a challenge and began showing off his new vegetarian dishes.

All around them, this family witnessed the rising toll. "Every week, I get a call about someone in the family who has passed," Nasra said. "Mustafa, too. I decided I am not going to wear black anymore. Otherwise, I will never take off my mourning clothes." Yet, here she sat, a few days after Mustafa's departure, in her black *abaya*. For forty days she would greet the many women and men who came from all across Iraq to praise Mustafa, to accept Allah's will, and to give her and the children some comfort.

Was Mustafa a victim of sanctions?

Each of us likely knows someone his age who was struck down by a heart attack. Heart disease is a common outcome of stressful living anywhere. So, it is not calculated among the diseases resulting from Iraq's embargo. But speak to any cardiologist in Iraq and he or she will tell you that there has been a doubling of the rate of heart attacks and tripling of the mortality rate among heart patients since 1991 because of the collapse of the health system.[4] Doctors no longer have the machines and medicines needed to treat these attacks.

Was Mustafa a victim of sanctions? Ask his forlorn wife and daughter, or his teenage son. Ask Mustafa's sister, Ferdous. (Mustafa was very proud of her cookbook, a tome she compiled twenty years earlier that remains the only cookbook documenting Iraq's unique cuisine.[5]) Ask the women at the Academy of Science, where Mustafa worked. Ask journalists at *Al-Jumhouriyah,* where he occasionally published his work. Was Mustafa killed by sanctions?

Across the nation, all Iraqis know that every one of them today—dead or alive—is a victim of the sanctions. It's simple and unequivocal for them, because the sanctions deprive the whole society of its intellectual strength and vigor, of its self-sufficiency, of its dignity. It's more than the grinding poverty. It's deprivation at every level. As the eminent economist

Amartya Sen explains, poverty created by deprivation of food and health means a deprivation of freedom.[6] Whatever political rights the Iraqi system has denied them, Iraqis once had the right of quality health care, education, and food. Now that has been taken away by the very powers that claim they set the standard for democracy and freedom.

Moreover, Iraqis have begun to understand that they are actually the targets of an ongoing war designed to destroy them. As Pam Africa, the prominent Philadelphia activist who has lead the campaign to free Mumia Abu-Jamal, says of police harassment of African Americans: "We are targets, not victims."

Not unexpectedly, with the accumulated effects of the deprivations and the feeling of being targeted, a malaise is overtaking the nation. This fact is behind the rising petty crime, the rampant and hitherto almost unknown corruption, the smuggling of museum antiquities, and the pillaging of archaeological sites. It is behind the readiness to betray one's friend, or to sell one's daughter. It is the source of a new greed, of unheard-of jealousy among brothers. It is the motive for the prevailing questions: how can I get out of here, and how can I get my child out?

Denis Halliday, the former head of the UN humanitarian program in Iraq, has spoken widely about the breakdown of Iraqi civil society, a breakdown that goes far beyond lack of food and medicines. (See Chapter 2.) The sanctions have penetrated into a sphere beyond the personal. The sanctions are rendering professional excellence obsolete; they are making knowledge redundant; they are making Iraq's great history irrelevant; they are mocking the value of its abundant oil resources. Those endowments, as much as Baath Party machinery, had accounted for indigenous Iraqi nationalism. Today, the Baath Party machinery and its military can still hold together a semblance of a society; they can offer farmers and merchants fortunes to produce wheat and to smuggle in essential light fixtures for the poor and luxuries for the elite; and they can spout a bizarre kind of nationalism that rings hollow to Iraqis and foreigners alike. But the real elements that made Iraq modern, dynamic, and capable are threadbare. The administration can organize, coerce, and order, but fewer Iraqis have hope and are able to plan; fewer can follow the example of Mustafa Al-Muhktar and others like him.

The US and Britain devised the embargo plan and maneuvered the UN into implementing it with alarming speed after the military invasion of Kuwait. Washington established a regime of worldwide compliance and ongoing policing that is truly formidable. Nine years later, this embargo remains rigidly enforced under US leadership, despite other nations' attempts to circumvent or ease it. Meanwhile, the terms of compliance keep shifting, so that no progress seems to be made toward an end. While smuggling and corruption continue to grow, a new small class of wealthy farmers and smugglers who work with the regime and are completely beholden to the party for their fortunes has emerged.

Periodically, the sanctions policy is discussed in the United Nations, but there is no serious debate about its removal. Compensation is paid out of Iraq's escrowed revenues in New York to Vietnamese, Sri Lankan, Egyptian, and other nationals who lost their jobs because of the Kuwait war. Iraq also pays for all UN operations related to the country—from the salaries of the sanctions committee at the UN headquarters to the Unscom inspectors who engaged in illegal spying while on duty in Iraq, to the $100,000-a-year salaries of hundreds of UN-appointed monitors who supervise distribution of the food that is permitted into Iraq. Iraqis are so outraged by the opulence they see exhibited by UN employees inside Iraq that their property has to be protected from public attacks and individual UN staff must carry special devices to protect themselves.

It is increasingly clear that the US and UK sanctions policy is a war not to remove a leader but to decimate a society. Kathy Kelly has rightly called the embargo "a weapon of mass destruction."[7] It is indeed just that. Its effect is to destroy Iraq's culture, modernity, and history.

Washington worked with Saddam Hussein before the invasion of Kuwait. The Iraqi leader was as despotic and as ambitious militarily during those years as he was in 1990. Iraq, moreover, never challenged or suggested anything but continued cooperation with Washington. Even though it was a leading critic of Israel, when Israeli planes attacked Iraq's Osirisk nuclear plant in 1981, Baghdad did not retaliate. But Washington was not satisfied with a military defeat at the end of the Gulf War. It had to get at the roots of the society, the people like Mustafa who made Iraq modern and forward-looking, people who wanted (and had the skills) to define another political path. Iraq had the technological and educational tools that could have established it as a pivotal regional leader.

This is not to say that one wanted to see Iraq's type of government flourish. The Baathist intolerance of individual liberties should be soundly rejected. But Iraq's leadership could have been a force of some significance, for example, in the non-aligned movement, in which Baghdad had been a major force; and it could have threatened US global economic interests or its domination of the United Nations. In that respect, Iraq represented an indigenous nationalist potential, and Washington decided it had to be neutralized militarily, technologically, and economically. Thus Iraqis with education, will, skills, and dreams became the targets. Institutions that taught, nourished, and supported them—such as museums, schools, medical colleges, fish hatcheries, the solar energy research center, clubs and seminars, and professional journals—had to be decimated, too.

In 1990, a high-ranking US military officer asked his planners and experts on Iraq "what is unique about Iraqi culture that they put very high value on [that our military could target]?"[8] The embargo is phase two of that bombing strategy. With it, Washington is telling men like Mustafa that his library will be sold and may disappear from the country, that his car will become useless, his phone will not work, and his life span will be halved. His educated children will not find work; or, with other hungry young men and women, they will go to the farms to dig potatoes; and the mosque will replace their electronics seminar.

The UN has instituted a relief program (paid for by Iraq) that ensures most of Iraq's population will not die of starvation. Yet Iraqis have become so weak that few can think beyond how to find enough food for their family. The oil-for-food scheme that the US government allowed the UN to put in place merely keeps famine at bay so Washington and its friends cannot be accused of genocide.

Was Mustafa just a victim? Or were he and the millions who have died or fled—infant or adult, woman or man, Kurd or Christian, teacher or student—targets?

Notes

1 Noam Chomsky, *Fateful Triangle: Israel, the United States, and the Palestinians*, updated ed. (Cambridge: South End Press Classics, 1999), p. x.
2 Chomsky, *Fateful Triangle*, p. xii.
3 Noam Chomsky, *Year 501: The Conquest Continues* (Boston: South End Press, 1993).
4 Based on author interviews with doctors at Kerbala General Hospital, Iraq, in 1995 and 1998.
5 Ferdous Al-Mukhtar and Naziha Adib, *Arabian Cuisine* (Surrey, UK: Surbiton/Laam Publishers, 1993).
6 See Amartya Sen, *Development as Freedom* (New York: Knopf, 1999).
7 Kathy Kelly, "Statement from Baghdad," February 23, 1998.
8 Rick Atkinson, "U.S. to Rely on Air Strikes if War Erupts," *Washington Post*, September 16, 1990, p A1.

Chapter 11

Sanctions: Killing a Country and a People

George Capaccio

On August 2, 1990, Iraq invaded Kuwait. Four days after the invasion, the United Nations instituted a comprehensive trade embargo against Iraq. Nine years later, it is still in place.

The stated purpose of the sanctions was to compel Iraq to withdraw from Kuwait without the "international community" having to resort to force of arms. In that respect, the strategy failed. In January 1991, the US government and its allies went to war. The "war" lasted only a few weeks, but it has contributed to the deaths of tens of thousands of Iraqis and left the country in ruins. No matter. Kuwait was "liberated." Yet the sanctions remained. Now their alleged purpose was to leverage Iraq to abide by the terms of UN Resolution 687. Among other demands, the resolution called for the dismantling of Iraq's "weapons of mass destruction."[1]

Once the bombing had stopped, the media and the government turned to other matters, forgetting the people of Iraq and their suffering in the aftermath of the Gulf War. In 1996, I decided to go to Iraq to witness the effects of war and six years of sanctions. From 1997 to 1999, I made six trips to Iraq with different organizations, each with its own mission. On two occasions, I traveled as a delegate with Voices in the Wilderness. I have also served on delegations sponsored by the American Friends Service Committee and Life for Relief and Development (a Muslim relief organization). In May 1998, I was one of more than eighty delegates with the Iraq Sanctions Challenge, which delivered millions of dollars of medicine to hospitals in Iraq. Most recently, in September 1999, I worked in Iraq under the auspices of the Middle East Council of Churches.

As an activist in the growing worldwide movement to lift sanctions against Iraq, I have traveled through south-central Iraq, as well as the UN-controlled governorates of the north. I have visited refugee camps, public hospitals, elementary and secondary schools, water treatment plants, and centers of culture and learning. Finally, I have become very close to several Iraqi families. They are an inseparable part of my own extended family. They are also a continual source of hope and inspiration in the struggle against sanctions and the system that keeps them in place.

Those who support sanctions generally argue that the government of Iraq is brutal and repressive and needs to be constrained; that a comprehensive trade embargo is the only way to compel that government to abide by the terms of UN Resolution 687; and that the suffering of the Iraqi people is largely due to the greed and corruption of the Baath Party regime of Saddam Hussein. When one refers to the growing body of evidence that points to sanctions as the major cause of malnutrition and infant mortality, one is likely to hear that Iraq can sell enough oil to meet the needs of its people under the terms of UN Resolution 986 (the "oil-for-food" deal).

Making tea: an interview with the FAO

During my second trip to Iraq, as a delegate with Voices in the Wilderness, I met with Mohammed Farah, Amir Khalil, and Yusef Ahmed Abdullah of the Food and Agriculture Organization (FAO), a UN agency with offices in Baghdad. We discussed the inadequacies of Resolution 986 and the complex interrelationship of all sectors of Iraqi society, particularly health and agriculture.

Mohammed Farah, the FAO coordinator for north Iraq, presented an overview of his agency's work since 1979: "We cover almost all agricultural activities, whether livestock, spare parts, spraying crops, veterinarian drugs, vaccination compounds."[2] As with every other aspect of life in Iraq, the production and distribution of food have been severely affected by sanctions. In the agricultural sector, Farah said, "there has been complete deterioration." He criticized aid programs that fail to address the complexity of the factors involved in food distribution:

> We can't bring in medicine without rehabilitating the hospitals. You can't give me seeds without giving me the fertilizer and the other inputs to agriculture. There should be a package approach to the problem.

Farah compared this approach to making tea:

> You give me the tea, you give me the pot, you give me the water, you give me the gas. If you don't give me such things, I cannot prepare a cup of tea. For me, in agriculture, you can give me five inputs, but if one is missing, I cannot use the five.

The FAO in Iraq has been authorized to conduct a crop-spraying program in the south. However, the agency has at its disposal only three helicopters. Each one is more than twenty years old. "Today, if there is an outbreak of any disease or infestation, we cannot do anything about it," Farah said. One pest that is poised to create an epidemic of disease and death is the Old World screwworm fly. This insect is a fly that lays up to 500 eggs on the body of an animal. The larvae are flesh-eating. If the animal is not treated quickly, it will die a horrible death. To date, according to the FAO officials we interviewed in January 1998, there have been more than 50,000 documented cases of screwworm infestation in Iraq.

Not only does the screwworm fly infest animals, it also lays its eggs in humans. Farah noted:

> The human cases we have seen are children in rural areas where hygienic conditions are low. What the fly usually does is crawl up the nose and lay its eggs in the frontal sinuses. So the child doesn't know what is happening until the maggots crawl out of his nose.

Control of the screwworm fly and treatment of infected animals and humans point to the need for a coordinated approach to the problems affecting Iraq and to the inadequacy of the UN's response to these problems. As Amir Khalil explained,

> The state veterinary infrastructure used to have cold storage chambers in each veterinary hospital in the provincial capitals. All these cold storage chambers no longer function because they've had no spare parts and they don't even have generators to provide electricity. This means that the veterinarians come from the field to Baghdad to fill up iceboxes with ice and vaccines and then drive back to the field.[3]

The spare parts aren't available because they are banned under the sanctions' "dual use" provisions.

Under the current terms of Resolution 986, unanimously passed by the Security Council on April 14, 1995, Iraq is permitted to sell oil to raise revenues for humanitarian spending controlled by the United Nations. In 1998, at the time of this interview, the ceiling for oil sales was set at $2 billion worth of oil every six months, though it was raised in 1999. Iraq receives oil-for-food revenue (all the money from these sales are held in an escrow account in the Bank of Paris in New York City) only after money is first paid to Kuwait as war reparation and to the UN to cover its daily operation costs in Iraq.[4] The remaining amount is simply not enough, Khalil argued, to address the complex relationship between poverty, infrastructure decay, and disease. His colleague Yusef Abdullah added:

> If you feed the population, but the water is contaminated, people will eat, get diarrhea, and die. At the same time, there are no medicines, so you get more mortality, even though you're distributing food. [If] you don't have electricity, you don't have water and sanitation, you don't have health.

With the collapse of the health care system and the veterinary diagnostic and control infrastructure, brucellosis (affecting cattle and causing a high fever in humans), tuberculosis, and anthrax, among other diseases, are becoming almost impossible to control. In addition, we were told, birth abnormalities are appearing in sheep, possibly due to the depleted uranium used during the Gulf War.

Our discussion repeatedly returned to the issue of sanctions. While they were careful to position themselves as professionals and technocrats who keep politics out of their work, all three clearly indicated their opposition to sanctions and their exasperation with the political impasse that made it extremely difficult for them to fulfill their mandate to increase food production.

Toward the end of our interview, Mohammed Farah held up a copy of a September 1995 FAO report, which compared Iraqi children with children in Sudan, Senegal, and other poor countries in terms of calories, body weight, and malnutrition.[5] "Iraq is falling below that standard," he noted.

Health care under sanctions

During the Gulf War in 1991, coalition forces dropped more than 85,000 tons of bombs on Iraq in a six-week period.[6] In addition to military targets, the aim of this massive aerial bombardment was the destruction of the country's life-support system, especially its ability to produce and distribute clean, potable water to its citizens. Because of sanctions, water and sewage treatment plants continue to operate at a critically reduced capacity. Children who drink untreated water in Iraq are at great risk. Water-borne diseases such as gastroenteritis, cholera, typhus, and typhoid fever, in combination with chronic and acute malnutrition and upper respiratory illness, have had severe consequences.

According to a 1999 Unicef study, "both the infant mortality rate (IMR) and the under-five mortality rate (U5MR) consistently show a major increase in mortality over the 10 years preceeding the survey.... These mortality results show a more than two-fold increase over a ten year time span."[7] A previous Unicef report found that "The increase in mortality reported in public hospitals for children under five years of age (an excess of 40,000 deaths yearly compared with 1989) is mainly due to diarrhea, pneumonia and malnutrition. In those over five years of age, the increase (an excess of some 50,000 deaths yearly compared with 1989) is associated with heart disease, hypertension, diabetes, cancer, liver, or kidney diseases."[8]

Concerning malnutrition, Unicef found: "Malnutrition was not a public health problem in Iraq prior to the embargo. Its extent became apparent by 1991 and the prevalence has increased greatly since then.... By 1997, it was estimated about one million children under five were chronically malnourished."[9] Poor diet, contaminated drinking water, and lack of sanitation are responsible for this growing incidence of malnutrition among Iraqi children. "Accessibility to food beyond the amounts provided through public rations is limited by soaring food prices.... At least 80 percent of a family's income is spent on food."[10]

By 1990, Iraq had developed one of the most efficient and effective health care systems in the Middle East. Thanks to the Gulf War and the ongoing sanctions, that health care system is now in ruins.

"They are all of them going to be dead"

As a delegate with various humanitarian organizations, I have spent much time on the pediatric and cancer wards of many public hospitals in Iraq—in the cities of Mosul and Arbil in the north, Baghdad in the central region, and Amara, Nasiriyah, and Basra in the south. Here one sees most clearly the destructive force of sanctions and their impact on the young. I have interviewed doctors and hospital administrators about the conditions under which they work. More important, I have met with hundreds of parents and witnessed firsthand what they and their children are suffering.

In one hospital in Mosul, on a winter's day, I stood in a cold room surrounded by children afflicted with septicemia, a blood disease. I turned to our guide, a member of the Iraqi Red Crescent Society, and asked him about the prognosis for these patients. Normally a calm, restrained man, he turned toward me with a look I had not until that moment seen on his face. He appeared exasperated by my question. "Sometimes you know because of the shortage of medicines, they are all of them going to be dead," he said.[11] Then he turned away.

On a previous trip to Iraq, I visited the Saddam Teaching Center in Baghdad and spoke to Dr. Muhammed Hillal, chief of pediatrics, who showed me the children's oncology unit. In Iraq, prior to 1990, he explained, the remission rate for leukemia and other forms of cancer was about 70 percent, comparable to the United States. Now, he said, it is between 6 and 7 percent. Dr. Hillal attributed the sharp increase in childhood cancer since the imposition of sanctions to the use of depleted uranium bullets and mortar shells by coalition forces in the Gulf War.[12]

For most families, medical treatment for leukemia is simply too expensive. At the same time, recently developed chemotherapeutic agents are rarely available in Iraq. Cancer is a death sentence for Iraqi children, for whom supportive—not curative—care is too often the only course of treatment available.

Dr. Hillal introduced me to a fourteen-year-old girl named Shaima. She lay on a blanket from home. A pathetic, collapsed blood bag hung from a pole above her. A needle punctured her wrist, which was thin and delicate, almost transparent. She looked up at me but was too weak to move, much less speak. Her mother and grandmother wept openly by her side. "She has Hodgkin's lymphoma," Dr. Hillal told me. "The family has sold everything for treatment. We do not have the necessary drugs to treat her. She has only two, possibly three days more."

In January 1998, I visited Al Karama Hospital in Baghdad. Our delegation met with the hospital director, Dr. Raad Yusufani. Dressed in a conservative suit, starched shirt, and dark tie, he guided us from ward to ward. Staff members stood at attention as soon as he entered. Dr. Yusufani rarely smiled. There was great sadness in his eyes. "We do our best," he told us in one of the hallways. "Determination is all we have left."[13]

The hospital's entire heating system had broken down and couldn't be repaired. We could see our breath as we followed our guide and met with patients and doctors. On the pediatric ward, the only source of warmth was a heater a family had provided. The parents pointed with pride toward a fluorescent lightbulb on the wall above their son's bed. They bought the bulb themselves. The hospital couldn't even afford to replace it.

On the dialysis and coronary care units, poor men and women huddled beneath woolen blankets. Some were sleeping. Others stared off into space or looked at us through stark, frightened eyes. "We have thirteen dialysis machines," Dr. Yusufani explained. "Only six are working. We can't get spare parts or purchase new machines."

Catheters for patients with renal disease must be reused. Cannula for IV transfusion is in short supply. So too are basic cleaning agents and disinfectants. In one room, the floor was spattered with blood. Bloody bandages and tubing filled a waste basket beside a patient's bed.

Faced with critical shortages of essential surgical supplies and equipment, doctors at Al Karama are able to perform only about six operations a week. The norm had been thirty before sanctions. "In the summer," continued the hospital's director, "we must operate without air conditioning. Sometimes it is 120 degrees Fahrenheit. With so little anesthesia and antibiotics, always we must decide which patients will live and which will die."

As we returned to his office, my eye caught sight of the charred remains of a library beside the main entrance. "Last year there was a fire," Dr. Yusufani told us. "It destroyed all of our medical books and journals. We cannot purchase new ones, nor can we afford to make photocopies."

Back in his office, we asked about the "oil-for-food" deal. "Has it brought any improvement?" Dr. Yusufani shook his head and smiled with just the slightest trace of irony. "It doesn't prolong life," he said. "It only makes life seem longer."

Speaking truth to power

I traveled to Iraq for the first time with Voices in the Wilderness in March 1997. At the end of our stay, our delegation met with officials at the US Embassy in Amman, Jordan. We informed them that we had openly broken the travel ban prohibiting American citizens from traveling to Iraq without government approval. While displaying enlarged photos of malnourished Iraqi children, we also described what we had witnessed.

When it was my turn to speak, I could see the dimly lit hospital rooms and hallways in Iraq where the cost of a single fluorescent bulb is prohibitive. I recalled the overcrowded pediatric wards I had recently visited. I told US Embassy officials about the conditions I had witnessed in Iraqi hospitals. Charlie Hefferman, the consul and first secretary, listened attentively and somewhat sympathetically. Steven Thibeault, the press attaché, explained, "My job is not to justify but to clarify US policy."[14]

The impact of sanctions on Iraq's educational system

On the streets of Baghdad and other cities, you see evidence of the thousands of Iraqi children who have dropped out of school to help support their families.[15] The collapse of the Iraqi economy, due to the embargo, has produced high unemployment, along with hyperinflation and devaluation of the local currency. With rising prices and a scarcity of decent jobs, families must often resort to extreme measures to earn a livable income. Taking their children out of school and putting them to work is one such measure. Prostitution is another.

In April 1999, I returned to Iraq, this time with a delegation of teachers sponsored by the American Friends Service Committee (AFSC). Our mission was to assess the impact of sanctions on Iraq's educational system. We visited elementary and secondary schools in south-central Iraq; met with teachers, principals, and officials in the Ministry of Education; and interviewed Unicef representative Anupama Rao Singh and UN humanitarian aid coordinator at the time, Hans von Sponeck.

The experience of the AFSC teacher delegation to Iraq bears out the findings of Unicef and other humanitarian agencies monitoring the impact of sanctions on the Iraqi population. On the basis of our work, we concluded that Iraq's ability to provide fully subsidized, quality education for all children has been seriously jeopardized by the embargo. While various non-governmental organizations—such as the Middle East Council of Churches, the United Nations Educational, Scientific, and Cultural Organization (Unesco), and Unicef—are involved in school rehabilitation programs, the learning and physical environments of most schools continue to deteriorate.

For additional information about conditions in Iraqi schools prior to 1990, I spoke with Dr. Karim Khudieri, a former secondary school teacher and dean of the College of Agriculture at the University of Baghdad. Dr. Khudieri now lives in Boston, where he had served as a professor of biology at Northeastern University before his retirement. Even during the Iran-Iraq War (1980–1988), according to Dr. Khudieri, the Iraqi government maintained its commitment to high-quality education.[16] "The government built schools, trained teachers, and provided textbooks to students free of charge ... graduates from high schools were accepted to universities all around the world." Children in the primary grades, explained Dr. Khudieri, received milk, cod liver oil, biscuits, hummus, fresh fruit, and vitamins on a daily basis. In addition, each child received an adequate supply of copy books, pencils, and erasers and a new textbook for each subject area at the beginning of the school year. Other Iraqi expatriates whom I have subsequently interviewed contend that Iraq's educational system began to decline during the 1980s as a consequence of the war with Iran. However, they agree that the 1991 Gulf War and the embargo certainly accelerated this decline and led to the current crisis.

After nine years of sanctions, only the desire to learn remains intact. All else is falling apart or has long since vanished. In each school we assessed, roughly the same situation prevailed. Iraqi teachers, once highly respected and well-paid professionals, now receive an average monthly salary of $3. In the past, by contrast, the salary was about $450. Moreover, teachers received benefits and cash advances with which to purchase land. Currently, teachers must either change professions or work a second job to supplement their income.

Because of a population increase and constraints on the building of new facilities, existing primary and secondary schools now utilize two shifts. Typically, one group of students attends classes from 8:00 in the morning until noon. A second shift begins at 12:30 and ends at 4:30 in the afternoon. The school year runs from September through May.

Shakir Taher, principal of the Al Bakr School for boys in Nasiriyah, graduated in 1990 from the University of Mosul with a degree in history and education. He has been a principal for five years. On the afternoon the delegation met with him, he had spent the morning selling cigarettes on the streets because his salary is insufficient to provide for the needs of his family.[17] His story, unfortunately, is not exceptional. Neither is the transformation his school has undergone since 1990. What has happened to the Al Bakr School is emblematic of what is taking place in schools throughout south-central Iraq.

Each classroom the delegation visited was nearly identical in terms of the kind of learning environment it provided (or failed to provide). There were no desks and no chairs, either for the students or the teachers. Most of the windows were broken. There were no supplies of any kind. Nothing hung on the walls—not even a chart, a poster, or a sample of student work. The school had no intercom system, computers, rulers, maps, globes, books, or stationery of any kind. The barrenness of the classrooms was unbroken, save for the appearance of a single green board and a tin can holding nuggets of chalk. Without chairs, the students, all boys, sat on their copy books or on bent metal scraps. A few "lucky" students hunched over the skeletal remains of an ancient desk. In each class there was only one torn, dilapidated textbook shared by all.

Besides having overcrowded classrooms, the school lacks even a rudimentary heating and cooling system. Previously, each room had its own stove. Now, when the cold weather comes, students sit on straw mats in unheated rooms. The windows must be covered with cardboard. In late spring, when temperatures are well above 100 degrees, there are no ceiling fans or air conditioning. As with all the schools visited by the AFSC delegation, sanitation facilities at Al Bakr School were minimal. They consisted of one toilet with a non-functioning urinal and an exposed, poorly maintained stall. A battered can under a dripping tap served as the school's one and only source of drinking water.

Principals, teachers, and government officials in the governorates of Basra, Amara, and Nasiriyah were unanimous in their opinion that every effort is being made to maintain high academic standards despite sanctions and to teach the same basic curriculum at the primary and secondary levels. Undoubtedly, teachers and administrators are doing their best under conditions of extreme deprivation. However, according to the director of Unicef in Baghdad, Anupama Rao Singh, there has been no systematic evaluation of academic standards since 1989.[18]

In separate interviews, Singh and Hans von Sponeck concurred that only 1 percent of oil revenues under UN Resolution 986 is allotted to education.[19] Given the severity of government cutbacks in education and the resulting shortages of instructional materials, along with the degradation of existing facilities, an entire generation of Iraqi children may not acquire the academic competence to which they are entitled under the Convention on the Rights of the Child.

Notably absent from every school the delegation visited in southern Iraq were medical facilities of any kind. There were no school nurses or pharmaceutical supplies, such as aspirin, Band-Aids, or antiseptic. Moreover, none of the schools were able to maintain any kind of food program. Many of the students came to school without having had breakfast.

In each school evaluated by the delegation, many of the students appeared visibly malnourished and stunted, particularly children from centers for "internally displaced persons." In these centers, which are in fact refugee camps, families subsist almost entirely on government food rations. These rations, given on a monthly basis, consist of white rice, flour, legumes, sugar, tea, powdered milk, and cooking oil.

Suham Said Sadoon, principal of the Ishtar School, estimated that between seven and eight students faint each day from lack of food.[20] She also noted an increase in cases of diarrhea, gastroenteritis, and skin allergies—medical problems the school is unable to address because of its lack of resources. Students with gastrointestinal problems must be sent home since the school has no toilets. In some cases, sick children are referred to a nearby clinic for treatment. Unfortunately, the clinic almost never has enough medicine on hand.

The way forward

For those who seek to end sanctions and the needless suffering of the Iraqi people, compassion is the first step. Organized opposition is the second. If we wish to effect positive change, we must unite and stand together against the policies and institutions that seek to "contain Saddam" by crushing his people. In the 1960s, hundreds of thousands of ordinary people came together to protest the war against Indochina. The war-makers heard their voices. It took time. It took struggle. It took sacrifice. But in the end the people won. The United States pulled its forces out of Vietnam.

The antiwar movement that surfaced in the 1960s was an expression of a politics of dissent deeply rooted in American culture and history. Today this tradition is once again asserting itself in response to the challenge of sanctions. People who oppose the sanctions against Iraq are not alone. They are part of an international community of activists and peacemakers who keep each other informed via the Internet; who organize marches and demonstrations in their towns and cities; who put pressure on their elected representatives; who challenge the mainstream media to present the truth of what is happening inside Iraq; who understand that an organized, committed group of individuals, guided by compassion and a keen sense of justice, can create a change of policies and put an end to the sanctions.

Notes

1 UN Security Council Resolution 687, section C, paragraphs 7–9. All UN resolutions cited are available online at http://www.un.org.
2 Mohammed Farah, author interview, Baghdad, January 7, 1998.
3 Amir Khalil, author interview, Baghdad, January 7, 1998.
4 See UN Office of the Iraq Program "Oil-for-food—The Basic Facts." Available at http://www.un.org/Depts/oip/reports/basfact.html.
5 UN Food and Agriculture Organization, *Evaluation of Food and Nutrition Situation in Iraq, Terminal Statement prepared for the Government of Iraq by the Food and Agriculture Organization of the United Nations* (Rome: FAO, 1995), p. 25. See section 4.
6 Michael T. Klare, "'Weapons of Mass Destruction in Operation Desert Storm," in *Collateral Damage: The 'New World Order' at Home and Abroad,* ed. Cynthia Peters (Boston: South End Press, 1992), p. 218.
7 Unicef press release, "Iraq Survey Shows 'Humanitarian Emergency,'" August 12, 1999 (Cf/doc/pr/1999/29). See Unicef and Government of Iraq Ministry of Health, *Child and Maternal Mortality Survey 1999: Preliminary*

Report (Baghdad: Unicef, 1999), Chapter 4, p. 9. Available online at http://www.unicef.org.

8 Unicef, *Situation Analysis of Children and Women in Iraq* (Baghdad: Unicef, 1997), part two, p. 42.

9 Unicef, *Situation Analysis of Children and Women in Iraq*, part two, p. 23.

10 Unicef, *Situation Analysis of Children and Women in Iraq*, part two, p. 29.

11 Dahar Al Zobai, author interview, Baghdad, January 9, 1998.

12 Dr. Muhammed Hillal, author interview, Baghdad, March 23, 1997. On depleted uranium, see Robert Fisk, Chapter 7, and Huda Ammash, Chapter 13.

13 Dr. Raad Yusufani, author interview, Baghdad, January 5, 1998.

14 Steven Thibeault, author interview, Amman, Jordan, March 26, 1997.

15 See Michael Yamashita's photograph of a four-year-old Iraqi child hammering chain links in *National Geographic* 196: 5 (November 1999): 15. See also Leon Barho, "Suffer the Children," *Ottawa Citizen,* February 15, 1999, p. B13.

16 Dr. Karim Khudieri, author interview, Wellesley, Massachusetts, April 20, 1999.

17 Shakir Taher, author interview, Nasiriyah, Iraq, April 8, 1999.

18 Anupama Rao Singh, author interview, Baghdad, April 4, 1999.

19 Hans von Sponeck, author interview, Baghdad, April 4, 1999.

20 Suham Said Sadoon, author interview, Amara, April 6, 1999.

Part 4

Documenting the Impact of Sanctions

Photographs of Iraqis who died in the US bombing of the Amariyah shelter (see pp. 115–16). Photo by Alan Pogue (July 1998).

Chapter 12

Sanctions, Food, Nutrition, and Health in Iraq

Dr. Peter L. Pellett

As a response to the invasion of Kuwait, the United Nations Security Council adopted Resolution 661 on August 6, 1990, imposing multilateral sanctions against Iraq. It is now clear that these sanctions have proved to be the most severe in history.

The government of Iraq immediately recognized that these international actions could destroy its ability to survive. Within weeks, the Ministry of Trade introduced national food rationing to feed the population despite the sanctions. The basic scheme, with its integral income subsidy, remains in place today and can be seen as the fundamental reason for Iraq's having been able to withstand the embargo for so long.

Initially sanctions were viewed as a short-term penalty to force Iraq to withdraw from Kuwait. The UN imposed a blanket ban on all imports and exports. As the Center for Economic and Social Rights (CESR) notes, the Security Council then "decided to allow only the import of 'supplies intended strictly for medical purposes, and, in humanitarian circumstances, foodstuffs.' It was left to the discretion of the sanctions committee, created under Resolution 661, to determine what constituted humanitarian circumstances." By March 1991, the United States and its allies "had driven Iraqi forces out of Kuwait by military force, in the process destroying or disabling most of Iraq's civilian infrastructure, including factories, electric power stations, and water treatment and sewage plants."[1] The cutoff in oil sales consequently devastated the economy of Iraq, which formerly had provided its citizens with some of the best social and health services in the Arab world.

The Security Council's decision to maintain sanctions despite the destruction of Iraq's civilian infrastructure during the Gulf War, and the inability, until late 1996, of Iraq and the council to agree on humanitarian exceptions to the sanctions, led to a steep increase in hunger, disease, and death throughout Iraqi society, especially among women, children, and the elderly. The population of Iraq, which formerly enjoyed some services comparable to those in the West, has suffered terrible hardship because of the sanctions. In effect, the population moved from the edge of first-world status to poor, third-world status with staggering speed.

In 1990, then–Central Intelligence Agency director William Webster said in testimony to Congress, "Our judgment has been and continues to be that there is no assurance or guarantee that economic hardships will compel Saddam to change his policies or lead to internal unrest that would threaten his regime."[2] The correctness of this prediction, generally ignored, can be seen from the fact that more than nine years of the most severe Security Council sanctions in history have not loosened the control of Saddam Hussein's government. Instead, they have devastated the most vulnerable sectors of Iraqi society, especially children. As the CESR has noted, there has been an astonishing lack of public debate over the UN's role in this massive violation of human rights, and particularly children's rights.[3] Then–UN Secretary-General Boutros Boutros-Ghali pointed out in 1995 that the international community had failed to confront "the ethical question of whether suffering inflicted on vulnerable groups in the target country is a legitimate means of exerting pressure on political leaders whose behavior is unlikely to be affected by the plight of their subjects."[4] We still do not have an answer. This silence is especially troubling in light of the post–cold war Security Council's frequent and uncritical use of sanctions as the preferred means to pressure states and maintain international peace and security.[5]

Iraq: country background

The Iraqi economy had been dominated by the oil sector from the early 1950s until the major cessation of exports in 1990. During this period, there had been an improving standard of living for the vast majority of the population, including very significant advances in the provision of health care. As a result of these improvements, the infant mortality rate in Iraq had declined from about 120 per 1,000 live births in 1960 to about 45 per 1,000 by the late 1980s. Following the imposition of sanctions in 1990, the infant mortality rate returned to more than 100 per 1,000 by 1998.[6] Economic decline proceeded very rapidly in the first half of the 1990s.

The total land area of Iraq is 43.5 million hectares (a hectare is equivalent to 2.47 acres), of which 91.2 percent is in south-central Iraq and only 8.8 percent is in the three autonomous northern governorates. Of the total land area, only 28 percent is arable, with much of the rest being desert. About 8 million hectares are located within the irrigated facilities, and 4 million hectares are rain-fed. The actual cultivated land area is still lower: 5.75 million hectares, of which 3 million are located in south-central Iraq and 2.75 million hectares are in the north.[7] In consequence, it is not surprising that food production is far more difficult in south-central Iraq, where the climate is also more extreme.

About 74 percent of the irrigated lands, mainly in south-central Iraq, have salinity problems; as a result, several thousand hectares are going out of cultivation annually. Although the agricultural sector was given high priority by the government to ensure food security through greater self-sufficiency, a high dependence on imported foods remains. Cereal production continues to decline, and domestic flour is frequently of poor quality. Major constraints on agricultural production include the lack of functioning agricultural machinery, particularly of essential replacement and spare parts, as well as high-quality seeds, fertilizers, pesticides, and herbicides, all of which have resulted in declines in output.

Livestock, poultry, and fish subsectors also suffer from severe setbacks because of shortages of machinery, equipment, spare parts, and essential veterinary drugs. A major recent problem, which could also threaten neighboring countries, is the spread of foot and mouth disease. This is an acute, highly contagious viral infection and is now present throughout Iraq. It affects cattle, buffalo, sheep, and goats, causing high morbidity and heavy losses in newly born animals from infected mothers. The factory that used to produce foot-and-mouth-disease vaccine was partially destroyed by the UN Special Commission (Unscom) biological weapons monitoring program.[8] In addition, Iraq's capacity for dealing with the disease, even with imported vaccine, has been limited and constrained by lack of adequate refrigeration and transport.

Food safety in Iraq is also a concern, especially for locally produced items. The food industry in Iraq was returned to the private sector in 1990, but total production remains only a fraction of the pre-1991 level. This has a variety of causes, including the lack of production equipment, raw materials, and packaging. It has been more profitable in recent years to import products, both legally and illegally, from the cheapest sources, than to produce locally. (These goods are often past their expiration dates or have been declared unfit for human consumption.) This is because many necessary materials, such as stainless steel, and certain chemicals are embargoed.

International food availability data from the UN Food and Agriculture Organization (FAO) is reported annually for more than 150 member nations.[9] Only in Iraq has there been such a precipitous decline in average availability over recent years. Daily availability dropped from 3,375 kilocalories per capita in 1987–1988 to 2,277 kilocalories in 1993–1995.[10] This was not due to generalized regional factors and conditions affecting production, such as the weather. Six neighboring countries all showed food energy supplies either increasing or remaining stable over the same period. Again, the direct and indirect effects of sanctions produced the observed decline in food energy availability. The daily availability of protein for Iraq fell from 67.7 grams to 43.3 grams during the same period, while values for the other countries either increased or remained stable.[11]

Food and nutrition evaluation missions

In addition to nutrition activities by UN agencies within Iraq, three missions visited Iraq in 1993, 1995, and 1997 under the auspices of the FAO. All three missions were similar in composition and terms of reference. Each mission comprised nutritionists, agriculturists, and agricultural economists whose task was to assess the crop and food availability situation and to investigate the nutritional status of the population in light of the ongoing sanctions.

The staff of UN agencies based in Baghdad and elsewhere in the country—including the United Nations Children's Fund (Unicef), the UN Development Program (UNDP), the World Food Program (WFP), and the World Health Organization (WHO)—and from the government agencies and non-governmental organizations (NGOs) involved in food and nutrition activities gave each mission full cooperation. We were able to visit all parts of the country, including the autonomous north. The three mission reports produced by the missions all demonstrated declines in food availability, significant increases in malnutrition, and severe deterioration in public health.[12] By the time of the 1997 mission, however, a significant change in emphasis was discernible in the position of the Iraqi government. The government openly acknowledged the seriousness of the food and nutrition situation. Because it had reached an agreement with the Security Council, an improved food ration was becoming available throughout the country through the oil-for-food program, based on Security Council Resolution 986.

Global considerations in food, health, and nutrition

Only in recent years have the political and socioeconomic dimensions of malnutrition received adequate attention.[13] As Table 1 shows, the causes of malnutrition are now discussed at three key levels: immediate causes, underlying causes, and basic causes.[14] In the past, nutritionists had usually limited their attention to immediate causes, such as lack of food or nutrients, and had been less appreciative of underlying and basic causes of malnutrition; nutrition professionals had generally hesitated to engage with the political dimensions of malnutrition because of difficulties in influencing these dynamics. Nevertheless, these basic political and economic causes of malnutrition are fundamental. Unless they are changed, it is unlikely that our actions in dealing with the immediate and underlying causes are likely to be successful, except in the very short term. The new international emphasis on relating nutrition to human rights recognizes the importance of these fundamental factors and may influence policies in the future.[15] In Iraq, the most fundamental factor influencing food, nutrition, and health in recent years has been the economic embargo.

Table 1: Levels of Determinants

Level	Determinants
Immediate Causes	Food Intake and Health
Underlying Causes	Income, Land, Water, Fuel, Education, Health Service Availability
Basic Causes	Resources, Economics, Politics

Source: See note 14.

A high correlation generally exists between wealth, expressed as gross national product (GNP), and a number of food availability and health indices. As wealth increases, there is increased availability of food energy; total protein and animal protein availability increases; child mortality declines; and life expectancy increases. Before 1990, Iraq could be classified among Group III nations with an annual GNP in excess of $3,000 per capita. Recent estimates for Iraq, following nine years of sanctions, place real GNP below $500 per capita. Iraq is now in Group I, among the poorest countries in the world.[16] Food, nutrition, and health indicators for Iraq have all declined to values appropriate to the new economic grouping.

The situation in Iraq

Prior to the Gulf War, Iraq had one of the highest per-capita food-availability ratings in the region, due to its relative prosperity and capacity to import large quantities of food, which met up to two-thirds of food requirements. The imposition of UN sanctions in August 1990 significantly constrained Iraq's ability to earn the foreign currency needed to import sufficient quantities of food to meet its needs. As a consequence, food shortages and malnutrition became progressively more severe and chronic. That food availability before the Gulf War was more than adequate has been corroborated by numerous nutrition assessments, including a nutrition survey of children under eight years old conducted in the Baghdad area in 1989 in which the distribution of weight and height was found to be similar to those of the international reference population.[17] Since this period, the nutritional health of the population has deteriorated significantly. This has been documented by a number of nutritional surveys undertaken between 1991 and 1997. Indeed, nutritional catastrophe has been avoided only by the widespread availability of the government food rations in south-central Iraq and by the presence of NGOs and foreign aid in the north.

A number of investigations have been undertaken into the state of nutrition and health in Iraq under the embargo. In addition to the three FAO missions, the Harvard Study Team undertook two large surveys—in 1991, immediately after the cessation of hostilities, and again, under a new name, the Center for Economic and Social Rights, in 1996.[18] The media gave greater attention to the 1995 FAO report because of the interest of Ramsey Clark and the International Action Center, which reprinted the report in the book *The Children Are Dying*.[19] Unicef, in association with the Iraqi Ministry of Health, has also undertaken nutritional assessment activities, as well as very recent examinations of child and maternal mortality rates over the whole period of the sanctions.[20]

Many NGOs have been active in the autonomous northern governorates, especially before the mid-1990s. There were also large quantities of Western aid specifically earmarked for the north. In contrast, in south-central Iraq, there has been very little NGO activity. Throughout the whole country, we continue to see the bizarre spectacle of the United Nations supporting punitive sanctions on the one hand but, on the other, being engaged in humanitarian relief—though at levels far below what is needed.

The government food ration and Resolution 986

Famine in Iraq has been prevented since the imposition of sanctions largely by a highly efficient public rationing system. Initially, the ration was funded, supplied, and administered solely by the Iraqi government.

However, the ration now follows the rules of Security Council Resolution 986. In south-central Iraq, the program is administered by the Iraqi government but is monitored by the World Food Program. In the three autonomous northern governorates, the complete program is administered by the WFP but is funded by Iraqi government oil revenues.

In April 1995, the UN Security Council adopted Resolution 986, the oil-for-food program, which permitted Iraqi oil sales to finance imports of food and other essential humanitarian supplies.[21] On May 20, 1996, the government of Iraq and the UN Secretariat signed a Memorandum of Understanding to implement this arrangement.[22] While highly significant, the oil-for-food program has served only to reduce, rather than end, civilian suffering in Iraq. The country is now permitted to sell more than $10 billion worth of oil annually to buy humanitarian supplies. All proceeds from such sales are placed in a UN-controlled bank account, to which Iraq has no access.

While the present annual revenue of more than $10 billion marks a significant increase from the original $4 billion, the distribution for expenditures remains similar to the original agreement. While 53 percent of the revenue is for food, medicine, and humanitarian supplies for the center and south, the arrangement requires Iraq to repay approximately 30 percent of revenues from permitted oil sales toward Gulf War reparations; 5–10 percent for UN operations in Iraq and the repair and maintenance of oil pipelines; and 13 percent for humanitarian supplies for the 3 million Kurds in northern Iraq.[23] It can thus be estimated that, on a per-capita basis, the north receives 50 percent more oil-for-food aid than the south-central area. In practice, only about one-half of the original revenue from oil sales is available for food and humanitarian supplies for the almost 18 million people dwelling in the areas administered by the Iraqi government. It is important to note also that this is not an "aid" program, since the extensive UN operations in Iraq are funded by Iraq's own oil revenues, not by the international community.

Although oil sales had commenced in late 1996, deliveries of food and medicine were still not meeting targets by summer 1997. Furthermore, the WFP was able to provide the full ration in only seven of the first twenty-four months. Shortages and delays have been due, in part, to the capricious nature of the rulings of the UN committee supervising sanctions in New York. The sanctions committee is required to approve every contract with the Iraqi government. It votes in secret and every member country has veto power. There have been strong suspicions of political motives at work in the approval of contracts, a situation that has been specifically condemned by Kofi Annan, the secretary-general of the United Nations.[24] Transportation and storage for such enormous quantities of food have also created delivery problems. The implementation of Resolution 986 has undoubtedly eased the food-supply situation in Iraq. Sustainable improvement in the nutritional well-being of the population will require, however, a substantial flow of resources into rehabilitation of the agriculture sector and the economy as a whole.

The basic ration nominally provides a minimum food basket for all Iraqi families. By 1995, as foreign exchange became more and more constrained, the ration was able to provide only about one-third of the food energy and protein compared with 1987–1989, declining from 53 percent of food energy to 34 percent in September 1994. The reduction was a result of both decreasing grain availability and the increasing cost burden it imposed on the government. While essential for survival, the ration, based as it is on cereals, has remained deficient in a number of minerals and vitamins, especially vitamins A and C.[25]

Certainly the ration under the first phase of Resolution 986 is considerably improved from earlier versions; but it remains low in a number of nutrients when compared with that available in 1988–1990 or with the estimated requirements for a young Iraqi adult male at a moderate level of physical activity. Animal protein remained lacking until some milk and cheese were added in the 1999 ration under the oil-for-food program. It is important to note that the food ration is made available at a price that is well below cost and is, therefore, a significant income subsidy. All additional foods beyond those provided by the ration—even when necessary to supply nutrient needs, such as animal protein, fruits, and vegetables—must be purchased at market prices. These foods, while generally available in the shops, are beyond the financial means of many families.

Child malnutrition

All three FAO missions visited pediatric hospitals throughout Iraq. Following visits to the hospital's directors, we consulted doctors, visited wards, examined medical records, and observed the general status of the hospitals, including drug and medicine availability. There were frequently severe limitations in supplies and medical services. Nutritional problems remain serious and widespread. We witnessed severe forms of malnutrition, such as kwashiorkor or marasmus, in pediatric wards throughout the country, evidenced by classically recognized signs such as edema (swelling) and severe wasting, especially visible in the face, ribs, and limbs. An illustration of marasmus is shown in Figure 1. This child from a Baghdad hospital was typical of many we saw throughout the country. Some children we examined weighed only about half of their desired weight for their age. Most also had gastroenteritis or diarrhea.

Malnourished children were frequently from large extended families with few wage earners. When possible, we questioned mothers concerning food availability and water sanitation. The food ration appeared to be universally available in Iraq. Family diet was almost completely cereal based, with children eating mainly rice water and thin soup. The typical disease profile for children was one of poor nutrition, diarrhea, and infection. Most of the malnourished children were initially admitted to the hospital to seek treatment for either acute respiratory or diarrheal infection. Children suffering from malnutrition without any infection were usually never brought to the hospitals, since most hospitals are not in a position to admit uncomplicated malnutrition cases. Numerous vitamin and mineral deficiencies have also been identified, with anemia being the most common and vitamin A deficiency the most serious.

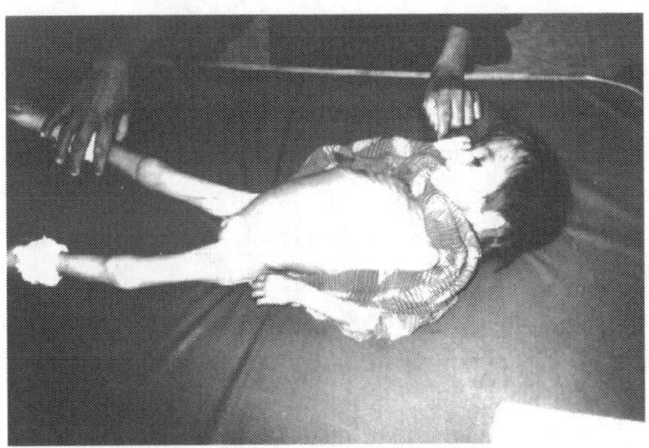

Malnourished child in Al-Mansur Pediatric Hospital, Baghdad, in July 1997. Photo by Peter L. Pellett.

In addition to observations in hospitals, the standard procedure for estimating the prevalence of malnutrition in the community is to weigh and measure children and then compare these data with an international reference.[26] Numerous surveys in Iraq have been undertaken by various organizations over the years.[27] In studies performed since the Gulf War, the degree of severe malnutrition ranged from 3 to 13 percent for wasting, 14 to 30 percent for undernutrition, and 12 to 32 percent for stunting.[28]

Observations by the 1997 FAO team showed widespread undernutrition in Baghdad, though to a lesser degree than in 1995. This survey also demonstrated that children between the ages of twelve and thirty-six months—that is, the weaning age group—were at greater risk of malnutrition than children in other age groups. A smaller group was surveyed in Kerbala, a provincial town some two hours from Baghdad. Here, the situation was worse than in Baghdad: 27 percent were stunted, 18 percent were underweight, and 5 percent were wasted. As many as 50 percent were mildly malnourished.[29]

Adult malnutrition

The 1997 FAO team also surveyed the nutritional status of adults. More than 1,000 adults had their weight and height measured and body mass index (BMI) calculated in Baghdad and Kerbala. Using agreed reference cutoff points (BMI below 18.5), significant levels of malnutrition were found among the Iraqi population, especially in adults younger than twenty-five years old who experienced reduced food availability and poor health conditions during their growing years. For example, 26 percent of young men were significantly underweight, compared with the less than 5 percent who are underweight in a normally nourished population.

Water sanitation

The water and sanitation system remains critical throughout the country, with the Basra area being the most serious. The basic reason is the lack of spare parts for equipment and machinery that cannot be purchased without foreign exchange. In addition, specific sanctions committee approval is required for many of the items, including chlorine for water purification. Many areas are grossly unhygienic. Under these circumstances, it is not surprising that there are many cases of infectious diseases, including typhoid fever, infective hepatitis, and gastroenteritis in the hot summer months. The hazards of water supply and sewage disposal affect all of Iraq but are more serious in the south-central area. The parallel problems of waterlogging and salinity of previously arable land, with consequent reduction in the area available for food production, have exacerbated health problems. Both are related to Iraq's inability to purchase new equipment and spare parts for pumps and equipment.

Unicef mortality data

The seriousness of the nutrition situation is confirmed from recent mortality data for Iraq reported by Unicef.[30] Table 2 lists values for under-five and infant mortality rates (deaths per thousand live births) for Iraq between 1960 and 1998. The data unequivocally demonstrate that the rates for both declined steadily from 1960 to 1990 but then increased after 1990 as the effects of sanctions were felt throughout society. Under-five mortality more than doubled from 56 (1984–1989) to 131 (1994–1999) for south-central Iraq, and rose from 80 (1984–1989) to 90 (1989–1994) but then decreased to 72 (1994–1999) in the autonomous northern region. Values in south-central Iraq are comparable to current rates in Malawi and Pakistan.[31] On the basis of the downward trends in mortality rates observed between 1960 and 1990, Unicef estimates that some 500,000 excess deaths of children under the age of five may have occurred during the period from 1991 to 1998.[32]

Table 2: Child Mortality in Iraq

Year	U5MR[a]	IMR[b]
1960	171	117
1970	127	90
1980	83	63
1990	50	40
1995	117	98
1998	125	103

Source: See note 30.
a: under-five mortality rate
b: infant (under-one) mortality rate

The differences between mortality rates between the north and south-central Iraq have been seized upon by some in the Western media as further evidence that "it's all Saddam Hussein's fault."[33] This is far from true. Indeed, all scientific evidence confirms that the economic embargo has directly and indirectly caused widespread suffering, malnutrition, and increased mortality, especially in the south-central region of the country. As the UN Security Council Panel on Humanitarian Issues has acknowledged: "Even if not all suffering in Iraq can be imputed to external factors, especially sanctions, the Iraqi people would not be undergoing such deprivations in the absence of the prolonged measures imposed by the Security Council and the effects of war."[34]

Reasons for the differences between the northern and south-central regions include the following:

• Prior to sanctions, Iraq was rich enough to fulfill the basic humanitarian needs of the whole population. Hence, the under-five mortality rate was low and declining throughout the country. In this period, the child mortality rate in the north had been higher than in south-central Iraq because the war with bordering Iran and internal conflict between the Kurds and the Baghdad government both brought about significant population displacements.

• Although the north comprises only 9 percent of the land area of Iraq, with 13 percent of the population, it contains about 48 percent of the cultivated arable land. Thus, the north was relatively more prosperous and had better food availability than the south-central region after the imposition of sanctions. In south-central Iraq, the government rationing system was able to provide an average of only about two-thirds of people's food energy needs before the oil-for-food program. In the north, the food needs of poorer people who did not have access to land was supported by the WFP. These allocations fully met the food needs of the vulnerable. In contrast, in the government-controlled area, the WFP was able to supply less than 20 percent of need, in part because donors had earmarked some food aid for the north only.

• International donor support has always been much greater for the north. For example, despite the then population distribution of some 2.9 million in the north and 17.7 million in the south, Unicef employed thirty-nine staff in the north and forty-five in the south in September 1996. In the same month, Unicef-procured supplies amounted to $528,063, with only $212,527 delivered in south-central Iraq. Because of this disparity in financial support, various UN agencies and NGOs were able to upgrade water-sanitation and health-sector needs in the north. In contrast, donations in south-central Iraq were very poor, and health and sanitation services have been in continuous decline.

• The Gulf War destroyed much of the infrastructure for electricity and water sanitation in south-central Iraq, which affected the ability of the government to provide safe drinking water to people living in this region. The ongoing US and UK bombing of Iraq has had a similar impact. In January 1999, one of the large power stations of Baghdad was hit, thus affecting the ability of the Iraqi government to rehabilitate the water sanitation system, especially since sanctions restrict the purchase of spare parts and even chlorine for water purification. In the north, in contrast, the infrastructure existing before sanctions was not destroyed by bombing. Furthermore, the weather conditions in the north are generally cooler, thus lessening the impact of pathogens on childhood morbidity, mortality, and nutritional status.

• The per-capita share of oil-for-food revenue is much higher in the north than in south-central Iraq, thus allowing agencies in the north to invest in long-term development plans and poverty alleviation programs. In contrast, the oil-for-food program has not met the emergency needs of Iraqis in the south; huge investment is still needed for the infrastructure and health care system.

In summary, the major effect of sanctions has been to induce nationwide poverty. This, in consequence, has produced malnutrition and increased mortality. When this is compounded by the destroyed electricity and water-sanitation infrastructure caused by bombing, high levels of malnutrition and increased mortality are inevitable. Let us acknowledge reality. The embargo was intended to hurt; because oil is the basis of the Iraqi economy, it has hurt the country enormously. Sanctions are designed to cause deprivation and poverty, and the greater the poverty induced, the greater the prevalence of malnutrition. Hence, more children die.

Sanctions and human rights

Violations of human rights caused by sanctions include elevated and excessive levels of malnutrition, increased mortality at all ages, and disruption and social devastation of a whole society. The increased mortality caused by the sanctions has even been highlighted in the establishment journal *Foreign Affairs*, which in a 1999 article estimated that Iraqi deaths from sanctions exceed the number "slain by all so-called weapons of mass destruction throughout history."[35]

Despite the many thousands of excess deaths caused by the Security Council sanctions against Iraq, the international community has still not addressed their legality in any serious manner.[36] While "only the Security Council is granted power to take specific enforcement actions to maintain peace and security," Article 24 of the UN Charter requires the Security Council to act in accordance with purposes and principles of the United Nations in its authority to maintain peace and security. Article 1, furthermore, requires the promotion of human rights as among the most fundamental purposes and principles, with the preamble to the charter specifically endorsing "fundamental human rights and the dignity and worth of the human person."[37] A basic question must then be asked: Should the Security Council be held to a higher standard than individual states, or should it be free to violate these principles in enforcing peace and security? Who polices the police?

Procedural duties require that the Security Council recognize, consider, and account for the impact of its actions on human rights.[38] In practice, though, the council has not created a commission or given funding to monitor this. Instead, such monitoring has been left to technical agencies such as the FAO, Unicef, the WHO, and the WFP, which have functioned quite independently of the Security Council. The Security Council should remain accountable to human rights principles regardless of the conduct of the Iraqi government. The rights of the population are not forfeited by a government's misconduct, particularly when the citizens do not have a voice in decision-making.

Sanctions have contributed to the violation of rights to health and an adequate standard of living, rights recognized in the Universal Declaration of Human Rights and the International Covenant on Economic, Social, and Cultural Rights. Indeed, the comprehensive sanctions violate the majority of the articles and many of the items in the preamble of the Universal Declaration. International law recognizes special rights for children, since they are uniquely vulnerable. Indeed, more countries have ratified the Convention on the Rights of the Child than any other human rights treaty in history. Yet deaths of children in Iraq have been a major consequence of sanctions, a fact accepted as justified by Secretary of State Albright. Interestingly, only two countries have not ratified the Convention on the Rights of the Child: Somalia and the United States.[39]

The sanctions violate yet another human right: the right to development. Under the oil-for-food program, Iraq is effectively being held as a vast refugee camp. Development is severely inhibited, if not outright prohibited. In the 1986 General Assembly vote on the Declaration of the Right to Development, a few countries abstained. However, only one country—the United States—voted against the declaration.[40]

Lack of development and the consequent poverty created is most certainly a key factor in the precipitation of malnutrition and high infant mortality, whether globally or in Iraq. The right to development and steps toward its attainment should be essential components of any human rights approach to food and nutrition policies and programs.[41]

Conclusion

The comprehensive embargo on Iraq has had a major effect on food availability, nutrition, and health, especially for children. This remains true even following implementation of the oil-for-food resolution. All recent food and nutrition surveys have described essentially the same story: widespread severe malnutrition in hospitals, malnourished children and undernourished adults in the towns, ever-changing food prices, increased mortality, and a general breakdown in the whole fabric of society.

Despite the severe consequences reported, the Western media have frequently ignored or downplayed the many accounts of major nutritional problems. Even when consideration is reluctantly given to the human costs of sanctions, attention is often diverted by claiming that deaths and deprivation in Iraq are caused not by United Nations actions but by the Iraqi government. The argument appears to be that sanctions are blameless and that resisting them is the evil.

Sanctions are designed to produce deprivation and poverty; hence it is not surprising that they bring about widespread malnutrition and increased mortality.

Sanctions, of course, are designed to give economic pain; but who, in practice, is being hurt? Not the power elite, not the new smugglers and sharp operators profiting from the current crisis, but the poor and vulnerable. In theory, with sanctions operating quietly in the background, economic distress throughout Iraqi society would cause a popular uprising and the regime would then be replaced simply and cheaply with one more to Washington's and London's liking.

Sanctions have not succeeded in their stated aim of overthrowing the regime. Indeed, they have probably strengthened the position of Saddam Hussein, not only within Iraq, but throughout the region.

Addendum September 3rd 2002

Little has changed in Iraq in the food, nutrition, and health situation over the last two years for most people, especially for the poor. Adequate amounts of items such as meat, milk, and vegetables remain too costly, given the parallel decline in the economy and the residual effects of the recent drought on the availability of crops and horticultural products, for many families to purchase to supplement their diet. Consequently, a significant portion of the population requires special attention, in particular the most vulnerable population groups—women and young children—whose coping strategies are quickly being eroded. The embargo has had a major effect on food availability, nutrition, and health, especially for children. As is now well recognized, even mild malnutrition leads to greater susceptibility to infectious diseases with increased mortality as a consequence of the poor water quality and deficient sanitation. Renewed warfare is, at the time of writing, an increasing threat and the potential civilian consequences of this, for the vulnerable majority of the population, are enormous. These consequences are likely to be far greater than they were in 1990 on account of the continuous decline in the overall infrastructure and the deterioration in health status that have both occurred as direct and indirect effects of the economic sanctions since 1990.

Notes

1 Center for Economic and Social Rights (CESR), *Unsanctioned Suffering: A Human Rights Assessment of United Nations Sanctions on Iraq* (New York: CESR, 1996), p. 5. See UN Security Council Resolution 661, articles 3–4. All UN resolutions cited are available online at http://www.un.org. See also Barton Gellman, "Allied Air War Struck Broadly in Iraq," *Washington Post,* June 23, 1991, p. A1.

2 William Webster, testimony before House Armed Services Committee, Federal News Service, December 5, 1990.

3 CESR, *Unsanctioned Suffering,* p. 1.

4 Barbara Crossette, "UN Chief Chides Security Council on Military Missions," *New York Times,* January 6, 1995, p. A3.

5 CESR, *Unsanctioned Suffering,* p. 1.

6 Unicef, "Child and Maternal Mortality Surveys: Southern and Central Iraq, August 1999" (http://www.unicef.org/reseval/pdfs/irqu5est.pdf). Hereafter Unicef 1999.

7 United Nations Food and Agriculture Organization (FAO), *Evaluation of the Food and Nutrition Situation: Iraq,* TCP/IRQ/6713 (Rome: FAO, 1997), p. 11. Hereafter FAO 1997. See also http://www.fao.org/giews.

8 See Scott Peterson, "Inside 'Germ Base' that UN Team Demolished," *Daily Telegraph,* February 21, 1998, p. 13.

9 UN Food and Agriculture Organization (FAO), *Food Balance Sheets 1961–1994,* FAOSTAT-PC: FAO Computerized Information Series, Version 3 (Rome, FAO, 1996). Hereafter FAOSTAT 1996.

10 FAO 1997, p. 35.

11 Source for these figures is FAOSTAT 1996.

12 See FAO 1997; FAO, *The Nutritional Status Assessment Mission to Iraq,* Technical Cooperation Program TCP/IRQ/2356e (Rome, FAO, 1993); and FAO, *Evaluation of the Food and Nutrition Situation in Iraq,* Technical Cooperation Program TCP/IRQ/4552 (Rome: FAO, 1995). Hereafter FAO 1993 and FAO 1995. See also http://www.fao.org/giews.

13 See FAO and World Health Organization (WHO), *International Conference on Nutrition: Nutrition and Development—A Global Assessment* (Rome: FAO, 1992).

14 U. Jonnson, "Towards an Improved Strategy for Nutrition Surveillance," *Food and Nutrition Bulletin* 16: 2 (1995): 102–11. See also Unicef, *The State of the World's Children 1998* (New York and Oxford: Oxford University Press, 1998). The full text of this report is available at http://www.unicef.org/sowc98/sowc98.pdf. Table 1 adapted from Unicef, *The State of the World's Children 1998,* pp. 23–25.

15 See United Nations Administrative Committee on Coordination, Sub-Committee on Nutrition (ACC/SCN), "Human Rights and Nutrition," *SCN News*, Vol. 18 (Geneva: ACC/SCN-World Health Organization, 1999); Unicef, *The State of the World's Children 1998*; and N.S. Scrimshaw, C.E. Taylor, and J.E. Gordon, *Interactions of Nutrition and Infection,* WHO Monograph Series No. 57 (Geneva: World Health Organization, 1968).

16 See Peter L. Pellett, "World Essential Amino Acid Supply with Special Attention to South-East Asia," *Food Nutrition Bulletin* 17: 3 (1996): 204–34.

17 See FAO 1993, p. 9 and Table 7.

18 See FAO, 1993, FAO 1995, and FAO 1997; CESR, *Unsanctioned Suffering*; and Harvard Study Team, *Public Health in Iraq After the Gulf War* (Cambridge: Harvard Study Team, 1991). See also Harvard Study Team, "Effect of the Gulf War on Infant and Child Mortality in Iraq," *New England Journal of Medicine* 325 (1992): 977–80.

19 See Ramsey Clark et al., *The Children Are Dying: The Impact of Sanctions on Iraq,* second ed. (New York: International Action Center and International Relief Association, 1998).

20 See Unicef 1999; Government of Iraq Ministry of Health and Unicef Iraq, *Nutritional Status Survey at Primary Health Centers during Polio National Immunization Days (PNID) in Iraq, April 12–14, 1997* (IRQ/97/169); Government of Iraq Ministry of Health, Unicef, and World Food Program Iraq, *Nutritional Status Survey at Primary Health Centers during Polio National Immunization Days (PNID) in Iraq, March 14–16, 1998*. Hereafter Nutritional Status Survey 1997 and Nutritional Status Survey 1998.

21 Stanley Meisler, "UN Allows Limited Sales of Iraqi Oil," *Los Angeles Times,* April 15, 1995, p. A1.

22 Robin Wright, "UN Will Let Iraq Sell Oil for Humanitarian Supplies," *Los Angeles Times,* May 21, 1996, p. A1; Roula Khalaf and Robert Corzine, "Iraq Food-for-Oil Deal Offers 'Something for Everyone,'" *Financial Times,* May 22, 1996, p. 4; and Anne Reifenberg, "Oil-for-Food Deal Won't Leave Much for Iraq's Needy," *Wall Street Journal,* May 23, 1996, p. A11.

23 See UN Office of the Iraq Program "Oil-for-food—The Basic Facts." Available at http://www.un.org/Depts/oip/reports/basfact.html.

24 Kofi Annan, "Annan Criticises Iraq Aid Delays," BBC News Online, October 27, 1999 (http://www.bbc.co.uk). Kofi Annan, Letter to the President of the Security Council, October 22, 1999 (S/1999/1086), p. 1; and Benon V. Sevan, Annex, Note to the Secretary-General from the

Executive Director of the Iraq Program, October 22, 1999 (S/1999/1066), pp. 2–4.

25 See FAO 1997, p. 11. Also see http://www.fao.org/giews.

26 The indicators most often used to measure health and nutrition status are body weight and height in relation to a subject's age and sex. The main anthropometric indices for international nutritional status assessment are: weight-for-height (W/H), height-for-age (H/A), weight-for-age (W/A), and Body Mass Index (BMI: weight in kilograms divided by the square of height in meters). Those including age (W/A and H/A) are only used for children and adolescents, while W/H and BMI can be used at all ages. Measurements must be compared with an acceptable standard.

27 See, for example, CESR, *Unsanctioned Suffering*; FAO 1993, FAO 1995, and FAO 1997; and references in note 20.

28 This is generally defined as more than two standard deviations (-2SD) below the median. Wasting is determined by weight-for-height, undernutrition by weight-for-age, and stunting by height-for-age.

29 Using the less stringent -1SD (standard deviations) criteria, as opposed to -2SD for the other figures.

30 Unicef press release, "Iraq Survey Shows 'Humanitarian Emergency,'" August 12, 1999 (Cf/doc/pr/1999/29). See Unicef and Government of Iraq Ministry of Health, *Child and Maternal Mortality Survey 1999: Preliminary Report* (Baghdad: Unicef, 1999). Available online at http://www.unicef.org. Table 2 based on Unicef 1999, unnumbered table "Child Mortality: Iraq." See also Charts 1–3.

31 United Nations Development Program, *Human Development Report 1999* (New York and Oxford: Oxford UP, 1999), Table 8, "Progress in Survival," pp. 170–71.

32 Unicef press release, "Iraq Survey Shows 'Humanitarian Emergency,'" p. 2.

33 See, for example, Barbara Crossette, "Children's Death Rate Rising in Iraqi Lands, Unicef Reports," *New York Times,* August 13, 1999, p. A6.

34 Unicef press release, "Iraq Survey Shows 'Humanitarian Emergency,'" p. 2.

35 John Mueller and Karl Mueller, "Sanctions of Mass Destruction," *Foreign Affairs* 78: 3 (May/June 1999): 43–53.

36 A special issue of the *Bulletin of the World Alliance of Nutrition and Human Rights,* "Food as a Weapon of War or for Political Purposes," provides a good introduction to the relevant considerations. See *WANAHR Bulletin* 7 (September 1998). CESR's *Unsanctioned Suffering* includes a review on international law and sanctions in Iraq (see pp. 33–41). Similar considerations were also part of the proceedings of the International Tribunal in Madrid, November 16–17, 1996. See Tribunal Internacional por crímenes contra la Humanidad cometidos por el Consejo de Seguridad de Naciones Unidas en Irak, *Guerra y sanctiones a Irak. Naciones Unidas y el "nuevo orden mundial,"* ed. Carlos Varea and Angeles Maestro (Madrid: Los Libros de la Catarata, 1997).

37 Available online at http://www.un.org.

38 Humanitarian law recognizes two basic principles termed *distinction* and *proportionality*: belligerents are required "to distinguish between civilians and combatants at all times," while the Geneva convention prohibits "any

attack which may be expected to cause incidental loss of civilian life and injury to civilians which would be excessive in relation to the concrete and military advantage anticipated." Thus comprehensive sanctions, which cause total economic collapse and the deaths of thousands of civilians, would appear to violate the principle of distinction (see CESR, *Unsanctioned Suffering*, pp. 33–41). However, lawyers will debate the detail. Is the entire population being targeted as a means to influence the regime? If so, this would be a clear violation. Alternatively, is the regime being targeted with unfortunate collateral damage to civilians? This, apparently, would be acceptable!

39 See Unicef, *The State of the World's Children 1998*.

40 The World Conference on Human Rights, the International Conference on Population and Development, the World Summit on Social Development, the Fourth World Conference on Women, and the World Food Summit have all affirmed the right to development. The United Nations Development Program (UNDP) has also adopted the concept of such a right in its development activities. See UNDP, "Integrating Human Rights with Sustainable Human Development" (http://magnet.undp.org/Docs/policy5.html), Annex 3.

41 This has not always been the case, even among nutritionists, however. The neglect of the Iraq situation is evident in the symposium on "Nutrition and Human Rights" held in Geneva in April 1999 and attended by high level representation from the UN and other organizations (published in *SCN News,* Vol. 18). While there were wide-ranging discussions on human rights and their relationships to malnutrition and increased mortality, the situation in Iraq—with more than 500,000 excess deaths of children (Unicef 1999) and documented extensive malnutrition—was not even mentioned and was only subsequently raised as an issue by an external reviewer of the conference documents. See Peter L. Pellett, "Commentary: A Human Rights Approach to Food and Nutrition Policies and Programmes," *SCN News,* Vol. 18, pp. 84–86.

Chapter 13

Toxic Pollution, the Gulf War, and Sanctions

The Impact on the Environment and Health in Iraq

Dr. Huda S. Ammash

The Gulf War ended in 1991, but the massive destruction linked to it continues. An unprecedented catastrophe resulting from a mixture of toxic radiological, chemical, and electromagnetic exposure is still causing substantial consequences to health and the environment, exacerbated by the sanctions imposed on Iraq. Much of Iraq has been turned into a polluted and radioactive environment.

The use of depleted uranium

In spite of the international treaties that prohibit "use of weapons or tactics which cause unnecessary or aggravated devastation or suffering … indiscriminate harm … to noncombatants … [and] widespread, long-term, and severe damage to the environment," more than 1 million rounds of weapons carrying depleted uranium (DU) were used against Iraqi troops in the Gulf War.[1] DU is radioactive waste used because of its capacity to destroy armor and other defenses.[2] Most of its radioactivity is attributed to uranium-238 and its daughters, mainly thorium-234 and protactinium-234.[3]

DU is both radiologically and chemically toxic to humans and other forms of life. A terrifying total of 320 to 350 tons of DU were fired, including 14,000 large-caliber (105 and 120 millimeter) and 940,000 small-caliber (25 and 30 millimeter) bullets. As much as 300 tons of expended DU ammunition remains scattered throughout Iraq and Kuwait.[4]

Upon impact, DU penetrators oxidize rapidly, spreading toxic uranium oxide dust particles. If a person inhales or ingests DU, it enters into the bloodstream and then can circulate throughout the whole body. Prolonged internal exposure to radiation may cause severe health problems, including cancers (mainly leukemia and lung and bone cancer); pulmonary and lypmh node fibrosis; pneumoconiosis; inhibition of reproductive activities; chromosomal changes; depletion of the body's immune system; and finally death.[5]

Aware of these dangers, US authorities warned prior to the war that the use of DU could have potential health and environmental consequences.[6]

DU pollution is also transferred to humans through water contaminated by soluble components of DU and through eating either contaminated plants or animals living on such contaminated plants.

In 1993, Iraqi researchers found the first evidence that DU was used in the war, when they successfully analyzed a specimen taken from an Iraqi tank that was destroyed by a DU bullet in the battlefield in the south of Iraq. When radioactivity of sites inside and outside the destroyed tanks was measured, researchers registered levels of 84 microroentgen per hour, twelve times the natural background of 7.1 to 7.9 microroentgen per hour. Researchers also detected elevated concentrations of U-238 chain, mainly thorium-234 and radium-226. These increases were associated with high concentrations of low-percentage (depleted) U-235. This proved beyond any doubt the existence of DU contamination.[7]

An Iraqi team including Dr. Suaad Al-Azawi and Dr. Baha'a El-Dean Marouf performed a comprehensive study to investigate the presence of DU in the battlefields in five regions of south-central Iraq: Zubair, Safwan, Sanam, and Southern and Northern Rumeila. In Sanam and Southern and Northern Rumeila, radioactivity around the destroyed tanks was 79.3 to 184.5 microroentgen per hour, compared with a natural background of 7.1 to 7.9 microroentgen per hour. Surface and ground water and sediments of stream channels were contaminated.[8] Professor Mikdam Saleh and Ahmed Mequar have also found significant levels of U-238 series in 154 plant and animal tissues.[9]

To investigate the presence of DU in the body of exposed persons, Dr. Hari Sharma, at the University of Waterloo in Canada, examined the amount of DU in the urine of Gulf War veterans.[10] The concentration of DU in twenty-four-hour urine samples of thirty veterans from the United States, United Kingdom, Canada, and Iraq ranged from 3 to 18 micrograms.[11] The concentration in urine specimens of Iraqi civilians in the southern city of Basra was 2 micrograms per day.

Dr. Neboysha Ljepojevic, a professor of physics at London University, studied the ratio of U-235 and U-238 in the urine of some Gulf War veterans by using delayed neutron counting, neutron activation, and two other mass spectrometric methods. The average excreted amount was 3 micrograms per day (1,000 times higher than normal values of natural uranium). Measurements confirmed beyond any doubt the presence of DU in the samples.[12]

It is well established that only 10 electron volts of energy is required to break DNA or other molecules in the body.[13] Since DU is a very forceful alpha particle emitter, of 4.2 million electron volts (MeV) per particle, one can estimate the deleterious consequences of such exposure on veterans and public health, especially increased risk of cancer.

Electromagnetic pollution

Electromagnetic pollution is the spread of unwanted electromagnetic fields in the environment. This type of pollution is particularly dangerous because it is often undetected. Electromagnetic pollution can cause pregnancy problems, anxiety, depression, and fatality. In Finland, heart failures, cardiovascular diseases, and cancers have increased in an area containing early detection radar systems. Increases in the incidence of leukemia and eye and skin diseases have been recorded among workers in other electromagnetic environments.[14]

During the forty-five days of the Gulf War, the Allies widely deployed electronic devices such as advanced radar systems and laser-guided missiles, which released high-frequency electromagnetic energy into the atmosphere. The effects of this electromagnetic pollution were exacerbated by the massive bombardment of Iraqi troops and infrastructure. A total of 88,000 tons of explosives were dropped on Iraq—an explosive tonnage judged equivalent to nearly five Hiroshima-sized atomic bombs.[15] As a result of the energy released by this bombing, ionization of the Iraqi atmosphere transpired. Normally oxygen in the air is a relatively weak oxidant. However, if enough energy is available, complete reduction of oxygen by univalent pathway occurs, causing the formation of unusual oxygen ions (radicals) such as superoxide.

These free radicals are toxic because they react with aquatic solutions of the human body, creating highly energetic chemical compounds.[16] The formation of electron flux from a variety of chemical reductions usually follows, causing oxygen reduction and further generation of more toxic free radicals inside the living cells. This can have dangerous consequences both at the cellular and organic levels, causing health disorders and life-threatening diseases, including cancers; heart, vascular, respiratory, and gastrointestinal diseases; and depletion of the immune system, which leads to the spread of infectious diseases.[17]

It is worth mentioning that under normal nutritional conditions, many enzymes function to protect the cells from such toxicities. Some vitamins and nutrients, such as vitamin E, betacarotene, ascorbic acid, and niacin are among those required for such protection.[18] Therefore, lack of such nutrients in daily diet of the Iraqis due to sanctions increases the harmful effects of this type of pollution.[19]

Chemical pollution

The massive and indiscriminate onslaught of the Gulf War extended far beyond military targets to include elements of Iraq's industry and social infrastructure. Targets in all of Iraq's main towns were comprehensively bombed, some repeatedly. Destruction of oil installations, pipelines, refineries, storage facilities, stations, and delivery vehicles caused the release of thousands of tons of toxic hydrocarbons and chemicals into the air, soil, and water resources. Rates of pollution are escalating because of the continuation of comprehensive sanctions, which has paralyzed efforts to control environmental degradation.

The release of toxic fumes and acid rains followed the bombardment of numerous Iraqi oil wells. Soot filled the atmosphere and black rain fell all over the country. Bombardment of industrial plants caused the leakage of sulfuric and phosphoric acids, ammonia, and insecticides.[20] The closure of gas purification and water treatment units due to the lack of spare parts means toxic gases and heavy metals are being discharged into the air and drinking water resources.

The maximum concentration of air pollutant measured as total suspended particles has increased in Baghdad by 705 percent.[21] Eight years after the war, the values are up to 1,330 micrograms per cubic meter, constituting 887 percent of the levels recommended by the World Health Organization (WHO). Concentration of toxic metals in these particles has also increased due to the effects of the ongoing war, fuel combustion, and industrial pollution. Lead increased from 2.5 micrograms per cubic meter in 1989 to 87 micrograms in 1997 (172 times WHO standards). Carbon monoxide increased to three times WHO-recommended values, reaching

67 parts per million. It is well established that some of these metals and gases induce, among other problems, genetic defects, cardiovascular damage, and cancer.[22]

In addition, the accumulation of solid home wastes and water swamps creating a suitable media for the growth of microbes, insects, and rodents has contributed to the spread of infectious diseases. Under these circumstances, it is clear that the Iraqi people are living through a health crisis of immense proportions.

The impact on the environment

The massive destruction of Iraq's infrastructure inevitably produced substantial damages to its flora, fauna, and food chain. Soil and soil productivity were destroyed or damaged. In particular, the military bombardment altered the physical conditions of surface soil and incinerated many areas' plant cover. This inevitably affected the seed bank, which in turn reduced the density and composition of Iraq's plant life. In other areas where the soil has been compacted or severely eroded, plants can no longer grow. New fields of sand dunes were created, with simultaneous increase of dust storms and dust falls.

Contamination of soil with heavy metals, for example nickel and vanadium, reduced permeability and aeration, hindering seed germination, pollination, and fertilization. The destruction wrought by the unremitting onslaught on Iraq's electric power plants destroyed critical saline drainage systems, thus inducing waterlogging and salination of soils. Other impacts on flora include change of habitat conditions, change of run-off and floristic composition, vulnerability of soil to wind and water erosion, and the burial of topsoil with unproductive substratum. Many endangered species, especially the trees of *Acacia gerrardi,* are threatened.

Since the components of the ecosystem were changed, Iraq has seen an increase in rodents and scorpions, which has caused considerable problems for health and agriculture.

Most important, many animals were killed during the war. Although large mammals escaped from the war zone, their breeding was adversely affected. Small animals and soil invertebrates, which cannot escape rapidly, were destroyed.[23]

The impact on public health

The result of such a multiplicity of toxic factors, compounded with malnutrition and lack of medical care, has been a dramatic deterioration of public health. Elevated rates of cancers, congenital abnormalities, genetic defects, infertility, renal and hepatic dysfunction, cardiovascular diseases, malnutrition, spread of infectious disease, and death have all occurred.

Similar syndromes have been noticed among Gulf War veterans.[24] Throughout Iraq, but especially in the south, an approximate fivefold rise in cancer has been recorded since the Gulf War.[25] Not only the rate of cancer in the population increased, but the pattern of cancer is also changing, especially for lymphoma and leukemia. The incidence of more than one cancer type in the same family was recorded among fifteen families in Basra in 1998.[26] In addition, new types of cancers are being recorded for the first time in Iraq, and there has been a measurable decrease in the average age of cancer victims.[27]

Among Iraqi veterans, 1,425 cancer cases were recorded during the period from 1991 to 1997. Lymphoma, leukemia, and lung cancer, respectively, formed the highest percentages (31.5, 21.8, and 14.7 percent). Brain, bone, liver, gastrointestinal, and pancreatic cancers were also recorded.[28]

Upon calculating the external and internal DU exposures of Iraqi and non-Iraqi Gulf War veterans, Ljepojevic estimates that there could be 3,000 to 21,000 additional cancers for every 100,000 veterans.[29]

Cancer is not the only medical problem that results from DU exposure. If DU or its derivatives reach the blood of pregnant women, it can pass through the placenta and cause damages to the fetus. Congenital abnormalities have increased in Iraq since the Gulf War. For example, Dr. Salma Al-Hafith has recorded a significant increase in the number of children born with various genetic malformations, including missing limbs, ears, and eyes.[30]

The dramatic impact of the war and sanctions can be seen in the huge number of children and adults dying from the spread of infectious diseases due to immunodeficiencies and the closure of waste water treatment units.[31] Although the country had been free of cholera and scabies, both are now affecting thousands of Iraqis. Incidence of malaria and leishmaniasis not only rose but spread to new governorates in which no cases have been recorded previously.[32] According to the WHO and the

Iraqi Ministry of Health, the rate of increase of various infectious diseases (many of them deadly) ranges from 1.6 to 10.9 times 1989 levels.[33]

It is important to emphasize that these statistics probably underestimate the scale of the health problem in Iraq, as hundreds of victims, especially in rural areas, die before reaching any hospital. Recorded disease figures represent the official in-patient and out-patient admissions to public hospitals only. Therefore, cases referred to private clinics are not included. In addition, a substantial number of cases are not included because they cannot be diagnosed properly: Iraq's medical system lacks proper diagnostic materials and spare parts, rendering many medical instruments useless.

As a result of all these factors, Iraqi death rates have increased significantly, with cancer representing a significant cause of mortality, especially in the south and among children. The latest survey carried out by Unicef concluded that a "major increase" in child mortality has occurred from 1989 to 1999. The infant mortality rate increased from 47 per 1,000 live births in 1989 to 108 per 1,000 in 1999. Death of children under five years old increased from 56 to 131 per 1,000 children.[34]

Conclusion

The impacts of depleted uranium, electromagnetic pollution, and the destruction of the Iraqi infrastructure—combined with malnutrition and lack of medical care due to the continuation of the sanctions—have already claimed the lives of hundreds of thousands of Iraqi people, and threaten many more. Though some estimate the harm to be many times greater than even that caused by the Chernobyl disaster, the long-term, prolonged effects of the war and sanctions on Iraq are yet to be seen.

Since these massively destructive conditions can be inflicted elsewhere, as can be seen in Nato's bombing and use of DU in Yugoslavia, and since the resulting pollutants are transferable far and wide by various means, their impact is not restricted to innocent Iraqis alone.[35]

Notes

1 Morley Safer, "DU," produced by Peter Klein, CBS, *60 Minutes,* December 26, 1999. See also two investigative reports by Bill Mesler: "The Pentagon's Radioactive Bullet," *The Nation* 263: 12 (October 21, 1996): 11–14 (available online at http://www.thenation/com/issue/961021/

1021mesl.htm), and "Pentagon Poison," *The Nation* 264: 20 (May 26, 1997): 17–22 (available online at http://www.thenation/com/issue/970526/0526mesl.htm). On international law, see Alyn Ware, "Depleted-Uranium Weapons and International Law," in *Metal of Dishonor: Depleted Uranium,* second ed., ed. Depleted Uranium Education Project (New York: International Action Center, 1999), p. 196.

2 See Naomi H. Harley et al., *A Review of the Scientific Literature as It Relates to Gulf War Illnesses, Volume 7: Depleted Uranium* (Santa Monica, California: RAND, 1999), pp. xiii and 1.

3 Rosalie Bertell, "Gulf War Veterans and Depleted Uranium," in Laka Foundation, *Depleted Uranium: A Post-War Disaster for Environment and Health* (Amsterdam: Laka Foundation, 1999), pp. 18–26. Available online at http://www.antenna.nl/wise/uranium/dhap99.html. See also Harley et al., *Depleted Uranium,* p. 5, and Table 1.1 (p. 3), Appendix A (p. 73), and Appendix B (p. 75).

4 Safer, "DU," December 26, 1999; Mesler, "The Pentagon's Radioactive Bullet," p. 13; and Dan Fahey, "Collateral Damage: How US Troops Were Exposed to Depleted Uranium During the Persian Gulf War," in *Metal of Dishonor,* p. 28.

5 US Department of Health and Human Services, Public Health Service, Agency for Toxic Substances and Disease Registry (ATSDR), "Toxicological Profile of Uranium: Draft for Public Comment" (Atlanta: Research Triangle Institute for ATSDR, 1997); Luigi Parmeggiani, *Encyclopedia of Occupational Health,* third ed. (Geneva: International Labor Organization, 1991), p. 2238; and US Army Environmental Policy Institute (AEPI), *Health and Enviornmental Consequences of Depleted Uranium Use by the US Army* (Atlanta: AEPI, 1995).

6 Science Applications International Corporation (SAIC) study, in M.E. Danesi, *Kinetic Energy Penetrator Long Term Strategy Study* (Picatinny Arsenal, New Jersey: US Army Armament, Munitions, and Chemical Command, 1990), Appendix D; UK Atomic Energy Authority, "Kuwait—Depleted Uranium Contamination," April 30, 1991; Safer, "DU," December 26, 1999; and Felicity Arbuthnot, "Poisoned Legacy," *New Internationalist* 316 (September 1999), p. 12.

7 Baha'a El-Dean Marouf, "Pollution with Depleted Uranium in Iraq," *Umm Al-Ma'ark*, Vol. 16 (1998): 129–34.

8 Baha'a El-Dean Marouf and W. Al-Hilli, *The Effect of the Use of Radioactive Weapons on Soil and Air in Selected Regions of the South of Iraq* (Baghdad: University of Baghdad College of Engineeering, 1998). See also Suaad Al-Azzawi and Muhamed Sagi, "The Effect of Radioactive Weapons on Surface and Ground Waters in Selected Regions of the South of Iraq," *Journal of the Arabic Universities* 6: 1 (1999): 81–117.

9 Mikdam M. Saleh and Ahmed J. Mequar, "The Effects of Using Depleted Uranium by the Allied Forces on Humans and the Biosphere in Selected Regions of the Southern Area of Iraq," International Scientific Symposium on the Use of Depleted Uranium and Its Impact on Humans and the Environment in Iraq, Baghdad, December 2–3, 1998.

10 Dr. Hari Sharma's research, reviewed by Dr. Ljepojevic, "Depleted Uranium Health Hazards," is available online at http://www.enadu.i.am;

Bertell, "Gulf War Veterans and Depleted Uranium," pp. 18–26; Arbuthnot, "Poisoned Legacy," p. 13; and Military Toxics Project, Press Release, "Military Toxics Project Confirms NATO is Using DU Munitions in Yugoslavia and Releases Results of Medical Study Indicating Potential for Fatal Cancers," May 4, 1999 (http://www.miltoxproj.org/kosovo.html); and Military Toxics Project, "Independent Pilot Medical Study on Persian Gulf Veterans Confirms Exposure to Depleted Uranium," Press Release, September 25, 1998 (http://www.necnp.org/iraqvets.htm).

11 Daniel Robicheau, "The Next Testing Site for Depleted Uranium Weaponry," in Laka Foundation, *Depleted Uranium,* pp. 27–28.

12 See note 10.

13 Bertell, "Gulf War Veterans and Depleted Uranium," pp. 18–26.

14 Eman Ahmed, "Radiation and Health: Search for the Truth," *Umm Al-Ma'ark,* Vol. 16 (1998): 135–41; and Audrey Magee, "Electromagnetic Radiation Linked to Cancer in Study," *Irish Times,* June 10, 1994, p. 5.

15 Eric Schmitt, "US Weighs the Value of Bombing to Coerce Iraq," *New York Times,* November 16, 1997, p. 1: 3, and Scott Shepard and Joseph Albright, "Allied Air Strikes Reportedly Shatter Iraq's War Machine," *Atlanta Journal and Constitution,* January 17, 1991, p. A1.

16 R.F. Del Maestro, "An Approach to Free Radicals in Medicine and Biology," *Physiology Scandanavia Supplement Acta* 492 (1980): 153–68; and R.F. Del Maestro, "The Influence of Oxygen Derived Free Radicals on in Vitro and in Vivo Model Systems," *Acta Universitasis Uppsaliensis* (1979).

17 Huda S. Ammash, "Impact of Gulf War Pollution in the Spread of Infectious Diseases in Iraq," Otto Anni di Emargo in Iraq, Italian Solidarity Foundation ("Soli Al-Mondo"), Rome, April 6, 1999. See also Huda S. Ammash, "The Effect of Selected Free Radical Generating Agents on Metabolic Processes in Bacteria and Mammals," Columbia: Universiy of Missouri, 1983.

18 W.A. Pryor, "The Role of Free Radical Reactions in Biological Systems," in *Free Radicals in Biology*, ed. W.A. Pryor et al. (New York: Academic Press, 1976), pp. 1–49; B. Halliwell, "Biochemical Mechanisms Accounting for the Toxic Action of Oxygen on Living Organisms," *Cell Biology International Reports* 2 (1978): 113–28.

19 Huda S. Ammash, "Infectious Diseases and Health Consequences Induced by Free Radicals Resulting from Irradiation and Ionization of the Atmopshere in Iraq," International Scientific Symposium on the Use of Depleted Uranium and Its Impact on Humans and the Environment in Iraq, Baghdad, December 2–3, 1998. Hereafter Ammash 1998.

20 Huda S. Ammash et al., "Electromagnetic, Chemical, and Microbial Pollution Resulting from War and Embargo, and Its Impact on the Environment and Health," *Journal of the [Iraqi] Academy of Science* 44: 1 (1997): 109–22. Hereafter Ammash et al. 1997.

21 Ammash et al. 1997.

22 Arwa Taka, Adnan Aifg, and Ahmed Al-Saddi, *Air Pollution in Baghdad City and Suburbs with Lead and Other Toxic Pollutants* (Baghdad: University of Baghdad College of Science, 1999).

23 Nabiel M. Alla El-Din et al., *A Rapid Assessment of the Impacts of the Iraqi-Kuwait Conflict on Terrestrial Ecosystems* (Baghdad: UNEP, 1991), Part I.

24 Robicheau, "The Next Testing Site for Depleted Uranium Weaponry," pp. 27–28. For useful reports, see the web site of the National Gulf War Resource Center (http://www.gulfweb.org). See also "Gulf War Veterans Illnesses," Committee on Government Reform and Oversight, US House of Representatives, House Report 105–388 (1997 Union Calendar 228); Mesler's reports cited in note 1; Safer, "DU," December 26, 1999; Seymour M. Hersh, *Against All Enemies: Gulf War Syndrome: The War Between America's Ailing Veterans and Their Government* (New York: Ballantine, 1998); Philip Shenon, "Army Knew in '91 of Chemical Weapons Dangers in Iraq," *New York Times,* February 24, 1997, p. A16; Haro Chakmakjian, "Uranium from Gulf War Weapons a Danger to Region: Scientists," Agence France Presse, December 3, 1998; and the articles by Robert Fisk in Chapter 7.

25 Muhaimeed Mad-Allah Al-Jebouri, presentation at Universiy of Tikrit, December 1998, cited in Arbuthnot, "Poisoned Legacy," p. 14; Iraqi Cancer Board, "Results of Iraqi Cancer Registry" (Baghdad: Iraqi Cancer Registry Center, 1976–1997).

26 Jawad Al-Ali, "Depleted Uranium and Its Impact on the Population of the Southern Region Iraq," in *Cancer Symposium* (Basra: Basra Health Administration, 1999).

27 Ahmed Hardan et al., "Diseases and Health Problems Resulting from Exposure of Iraq to Ionizing Radiation of Depleted Uranium," International Scientific Symposium on the Use of Depleted Uranium and Its Impact on Humans and the Environment in Iraq, Baghdad, December 2–3, 1998. Hereafter Hardan et al. 1998.

28 Hardan et al. 1998.

29 See note 10.

30 Salma Al-Hafith, "Child Abnormalities in Iraq," International Scientific Symposium on the Use of Depleted Uranium and Its Impact on Humans and the Environment in Iraq, Baghdad, December 2–3, 1998.

31 Ammash et al. 1997.

32 Ammash 1998.

33 WHO Resource Center, *Health Conditions of the Population in Iraq Since the Gulf Crisis* (Geneva: WHO, 1996). Available online at http://www.who.int. Also based on reports from Iraq's Ministry of Health, Department of Biostatistics, Baghdad, 1996.

34 See Unicef and Government of Iraq Ministry of Health, *Child and Maternal Mortality Survey 1999: Preliminary Report* (Baghdad: Unicef, 1999). Available online at http://www.unicef.org. See also Unicef press release, "Iraq Survey Shows 'Humanitarian Emergency,'" August 12, 1999 (Cf/doc/pr/1999/29), p. 2.

35 See Robert Fisk, "US 'Lost Count of Uranium Shells Fired in Kosovo,'" *The Independent,* November 22, 1999, p. 13; Robert Fisk, "Exposed: The Deadly Legacy of Nato Strikes in Kosovo," *The Independent,* October 4, 1999, p. 1; and J.J. Richardson, "Depleted Uranium: The Invisible Threat," *Mother Jones* MoJo Wire, June 23, 1999 (available online at http://www.motherjones.com).

Part 5

Activist Responses

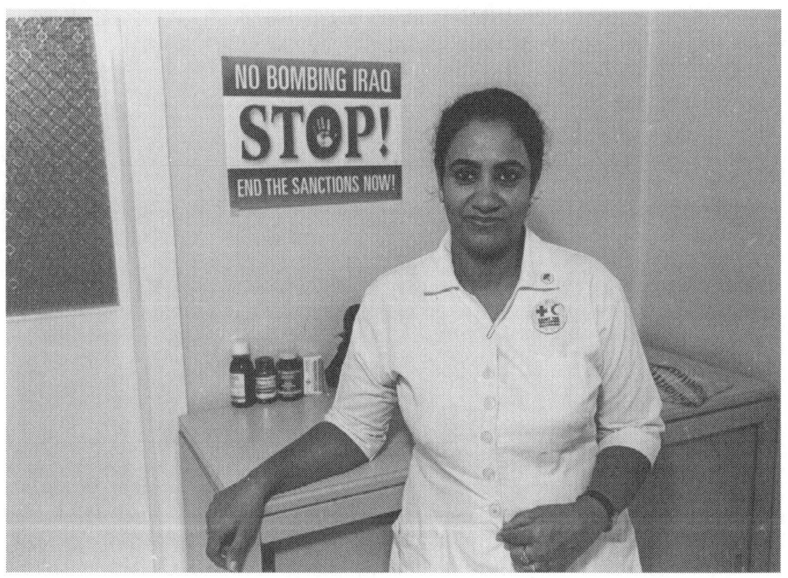

An Iraqi nurse at a Basra hospital for the rehydration of children. Bridges to Baghdad and other international solidarity groups helped finance the hospital. Photo by Alan Pogue (July 1998).

Chapter 14

Sanctions Are Weapons of Mass Destruction

Noam Chomsky, Edward S. Herman, Edward W. Said, and Howard Zinn

with Angela Davis, Robert Jensen, June Jordan, William Keach, Carlos Muñoz, Jr., and Sharon Smith

We the undersigned call upon the United States government to end sanctions against the people of Iraq.

At the end of 1998 and again in 1999, the United States once again rained bombs on the people of Iraq. But even when the bombs stop falling, the US war against the people of Iraq continues—through the United Nations harsh sanctions on Iraq, which are the direct result of US policy.

This month, US policy will kill 4,500 Iraqi children under the age of five, according to United Nations studies, just as it did last month and the month before that all the way back to 1991. Since the end of the Gulf War, more than 1 million Iraqis have died as a direct result of the UN sanctions on Iraq.

To oppose the sanctions is not equivalent to supporting the regime of Saddam Hussein. To oppose the sanctions is to support the Iraqi people. Saddam Hussein is a murderous dictator who promotes those who are loyal to him and kills all those who voice opposition to his regime. But throughout the 1980s, when it suited US strategic interests in the Middle East, the US government was more than willing to ignore Saddam Hussein's brutality. In fact, US and European companies provided Iraq with materials used to produce Saddam Hussein's "weapons of mass destruction." Moreover, the sanctions have not affected the lifestyle of Saddam Hussein or his inner circle. Food and medicine are available for those who can afford it. The sanctions hurt only the Iraqi people.

The sanctions are weapons of mass destruction. When a UN inspections team visited Iraq to survey the damage from the Gulf War in March

1991, it concluded that the bombing has reduced Iraq to a "pre-industrial age." The team said at that time that if the sanctions were not lifted, the country faced "immediate catastrophe."[1] Yet the sanctions have continued for the last seven years, preventing Iraq from obtaining the hard currency to buy basic foodstuffs and medicines—or to rebuild its infrastructure. The oil-for-food deal that allows Iraq to sell $5.26 billion of its oil every six months has had only marginal effects. The United Nations takes one-third of all oil revenues for war reparations and its own expenses.[2] The oil-for-food program does not generate enough money to feed adequately a population of 22 million. Raising the ceiling would not help. The refineries were bombed during the war and need to be rebuilt—even now, Iraq is unable to produce all the oil it is allowed to. In October 1998, Denis Halliday, the UN coordinator for humanitarian aid to Iraq, resigned in protest, arguing that the sanctions "are starving to death 6,000 Iraqi infants every month, ignoring the human rights of ordinary Iraqis and turning a whole generation against the West."[3]

The sanctions also prevent Iraq from importing many basic necessities. Most pesticides and fertilizer are banned because of their potential military use. Raw sewage is pumped continuously into water that people end up drinking because Iraq's water treatment plants were blown up by US bombs in 1991—and most have never been repaired. Yet chlorine is banned under the sanctions because it also could be of military use. Typhoid, dysentery, and cholera have reached epidemic proportions. Farid Zarif, deputy director of the UN humanitarian aid program in Baghdad, argued recently: "We are told that pencils are forbidden because carbon could be extracted from them that might be used to coat airplanes and make them invisible to radar. I am not a military expert, but I find it very disturbing that because of this objection, we cannot give pencils to Iraqi schoolchildren."[4]

For the past several years, individuals and groups have been delivering medicine and other supplies to Iraq in defiance of the US blockade. Now, members of one of those groups, Chicago-based Voices in the Wilderness, have been threatened with massive fines by the federal government for "exportation of donated goods, including medical supplies and toys, to Iraq absent specific prior authorization."[5] Our government is harassing a peace group that takes medicine and toys to dying children: we owe these courageous activists our support.

This is not foreign policy—it is state-sanctioned mass murder. The Iraqi people are suffering because of the actions of both the Iraqi and US governments, but our moral responsibility lies here in the United States. If we remain silent, we are condoning a genocide that is being perpetrated in the name of peace in the Middle East, a mass slaughter that is being perpetrated in our name.

This statement appeared in the New York Times *with the names of the first 1,000 signatories on March 28, 1999. It has also appeared in* The Progressive *in June 1999.*

Notes

1 Martti Ahtisaari, *The Impact of War on Iraq: Report to the Secretary-General on Humanitarian Needs in Iraq in the Immediate Post-Crisis Environment, March 20, 1991* (Westfield, New Jersey: Open Magazine Pamphlet Series 7, 1991), p. 5.

2 See UN Office of the Iraq Program, "Oil-for-food—The Basic Facts." Available at http://www.un.org/Depts/oip/reports/basfact.html.

3 Stephen Kinzer, "Smart Bombs, Dumb Sanctions," *New York Times,* January 3, 1999, p. 4: 4.

4 Kinzer, "Smart Bombs, Dumb Sanctions," p. 4: 4.

5 R. Richard Newcomb, Director, Office of Foreign Assets Control, "Prepenalty Notice," OFAC Nos. IQ-162016 and IQ-162433, December 3, 1998 (http://www.nonviolence.org/vitw/htv2.html).

Chapter 15

Building the Movement to End Sanctions

Sharon Smith

For 12 long years, sanctions against Iraq have been strangling its population. By the time the US and British militaries began the most recent bombing campaign against Iraq at the end of 1998—a campaign that still continues and which could soon involve another massive aerial campaign or even a ground invasion or occupation—more than 1 million Iraqis, many of them children, had died as a result of the United Nations sanctions on Iraq and the effects of the Persian Gulf War.[1]

After launching more than 300 cruise missiles and dropping hundreds of bombs in December 1998, the United States claimed (apparently failing to see the irony) that the four-day bombardment was needed to stop Saddam Hussein from developing "weapons of mass destruction."[2] Today, we hear these arguments used to justify "pre-emptive" strikes against Iraq.

US foreign policy toward Iraq has consisted of a two-pronged brutal campaign—deadly sanctions interspersed with bombing—since the end of the Persian Gulf War in 1991. For most of this time, mainstream newspapers across the United States have barely mentioned the sanctions, except perhaps as a passing comment while reporting the latest bombing raid or an upcoming discussion on the UN Security Council.

This should not be too surprising, given the role played by the US news media during the Gulf War. During that war, reporters (often wearing US army fatigues and surrounded by army vehicles) were complicit in the government's efforts to withhold information about the number of Iraqi casualties (coldly reported as "collateral damage," as if real people were not being killed) and the annihilation of Iraq's infrastructure. How could those of us not schooled in military jargon have guessed that within the "military theater" were oil production facilities and water sanitation plants? The round-the-clock coverage provided by the competing networks (each with its unique designer logo and theme song) managed to leave out the most important facts: that tens of thousands of Iraqis were killed after six weeks of carpet-bombing; that "smart bombs" more often than not missed their targets; and that, by the end of the war, Iraq had been reduced to a "pre-industrial age," according to a UN inspections team that visited the country in March 1991.[3]

Individual activists deserve credit for whatever information about the human toll of the sanctions and the bombing raids has filtered to the general public. Individuals such as former attorney general Ramsey Clark, along with the International Action Center, have visited Iraq periodically, each time warning of the mounting death toll.[4] In fall 1998, the UN coordinator for humanitarian aid to Iraq, Denis Halliday, resigned in protest, arguing that the sanctions "are starving to death 6,000 Iraqi infants every month."[5] Halliday has since campaigned against the sanctions, as has his successor as humanitarian coordinator in Iraq, Hans von Sponeck, who also resigned to express his opposition to the embargo.

Heroic individuals from the Chicago-based Voices in the Wilderness have defied the sanctions and hand-delivered medicine and supplies to Iraq. The US government responded in 1998 by charging Voices with "exportation of donated goods, including medical supplies and toys, to Iraq absent specific prior authorization," and imposing a $160,000 fine against the small organization. Voices member Bart Sacks, an activist in Seattle, was levied, along with Reverend Randall Mullins, with a $10,000 fine in spring 2002. Both have refused to pay the fine and instead pledged to raise $10,000 for children's medicine. Sacks and Voices in the Wilderness met their goal within only one week, after more than 500 people mailed in checks.[6]

It is a crime, apparently, to bring medicine and toys to dying children. After the original fine, Voices member Mike Bremer said that the organization would pose the question to the court: "If you believe in freedom, isn't it a basic freedom for any human being to go anywhere in the world to save a dying child's life?"[7]

Activists from Voices in the Wilderness–UK and other organizations around the world have engaged in similar efforts, while also working to change government policy toward Iraq and end the sanctions altogether.

Nevertheless, protests have been few and far between, considering the scale of the carnage—and the fact that the American and British governments are responsible for imposing the sanctions and leading the bombing raids. The silence, to be sure, has been deafening to all those who have known the truth about the sanctions against Iraq: that the *sanctions* are weapons of mass destruction, devastating an entire population and killing thousands more with each passing month.

Too few of us have been given the opportunity to view photographs taken of the devastation among ordinary Iraqis. Anyone who has seen them will be forever haunted by the suffering faces of Iraqi children, wasting away in hospitals without medicine or antiseptics, waiting for death; the quiet desperation of their parents, unable to do anything more than hold their children while they die; and the visible pain of a generation of children who have known nothing but deprivation.

Breaking the silence

The four-day bombing of Iraq in December 1998 spurred a large number of activists into action. Organizations such as the Iraq Action Coalition began to gain a wider hearing. By the hundreds and even thousands, demonstrators protested the December bombings in cities across the United States and the United Kingdom. Thousands of people with email received a "Call to Action" against the Iraq sanctions in January 1999, signed by Noam Chomsky, Howard Zinn, Edward Said, and Edward Herman. It was an appeal to activists which read, in part: "First, we must organize and make this issue a priority, just as Americans organized to stop the war in Vietnam.... We need a national campaign to lift the sanctions."[8]

The call to action was initiated and widely distributed by Robert Jensen, a professor at the University of Texas at Austin, and Austin-based activists Rahul Mahajan and Romi Mahajan. It inspired a small group of people to launch a signature campaign calling for an end to the sanctions against Iraq. We envisioned a campaign to place a full-page signature ad in the *New York Times* as a modest attempt to educate the public about the human toll of the Iraq sanctions and the growing opposition to them. If the mainstream media refuses to report the truth, activists can at least buy a page in the newspaper to put forward the facts.

Our goal was to educate, but the experience of building support for the ad also educated us. We were surprised by the support for the campaign that actually existed within the general population. Jensen, Chomsky, Zinn, Said, and Herman quickly agreed to be part of an advisory board to sponsor the ad. Within weeks, they were joined by William Keach, a professor at Brown University; Carlos Muñoz, Jr., and June Jordan from the

University of California at Berkeley; and Angela Davis from the University of California at Santa Cruz.[9]

A regular full-page ad in the *New York Times* costs $81,000—a frightening figure. We opted for a "stand-by" ad for "only" $34,000, which meant that we had to forfeit the right to choose the date the ad would appear. Our hopes for one or two generous contributions from Hollywood celebrities with left-wing sympathies or perhaps a liberal foundation to fund the cost of the ad went unfulfilled.

As it turned out, though, we had no trouble financing the cost of the ad. After an initial outreach effort, the campaign began to build itself by word of mouth. Checks accompanied by strong statements of support began streaming in—small amounts, for the most part—from professors, students, and people from all walks of life who dug into their own pockets and added their names to the statement. Small groups of activists from campuses, local peace networks, and religious groups took collections. All told, the statement drew the support of more than 1,500 people who were looking for an opportunity to voice their opposition to the sanctions against Iraq. The response—like the response to Voice's 2002 campaign to raise money for Iraqi children, rather than for the fines levied against Sacks and Mullins—showed the potential for building a grassroots movement in opposition to the barbaric policy against the Iraqi people.

The United Nations takes note

One morning—about a month after we began circulating the statement—I was surprised to be told by a co-worker that "John Mills from the United Nations" was waiting to speak to me on the telephone. Frankly, I had not expected the United Nations to be aware of the signature ad, much less take any interest in it.

Mills, as it turns out, was very interested, and quite perturbed. He abruptly informed me that the statement contained "numerous errors" regarding the list of supplies banned from entering Iraq under the sanctions regime, which bars many "dual use" items that allegedly could have military applications. He was particularly annoyed, he said, that the statement quoted Farid Zarif, deputy director of the humanitarian aid program in Baghdad, as saying, "We are told that pencils are forbidden because carbon could be extracted from them that might be used to coat airplanes and make them invisible to radar. I am not a military expert, but

I find it very disturbing that because of this objection, we cannot give pencils to Iraqi school children."[10]

Mills claimed that Zarif never made such a statement, implying that some sort of legal action might be undertaken if the quote were not removed. I reminded Mills that the quote had first appeared a few months earlier in a *New York Times* article, which I remembered had been cleverly titled, "Smart Bombs, Dumb Sanctions."[11] What better authority was there than the deputy director of the UN's humanitarian aid program to describe the human cost of the dual-use restrictions of the sanctions? Not only had the article appeared in a mainstream newspaper, I pointed out, but the *Times* had never printed a retraction. This seemed to annoy Mills even more. "You must know that you can't believe everything you read in the press," he remarked (perhaps appealing to what he assumed would be my instinctive left-wing mistrust of the mass media). In fact, Mills said, so many lies about the sanctions are printed daily in newspapers throughout the world that the New York office of the United Nations cannot keep up with them to demand retractions.

I reminded him that Denis Halliday, who had recently resigned as the UN's coordinator for humanitarian aid to Iraq, had endorsed the statement and asked, "Are you saying that there are plenty of pencils for Iraqi children?"

"No, I am not," Mills retorted angrily. He seemed to think that a bit of bluff and bluster on his part might compensate for the barrage of evidence to the contrary. He insisted, however, that Zarif denied ever claiming to *New York Times* reporters that pencils are banned in Iraq.

There was only one way to resolve the situation. I agreed to contact Stephen Kinzer, the author of the *Times* article in question, to ask him if he stood by the quote. If he stood by the quote, it would stay; otherwise, we would remove it. I received the reply within a matter of hours.

> Dear Ms. Smith:
>
> I received your note. Sounds like poor Mr. Zarif may be getting into trouble, but that's what you get for talking to reporters.
>
> For the record, I stand by the quote without any hesitation. I can still remember Zarif holding up a pencil and giving it to me.
>
> Give my regards to Howard Zinn, he was a professor of mine at Boston University.
>
> Best wishes,
> Stephen Kinzer[12]

The quote stood. On March 28, 1999, the statement appeared as a full-page signature ad in the *New York Times*, accompanied by the names of the first 1,000 people who had endorsed it.[13]

All told, more than 1,500 individuals signed on to the statement. Besides Halliday, they included British Labor MP Tony Benn; the Uruguayan writer and critic Eduardo Galeano; authors Tillie Olsen, Harold Pinter, and Kurt Vonnegut Jr.; journalists Barbara Ehrenreich and Katha Pollitt; Father Roy Bourgeois of School of the Americas Watch; and Bishop Thomas Gumbleton of Detroit. Perhaps most important, hundreds of individuals responded to the appeal by asking how they can could become more involved in efforts to end the sanctions.

Silence should not be mistaken for acquiescence. The lack of widespread, visible protest today does not equal mass support for the sanctions against Iraq. There is a small but growing movement against the Iraq sanctions. More than 275 people from around the United States and Canada attended the first national organizing conference on Iraq in Ann Arbor, Michigan, in October 1999. These individuals represented small networks of community, Arab-American, peace, and other activists, as well as large national organizations like the American-Arab Anti-Discrimination Committee and the American Friends Service Committee. Activists also organized protests in Washington, DC, for the tenth anniversary of sanctions in August 2000, and joined the April 2002 protests in Washington DC against the Israeli occupation of Palestine and the "war on terrorism." The response to the signature ad campaign and to the Voices in the Wilderness appeal for Sacks and Mullins are two small measures of the broad opposition to US policy in Iraq, and point to the potential for something much larger. In September 2002 we had a taste of that movement when hundreds of thousands of people worldwide joined together to march against a war in Iraq.[14]

Movements start small

Mass movements do not spring up overnight. They are built over a period of years—sometimes many years—by individual people with a strong sense of commitment and a long-term view of their goals. The civil rights movement that brought hundreds of thousands of people into active participation in the course of the 1960s was built on a foundation laid by committed activists over many years. Rosa Parks, for example, became a symbol of the civil rights movement in 1955 when she refused to give up her bus seat to a white man and helped to lead the Montgomery bus boycott. It was not the first time she had attempted to claim her rightful place on a bus: 11 years prior Parks had refused to enter through the back door and was thrown off the bus. But after her arrest in 1955, the forty-three-year-old seamstress, who had long been active in the Montgomery chapter of the National Association for the Advancement of Colored People, with the chapter's youth council, agreed to help organize a bus boycott on her behalf for the purpose of breaking segregation laws. Within a matter of days, tens of thousands of black people were actively involved in building the boycott. Fifty thousand Montgomery blacks took part in the bus boycott over the next year.[15]

The same is true of opposition to the Vietnam War. Between 1961 and 1964, only handfuls of protesters voiced opposition to the war. Even the main organization of campus activists, Students for a Democratic Society (SDS), did not immediately seize on the war as an organizing issue. The SDS national council meeting in December 1964 rejected a proposal by Todd Gitlin that the organization produce a "We won't go" statement to protest the Vietnam War. Only after hours of debate did the council decide to organize a march against the war in April of the coming year.[16] The first antiwar demonstration, held in 1964 in New York, drew only 600 people. But the numbers grew steadily over the following years. The April 1965 march planned by SDS drew 20,000. A year later, 400,000 demonstrated against the Vietnam War in New York. Six months after that, 100,000 demonstrated in Washington, DC, and 30,000 marched on the Pentagon, which was guarded by armed troops.[17]

It is easy to think of the 1960s as a different era, when the mass of the population supported the goals of civil rights and opposition to the war. But this was not the case until well after these issues had developed into mass movements. When Rosa Parks refused to give up her seat to a white man in 1955, she was breaking the law. The Montgomery boycott itself was illegal, according to a city ordinance. Moreover, civil rights activists in the North, as well as the South, were confronted by a well-organized and violent racist opposition. It took nearly a year before the US Supreme Court ruled to outlaw segregation on city buses.[18] Even after this victory, however, racists launched a series of violent attacks on civil rights activists in Montgomery. Churches and homes were bombed and activists were shot. This was the climate in which the civil rights movement was launched.

The antiwar movement was also swimming against majority opinion in its early stages. Eighty-three percent of the US public supported the escalation of the bombing of North Vietnam in 1965.[19] As the war dragged on, however, the growth of the antiwar movement began to have a deeper impact on public sentiment. By 1968, the number of people describing themselves as "doves" nearly equaled those describing themselves as "hawks" in relation to the war.[20]

After the US invasion of Cambodia in 1970, unrest on college campuses grew into a national student strike. During the month of May, protests were organized at nearly 1,350 campuses, with up to half of all US college students participating. More than 500 colleges were shut down by student strikes against the war.[21]

By 1970, union leaders began to speak out against the war and rank-and-file workers began joining antiwar protests in much larger numbers. After the National Guard and police fired on student protesters at Kent State University and Jackson State College in May 1970, killing a total of six students and wounding twenty-one, the General Executive Board of the United Electrical, Radio, and Machine Workers issued a statement calling the killings "a tragic product of an Administration in Washington which has made escalation of war abroad and repression at home its most distinguishing characteristics."[22]

By April 1971, a Harris poll found that a majority of people in the United States believed the war was "morally wrong." "The tide of American public opinion has now turned decisively against the war," Louis Harris declared.[23]

Viewed in this historical context, the possibility for building a movement to end the barbaric policies against the people of Iraq—and other nations terrorized by the US military and its open-ended "war on terrorism"—does not appear to be as daunting.

Iraq and the "war on terrorism" — Building a movement today

By summer 2002 preparations were underway for another full-scale military invasion of Iraq—with the goal of "regime change" clearly stated, even if the timetable was yet to be determined. As the US prepares to increase the devastation it inflicts on Iraq, the movement to oppose these plans must continue to build. It will not be easy. In the face of virtually unanimous international opposition, the Bush administration has asserted its right to launch a "pre-emptive strike" against Baghdad—demonstrating its belief that the world's sole superpower is exempted from the constraints of international law. No fewer than four military options for invasion under consideration were "leaked" to the mass media, some involving as many as 250,000 U.S. troops. Even a so-called "inside-out" strategy was under consideration—first bombing Baghdad, a city of more than four million people, to prompt a collapse of the Iraqi regime.[24]

The Bush administration has attempted to frame a new war against Iraq as a component of the US "war on terrorism." In so doing, however, the United States has exposed just how little its open-ended war has to do with seeking justice for the victims of the atrocities of September 11. Instead, these plans have everything to do with strengthening US dominance over the rest of the world. No credible evidence has yet emerged to link Iraq with the al-Qaeda terrorist network or the deadly anthrax attacks of fall 2001, so the US government has resurrected its old rallying cry to justify a new war against Iraq: that Saddam Hussein possesses weapons of mass destruction and used chemical weapons "against his own people" (neglecting to mention that the US supported him in the 1980s, when he did so).[25] The privilege of deploying weapons of mass destruction apparently belongs only to the United States and its allies-of-the-moment.

Well before September 11, members of the Bush administration were searching for a reason to escalate the bombing in Iraq. Assistant Secretary of Defense Paul Wolfowitz was among the first of the administration hawks to take to the airwaves to call for a war against multiple targets, including Iraq, in retaliation for September 11.[26] (For the most part, the mainstream media neglected to mention Wolfowitz' public statements prior to September 11, such as those calling for the United States to strike Baghdad as soon as "we find the right way to do it."[27]) The war against terrorism provided the US with the excuse it was looking for, with the mass media dutifully whipping up anti-Iraq hysteria to justify it.

Despite the widespread international outcry, domestic voices of principled opposition to the coming war have remained on the margins. Throughout the summer of 2002, the loudest critics of Bush's plan to invade Iraq were from the right, not the left. An array of Republicans, including outgoing House Majority Whip Dick Armey; Brent Scowcroft, who served as national security adviser during the 1991 war against Iraq; and even former secretary of state Henry Kissinger voiced strong criticism.[28] These critics, however, did not challenge the imperialist aims of the US government, but questioned whether a premature rush to war against Iraq might endanger those aims. The question was, in other words, not whether to force a regime change in Iraq, but when and how best to do so. "An attack on Iraq at this time would seriously jeopardize, if not destroy, the global counterterrorist campaign we have undertaken," warned Scowcroft in an opinion piece in the *Wall Street Journal.*[29]

As a group, the Democrats have aided and abetted the Bush administration's war aims since September 11. The Senate Foreign Relations Committee—which is chaired by Democratic Senator Joe Biden—invited no dissenters to speak when it held hearings on Iraq on July 31 and August 1. Missing were former UN humanitarian coordinators Denis Halliday and Hans von Sponeck, who could have testified to the ongoing human toll of the sanctions. Also missing was Scott Ritter, the Marine veteran and Republican who led the UN weapons inspection team until it was withdrawn in advance of the US bombing in December 1998. Ritter, an outspoken opponent of another war against Iraq, has argued, "To date, the Bush administration has been unable—or unwilling—to back up its rhetoric concerning the Iraqi threat with any substantive facts."[30]And Democrats, of course, helped to carry the October 2002 House and Senate resolutions authorizing Bush to strike Iraq.

A strong opposition to the expanding war on terrorism has yet to be built inside the United States. Immediately upon taking office, George W. Bush launched a frontal assault on all things liberal—as if he had a popular mandate for a return to the Reagan era, when, in fact, he had stolen the election. Using the September 11 attacks as justification, the Bush administration aggressively seized the opportunity to undertake a US military onslaught abroad and an ideological rampage at home. The mass of the population, seeking symbols of solidarity and solace as they mourned the deaths of thousands of innocent civilians in the World Trade Center attacks, were offered only American flags and calls for revenge by the war-mongers swarming the mass media. Many on the left were confused about how to react to the war, initially embracing the American flag and allowing the United States to cloak its real war aims in calls for "justice" for the victims of September 11. This confusion prevented many on the left from mounting a clear opposition to the bombing of Afghanistan. With breathtaking speed, the Bush administration used the opportunity to pass the USA PATRIOT Act, institute military tribunals, detain more than 1,000 Arabs and Muslims, and round up and deport scores of immigrants.[31]

The swift US victory in the initial phase of the war, however, has led to a significant erosion of support for the Bush administration. Heady with its own success, the Bush administration quickly reached further, both abroad and at home. Bush's list of potential military targets reaches not only to Iraq, but as far as North Korea, Malaysia, Georgia, and Colombia.[32] Each new target makes it that much more difficult to sustain the justification of September 11 among growing segments of the population.

Information emanating from Afghanistan itself has eroded support for the war. The return to warlord rule in Afghanistan as a result of the US victory there has given the lie to Bush's claim that the United States ushered in an era of democracy when it defeated the Taliban. News that Afghan courts will continue to enforce a strict interpretation of Sharia law—for example, imprisoning (rather than executing, as under the Taliban) women who run away from their husbands—has replaced the image of smiling women tearing off their burqas as US troops entered Kabul in December 2001.[33] Six months after the fall of the Taliban, more than half the Afghan population remained in need of emergency food aid. Yet the United States still poured the bulk of its aid money into military operations—demonstrating that its air food drops to starving Afghans as it was bombing them in the autumn of 2001 was nothing more than a public relations stunt.[34]

At home, the speed and arrogance with which the Bush administration has discarded basic civil rights in the name of national security has led to a growing public outcry. As Alexander Cockburn and Jeffrey St. Clair wrote in *CounterPunch,* "At the rate things are going, it won't be long before labor organizers are being thrown into military prisons, [or] held without warrant as 'enemy combatants.'" In fact, as Cockburn and St. Clair reported, in the midst of negotiations between the West Coast Longshoremen's Union and the Pacific Maritime Association, Tom Ridge, director of the Office of Homeland Security, phoned union leader Jim Spinosa to pressure him not to call a strike.[35] President Bush even threatened to replace strikers with Navy personnel—an action only permitted during wartime. Union leaders were told that Bush has declared that "a state of war exists and will go on indefinitely." Indeed, the Bush administration took advantage of a management-ordered lockout to invoke the Taft-Hartley Act on October 8 to eliminate the possibility of a strike for 80 days.[36]

The ongoing spectacle of Enron and other corporate thieves walking away with millions while ordinary workers suffer the effects of recession has brought a return of class anger. Stanley Greenberg, pollster for National Public Radio, writing in the August 5, 2002, *New York Times,* described the angry mood of voters in advance of November 2002 elections. According to Greenberg, recent polls show that roughly 75 percent of voters said they are very angry about Enron; the same percentage was also "very angry about chief executives taking lavish bonuses and perks as their companies fail and pensions lose value." Moreover, the issues most concerning voters in the November 2002 election did not include terrorism. They were, in order of importance: the economy and jobs (35 percent); Social Security and Medicare (24 percent); education (23 percent); and affordable health care (21 percent).[37]

As the US prepares for another war against Iraq, the potential to build a broader anti-war movement has grown. Even opinion polls showing overwhelming support for going to war against Iraq demonstrate this potential. In an August 2002 ABC News and *Washington Post* opinion poll, 69 percent of those surveyed supported military action against Iraq, but the number dropped to 54 percent if US allies opposed the war. While 57 percent supported the US using ground troops to invade Iraq, that number dropped to only 40 percent—and opposition rose to 51 percent—if it would cause "significant" US casualties.[38] The survey did not ask how respondents would feel about the likelihood of a "significant" number of Iraqi casualties. Nor did it ask how respondents felt about shouldering the cost of the war to the tune of billions of dollars, or paying sharply higher gasoline prices that would be the likely result. A late summer Pew Research Center opinion poll showed only 37 percent of those surveyed believe that the president has clearly explained the reasons for forcibly ending Saddam Hussein's rule.[39] The vast majority of people in the United States—just like the people of the United Kingdom, Bush's closest ally in the war on Iraq—will gain nothing from expanding the war on terrorism to Iraq.

Support for war on Iraq rises to 65 percent if the US launches a multilateral war (the figure for Europeans rises to 60 percent), according to a summer 2002 survey commissioned by the Chicago Council on Foreign Relations and the German Marshall Fund.[40] But UN support will not justify a new war against Iraq. After all, the UN Security Council backed the 1991 Gulf War and has sponsored 12 years of sanctions. It will be up to the anti-war movement to tell the truth about the US government's murderous record in Iraq, and to help larger numbers of people to learn the facts about US foreign policy. Through its war on Afghanistan, the United States established military bases in Afghanistan, Pakistan, Kyrgyzstan, Uzbekistan, and Tajikistan, and a presence in Kazakstan— corresponding exactly to the routes of planned American oil pipelines from the Caspian Oil Basin.[41] The overthrow of Saddam Hussein would give the United States control over Iraq's vast oil reserves, second only to those of

Saudi Arabia. To achieve these strategic goals, the US government has killed thousands of Afghans and many more Iraqis; and is going down a path that will kill even more.

Most people in the United States have no idea of the atrocities that have been committed in their name. The scale of suffering that is taking place would horrify the vast majority, if only they knew what abuses and crimes their tax dollars were funding. This knowledge would also expose the utter hypocrisy of Bush's charges about Saddam Hussein's "weapons of mass destruction." When it comes to inflicting mass destruction, the United States is second to none.

Moving forward

Those of us who live inside the countries most responsible for such militarism and state terrorism bear a certain responsibility. Whether or not a movement is built here can make a vital difference to those struggling for hope and freedom elsewhere in the world. The Vietnam antiwar movement showed that clearly.

On a wide variety of social issues, the US population stands clearly to the left of the politicians who run the US government, even at a time without clear mass movements and when the government is cynically using patriotism—as well as intimidation and violation of civil liberties—to advance its agenda. The time is ripe for building a mass movement to channel this discontent.

As we saw with the civil rights movement and the anti-Vietnam War movement, a small group of activists can prepare the ground for a mass movement. Those who are fighting for justice today are helping to pave the way for larger numbers tomorrow. We can break the silence and build an opposition to sanctions and a renewed war. If we build as broadly as possible, and reach out to the many people who are already dissatisfied and searching for alternatives, our numbers will grow.

Around the country, anti-sanctions activists have shown that they can reach much wider audiences with their message. When people learn about the reality of life in Iraq, and are armed with some basic arguments against the myths peddled by the media about what is happening there, they can quickly become convinced to get involved. A handful of organized antiwar activists not only publicly humiliated Madeleine Albright and other top US officials at a February 1998 "town meeting" in Columbus, Ohio, to mobilize support for US bombing of Iraq; they constrained the ability of the United States to intervene at that time. The activists posed questions to Albright about the contradiction of the United States government supporting the brutal dictatorship of General Suharto in Indonesia while claiming we had to go to war against a dictator in Iraq, one who, Albright neglected to mention, the US government had helped to arm. The protest was broadcast internationally by CNN.[42]

Activists can also hold their own town meetings or teach-ins to discuss the real impact of sanctions. Invite a speaker from Voices in the Wilderness or one of the other groups that has sent delegations to Iraq. (See "Resources" for contact information.) These speakers can put a human face on the impact of sanctions and help motivate others to take part in anti-sanctions activities. Contact Arab-American, religious, student, labor, and veterans' organizations that might also sponsor and bring out people for the meeting.

Student activists have successfully passed resolutions against sanctions at more than a dozen campuses. Others have successfully pressed their local newspaper to run articles or opinion pieces on the crisis in Iraq, including powerful reports with photographs documenting the human toll of the sanctions. Some groups have held creative demonstrations at their local post offices highlighting the fact that it is not possible to send relief materials to Iraq. When the packages are refused, they ship the materials with a note to the White House, the State Department, or their local senator. Other campus groups have assembled samples of the many household, medical, and educational items prevented from entering Iraq due to the sanctions to illustrate how they have caused deprivation and disruption to the lives of Iraqi civilians. Members of Voices in the Wilderness and other groups have openly violated the sanctions to expose the hypocrisy and brutality of the governments that back them.

In January and February 2000, activists from around the country protested in New York and Washington, some of them staging a hunger strike to dramatize the impact of sanctions and to pressure Congress to lift sanctions. The protests culminated on February 14 outside the United States Mission to the United Nations; eighty-six nonviolent demonstrators were arrested.[43] Under grassroots pressure, 70 representatives signed a congressional letter challenging economic sanctions in 2000.[44]

On August 6, 2002, six members of Voices in the Wilderness fasted in front of United Nations compound in Baghdad to mark the twelfth anniversary of the imposition of the sanctions holding banners that said, "Drop sanctions, not bombs."[45] Across the US, activists opposed to Bush's plan for "regime change" in Iraq organized protests during the summer and fall of 2002. Some 1,300 protesters chanting anti-war slogans were pepper-sprayed in Portland, Oregon, outside Bush's appearance at a Republican fundraiser, and anti-war activists demonstrated at virtually every stop Bush made in California.[46] On August 30, 80 war protesters rallied outside US Senator John Kerry's office in downtown Boston.[47] On September 5, 400 protesters, mostly teenagers, protested against war in Iraq outside a $1,000 a plate luncheon for US Representative Anne Northup attended by Bush.[48] At September 11 commemorations from coast to coast, participants spoke out against the war—joined in many places by Peaceful Tomorrows, the peace advocacy group of families of September 11 victims. In Oakland, California, some activists carried signs and wore stickers carrying the message, "Our grief is not a cry for war."[49] On September 28, London marched against the war, with reports of 150,000 to 400,000 people participating, while 100,000 took to the streets in Rome and thousands voiced their opposition to a war in Iraq during protests against the IMF and World Bank in Washington, DC, the same weekend.[50]

These examples show the potential that exists. There will be ups and downs along the way. But handfuls of civil rights activists helped to build a movement that brought down racial segregation laws. Small numbers of activists eventually built a mass antiwar movement that supported a national liberation force in a tiny impoverished country and defeated the world's biggest superpower. We can build a movement to end the sanctions and the war against the Iraqi people.

Notes

1 Matthew Rothschild, interview with Denis Halliday, *The Progressive* 63: 2 (February 1999): 26.

2 Dana Priest, "US Commander Unsure of How Long Iraq Will Need to Rebuild," *Washington Post*, December 22, 1998, p. A31.

3 Martti Ahtisaari, *The Impact of War on Iraq: Report to the Secretary-General on Humanitarian Needs in Iraq in the Immediate Post-Crisis Environment, March 20, 1991* (Westfield, New Jersey: Open Magazine Pamphlet Series 7, 1991), p. 5. See also Patrick Cockburn, "Pentagon Revises Gulf War Scorecard," *The Independent*, April 14, 1992, p. 12, and Michael T. Klare, "'Weapons of Mass Destruction in Operation Desert Storm," in *Collateral Damage: The 'New World Order' at Home and Abroad*, ed. Cynthia Peters (Boston: South End Press, 1992), pp. 218–20.

4 See Ramsey Clark et al., *The Children Are Dying: The Impact of Sanctions on Iraq,* second edition (New York: International Action Center and International Relief Association, 1998).

5 Stephen Kinzer, "Smart Bombs, Dumb Sanctions," *New York Times*, January 3, 1999, p. 4: 4.

6 R. Richard Newcomb, Director, Office of Foreign Assets Control, "Prepenalty Notice," OFAC Nos. IQ-162016 and IQ-162433, December 3, 1998. See also Voices in the Wilderness, "VitW update—New Fine Imposed," press release, June 29, 2002. Available online at http://www.nonviolence.org/vitw.

7 Sharon Smith, "Oil on Troubled Waters," *Socialist Review* 227 (February 1999), p. 11; and "Government Targets Peace Group," *Socialist Worker*, January 1, 1999, p. 6.

8 The text of the original call is available online at the Voices in the Wilderness website (http://www.nonviolence.org/vitw/pages/48.htm). See also Chapter 14.

9 Alan Pogue of the Texas Center for Documentary Photography in Austin (alanpogue@mac.com), graciously donated the powerful photograph we used in the ad. Gabe Huck from the Chicago Archdiocese agreed to help design the ad with a co-worker. Anthony Arnove and Phil Gasper, a professor at the College of Notre Dame in California, agreed to help outreach for signatures and donations. I coordinated the ad, with the help of Elizabeth Schulte and Chris Hodge. John Solimine designed a web page.

10 Kinzer, "Smart Bombs, Dumb Sanctions."

11 Kinzer, "Smart Bombs, Dumb Sanctions."

12 Stephen Kinzer, personal correspondence, March 2, 1999.

13 *New York Times*, March 28, 1999. The ad appeared on different pages in regional and national editions.

14 BBC, "Protesters Stage Anti-War Rally," September 28, 2002 (http://news.bbc.co.uk/2/hi/uk_news/politics/2285861.stm).

15 Juan Williams, *Eyes on the Prize: America's Civil Rights Years, 1954–1965* (New York: Penguin, 1987), pp. 59–89.

16 Tom Wells, *The War Within: America's Battle over Vietnam* (Berkeley: University of California Press, 1994), pp. 13–14.

17 Chris Harman, *The Fire Last Time: 1968 and After,* second edition (Chicago and London: Bookmarks, 1998), pp. 65, 70–71.

18 Howard Zinn, *A People's History of the United States: 1492–Present* (New York: HarperCollins, 1999), pp. 450–51.

19 Wells, *The War Within*, p. 20.

20 Wells, *The War Within*, p. 253.

21 Wells, *The War Within*, p. 425; Zinn, *A People's History of the United States*, pp. 490–91; and Harman, *The Fire Last Time*, pp. 168–69.

22 Wells, *The War Within*, p. 427. See also Jerry Lembcke, *The Spitting Image: Myth, Memory, and the Legacy of Vietnam* (New York: New York University Press, 1998).

23 Wells, *The War Within*, p. 491.

24 David E. Sanger and Thom Shanker, "U.S. Exploring Baghdad Strike As Iraq Option," *New York Times*, July 29, 2002, p. A1.

25 Patrick Tyler, "Officers Say U.S. Aided Iraq in War Despite Use of Gas," *New York Times*, August 18, 2002 p.1: 1. Nafeez Mosaddeq Ahmed, "The 1991 Gulf Massacre: The Historical and Strategic Context of Western Terrorism in the Gulf," Media Monitors Network, October 2, 2001. Available online at www.geocities.com/iraqinfo.html.

26 Sharon Smith, "Targeting Iraq: U.S. Hypocrisy and Media Lies," *International Socialist Review*, 20 (November–December 2001): 60.

27 Karen DeYoung and Rick Weiss, "U.S. Seems toEase Rhetoric on Iraq," *Washington Post*, October 24, 2001, p. 17.

28 Julian Borger and Richard Norton-Taylor, "U.S. Adviser Warns of Armegeddon," *Guardian*, August 16, 2002, p. 1. Editorial, "This is Opposition?" *Wall Street Journal*, August 19, 2002, p. A12.

29 *Wall Street Journal*, August 15, 2002.

30 Normon Solomon, "Fending Off the Threat of Peace," August 8, 2002.

31 The attacks are summarized in "The War on Civil Liberties," *The New York Times*, September 10, 2002, P. A24.

32 Gary Leupp, " 'Train and Equip' for What?" *CounterPunch*, May 29, 2002. Gary Leupp, "Red Targets in the 'War on Terrorism,'" *CounterPunch*, June 19, 2002.

33 Sharon Smith, "Afghanistan's Rigged Democracy," *International Socialist Review*, 24 (July–August 2002): 14.

34 Smith, "Afghanistan's Rigged Democracy." Elizabeth A. Neuffer, "Food Drops Found to do Little Good," *Boston Globe*, March 26, 2002, p. A1.

35 Alexander Cockburn and Jeffrey St. Clair, "Strikers as Terrorists?" *CounterPunch*, June 27, 2002.

36 David Bacon, "Unions Fear 'War on Terror' will Overcome Right to Strike," Inter Press Service, August 10, 2002, p. 40. David E. Sanger and Steven Greenhouse, "President Invokes Taft-Hartley Act to Open 29 Ports," *New York Times*, October 9, 2002. P. A1.

37 Stanley B. Greenberg, "What Voters Want," *New York Times*, August 5, 2002, p. A15.

38 "Poll Suggests U.S. Public Sharply Divided on Iraq," Associated Press, August 13, 2002. Duncan Campbell, "Threats of War," *Guardian,* August 16, 2002, p. 15.

39 Charles M. Madigan, "Poll: U.S. Public Leery of War on Iraq," *Chicago Tribune*, September 5, 2002.

40 Cited in Stacy Humes Schulz, "US Was Partly to Blame 'For Attacks,'" *Financial Times*, September 4, 2002, p. 5, and Paul Hofheinz and John Harwood, "An Attack Backed by U.N. Is Finding Favor," *Wall Street Journal*, August 4, 2002, p. A18.

41 Eric Margolis, "War on Terror Masks Bush's Grand Strategy," *Toronto Sun*, March 10, 2002.

42 See Mark Tran, "Slogans Evoke Vietnam Spirit," *Guardian*, February 23, 1998, p. 10.

43 See Fellowship of Reconciliation and Voices in the Wilderness press release, "86 Arrested in Protest of Economic Sanctions Against Iraq," February 14, 2000.

44 See the Education for Peace in Iraq Center (EPIC) website (http://epic-usa.org).

45 Sameer N. Yacoub, "American Activists Start Fasting to Protest U.N. Sanctions and U.S. War Plans," Associated Press, August 7, 2002.

46 Maxine Bernstein, "Police Tactics Rekindle Criticism [of] the Police," *The Oregonian*, August 24, 2002, p. A1.

47 Chris Tangney, "Antiwar Protesters Picket Kerry's Office," *Boston Globe*, August 31, 2002, p. B3.

48 Associated Press State and Local Wire, "Hundreds Rally to Protest President's Visit," September 5, 2002.

49 Charles Burress and Jim Doyle, "Bay Area Marchers Call for Peace," *San Francisco Chronicle*, September 9, 2002, p. A11.

50 Rebecca Allison, "Anti-war Marchers Evokes Spirit of CND," *Guardian*, September 30, 2002, p. 4, CNN, "London and Rome Host Anti-war Rallies," September 28, 2002. (http://europe.cnn.com/2002/WORLD/europe/09/28/london.march), and Manny Fernandez and Montel Reel, "Against War, a Peaceful March," *Washington Post*, September 30, 2002, p. B1. See also note 14.

Afterword to the Second Edition of Iraq Under Siege

No to War on Iraq

Denis J. Halliday

As the essays in *Iraq Under Siege: The Deadly Impact of Sanctions and War* show, sanctions are a form of warfare—slow, painful, and murderous. Economic sanctions, like war itself, are a form of state terrorism. It is much easier to blame Iraqi president Saddam Hussein for the suffering in Iraq than to look at the US government's involvement; its use of deadly weapons against civilians during the Gulf War, including those containing depleted uranium; and the deliberate destruction of civilian infrastructure resulting in an unsafe water supply that carries fatal diseases to a most vulnerable population.

We must bring about an attitude change in the United States, the United Kingdom, and the United Nations. We must end this so-called containment policy of tortuous economic sanctions. Instead, why not implement paragraph 14 of UN Resolution 687, which obliges the United States and the other arms traders of the UN Security Council to remove all weapons of mass destruction from the entire region? That would ease the current crisis. We know full well that if Washington would drop its plan for war on Iraq and the removal of Hussein, and if the economic embargo would be terminated, the government of Iraq would facilitate UN arms inspections, thus allowing the people of Iraq to live and their economy to be rebuilt.

The story of Iraq is one of innocent civilians who are being collectively punished—regardless of international law—by a United Nations Security Council driven by Washington and London. With support from Canada and my own country, Ireland, the UN continues to punish innocent Iraqis, even after 12 long years and massive loss of life. We in the Western democracies have to accept full responsibility for ending this disaster. But instead Washington is now ready to attack Iraq again—bombing its heavily populated towns and cities still more because it considers its president "evil."

This is dangerous and simplistic thinking. It makes one wonder, who is next?

The new regime in Washington is calling for a "pre-emptive" military attack on Iraq—a totally illegal concept under international law. US might is not right. The United States is not above international law. There is no evidence, no justification for US planes to bomb the towns and cities of Iraq—towns and cities populated by children, their parents, and their families— families like yours and mine.

We must end the sanctions on Iraq. Instead of being subjected to war and refugee conditions in their own country, Iraqis have a right—a human right—to employment, education, health care, and a functioning civilian infrastructure. They must be allowed to make their own choices—even if Washington does not agree with them—and change their system of governance how and when they are ready to do so. Give Iraqis back their lives, and they will address the wrongs that exist—as they see them.

We must end a foreign policy that neglects fundamental human rights. We must end our arms manufacture and sales—that most profitable trade for the United States and the other permanent members of the UN Security Council (ironically the same member states charged with peace and security).

We must demand that the United States cease its war on the people of Iraq—drop its legislation of assassination, its propaganda and misinformation, its overt and self-serving military aggression. Unless we organize to prevent it, another American war in the Middle East may lead to total catastrophe for all peoples living in the region.

Resources

Organizations Working to End Sanctions on Iraq

American Friends Service Committee
1501 Cherry Street
Philadelphia, PA 19102-1429
Phone: 215-241-7170
Fax: 215-241-7177
askaboutiraq@afsc.org
www.afsc.org/iraq

American-Arab Anti-Discrimination Committee
4201 Connecticut Avenue NW, Suite 300
Washington, DC 20008-1158
Phone: 202-244-2990
Fax: 202-244-3196
adc@adc.org
www.adc.org

Boston Mobilization
971 Commonwealth Avenue, Suite 20
Boston, MA 02215-1305
Phone: 617-782-2313
Fax: 617-354-2146
bostoncan@hotmail.com
www.bostonmobilization.org/

Campaign Against Sanctions on Iraq (CASI)
Cambridge University Students' Union
11-12 Trumpington Street
Cambridge CB2 1QA UK
info@casi.org.uk
http://welcome.to/casi/

Canadian Network to End Sanctions on Iraq
c/o Kairos (Canadian Ecumenical Justice Initiatives)
947 Queen Street E., Suite 205
Toronto, ON M4M 1J9 Canada
canesi@canesi.org
www.canesi.org

Citizens Concerned for the People of Iraq
c/o Western Washington Fellowship of Reconcilliation
225 North 70th Street
Seattle, WA 98103-5003
Phone: (206) 789-5565
info@endiraqsanctions.org
www.scn.org/ccpi

Education for Peace in Iraq Center (EPIC)
1101 Pennsylvania Avenue SE
Washington, DC 20003-2229
Phone: 202-543-6176
Fax: 202-543-0725
epicenter@igc.org
epic-usa.org

Fellowship of Reconciliation
PO Box 271
Nyack, NY 10960-0271
Phone: 845-358-4601
Fax: 845-358-4924
iraq@forusa.org
www.forusa.org

International Socialist Organization
PO Box 16085
Chicago, IL 60616-0085
Phone: 773-583-5069
Fax: 773-583-6144
contact@internationalsocialist.org
www.internationalsocialist.org

Iraq Action Coalition
7309 Haymarket Lane
Raleigh, NC 27615-5432
Phone: 919-604-7777
Fax: 919-846.7422
iac@leb.net
www.iraqaction.org

Iraq Resource Information Site (IRIS)
iris_author@yahoo.com
www.geocities.com/iraqinfo

Iraq Sanctions Challenge
International Action Center
39 West 14th Street, Room 206
New York, NY 10011-7489
Phone: 212-633-6646
Fax: 212-633-2889
iacenter@action-mail.org
www.iacenter.org

Iraq Speaker's Bureau
Education for Peace in Iraq Center (EPIC)
1101 Pennsylvania Avenue SE
Washington, DC 20003-2229
Phone: 202-543-6176
Fax: 202-543-0725
isb@igc.org
iraqspeakers.org/

Labour Against the War
PO Box 2378
London E5 9QU UK
Phone: (011-44)1208-985-6597
Fax: (011-44) 1208-985-6785

latw@gn.apc.org
www.labouragainstthewar.org.uk

Mennonite Central Committee
PO Box 500
Akron, PA 17501-0500
Phone: 717-859-1151
mailbox@mcc.org
www.mcc.org/areaserv/middleeast/iraq/

National Gulf War Resource Center
8605 Cameron Street, Suite 400
Silver Spring, MD 20910-3718
Phone: 800-882-1316 x162
Fax: 202-628-5880
hq@ngwrc.org
www.ngwrc.org/

National Network to End the War on Iraq
457 Kingsley Avenue
Palo Alto, CA 94301-3222
nnewai1@yahoo.com
www.endthewar.org

Pax Christi USA
National Catholic Peace Movement
532 West Eighth Street
Erie, PA 16502-1343
Phone: 814-453-4955
Fax: 814-452-4784
info@paxchristiusa.org
www.paxchristiusa.org

Peace Action
1819 H Street NW, Suite 420
Washington, DC 20006-3603
Phone: 202-862-9740 x3002
Fax: 202-862-9762
vgosse@peace-action.org
www.peace-action.org/home/iraq/getactive.html

Quaker Friends General Conference
1216 Arch Street, Suite 2B
Philadelphia, PA 19107-2835
Phone: 215-561-1700
Fax: 215-561-0759
friends@fgc.quaker.org
www.fgcquaker.org

Voices in the Wilderness
1460 West Carmen Avenue
Chicago, IL 60640-2813
Phone: 773-784-8065
Fax: 773-784-8837
info@vitw.org
www.nonviolence.org/vitw

Voices in the Wilderness UK
5 Caledonian Road
King's Cross, London N1 9DX UK
Phone: (011-44) 1-845-458-2564
voices@viwuk.freeserve.co.uk
www.viwuk.freeserve.co.uk/

Women's International League for Peace and Freedom
1213 Race Street
Philadelphia, PA 19107-1691
Phone: 215-563-7110
Fax: 215-563-5527
wilpf@wilpf.org
www.wilpf.org

Information Resources

Alternative Radio
David Barsamian
PO Box 551
Boulder, CO 80306-0551
Phone: 800-444-1977
Fax: 303-546-0592
ar@orci.com
www.alternativeradio.org

Democracy Now!
87 Lafayette Street - 2nd Floor
New York, NY 10005-3902
Phone: 212-209-2999
Fax: 212-219-0128
mail@democracynow.org
www.democracynow.org

Foreign Policy In Focus
Institute for Policy Studies
733 15th Street NW, Suite 1020
Washington, DC 20005-2112
Phone: 202-234-9382
Fax: 202-387-7915
fpif@ips-dc.org
www.foreignpolicy-infocus.org

Global Policy Forum
777 United Nations Plaza, 7G
New York, NY 10017-3521
Phone: 212-557-3161
Fax: 212-557-3165
globalpolicy@globalpolicy.org
www.globalpolicy.org

"Greetings From Missile Street" Video
Joe Public Films
PO Box 1295-1295
Dover, NH 03821
coffeeanon@yahoo.com
www.joepublicfilms.com

International Socialist Review
PO Box 258082
Chicago, IL 60625-8082
Phone: 773-583-7884
Fax: 773-583-6144
info@isreview.org
www.isreview.org

Middle East Report
Middle East Research and Information Project (MERIP)
1500 Massachusetts Avenue NW, Suite 119
Washington, DC 20005-1814
Phone: 202-223-3677
Fax: 202-223-3604
ctoensing@merip.org.
www.merip.org

New Internationalist
55 Rectory Road
Oxford OX4 1BW UK
Phone: (011-44) 1-865-728-181
Fax: (011-44) 1-865-793-152
www.newint.org/

No War Collective
worker-nowar@lists.tao.ca
www.nowarcollective.com

"Paying the Price: Killing the Children of Iraq" Video
Bullfrog Films
PO Box 149
Oley, PA 19547-0149
Phone: 610-779-8226
Fax: 610-370-1978
www.bullfrogfilms.com/catalog/pay.html

The Progressive
409 East Main Street
Madison, WI 53703-2863
Phone: 608-257-4626
Fax: 608-257-3373
editorial@progressive.org
www.progressive.org

Socialist Worker
PO Box 16085
Chicago, IL 60616-0085
Phone: 773-583-5069
Fax: 773-583-6144
letters@socialistworker.org
socialistworker.org

War Times
1230 Market Street, PMB 409
San Francisco, CA 94102-4801
Phone: 510-869-5156
editorial@war-times.org
www.war-times.org

Z Magazine
18 Millfield Street
Woods Hole, MA 02543-1122
Phone: 508-548-9063
Fax: 508-457-0626
lydia.sargent@zmag.org
www.zmag.org

Z Net Iraq Watch
18 Millfield Street
Woods Hole, MA 02543-1122
Phone: 508-548-9063
Fax: 508-457-0626
sysop@zmag.org
www.zmag.org

About the Authors

Ali Abunimah

A media analyst and activist, and frequent commentator on Palestine and the Middle East, Abunimah is vice president of the Arab American Action Network, a Chicago-based social service and advocacy organization, and co-founder of The Electronic Intifada website (electronicintifada.net).

Dr. Huda S. Ammash

Ammash is an environmental biologist and professor at Baghdad University and is a researcher at the Iraqi Academy of Science. Ammash earned her Ph.D. from the University of Missouri. She has conducted extensive research and written numerous scientific papers on the environmental and biological impact of sanctions.

Anthony Arnove

Arnove worked for seven years as an editor at South End Press before becoming a freelance editor and writer. A regular contributor to ZNet, his writing has appeared in *The Nation, International Socialist Review, Monthly Review, Socialist Worker, Z Magazine, In These Times, Financial Times,* and other publications. An activist based in Brooklyn, New York, he is a member of the International Socialist Organization and the National Writers Union. He contributed to *The Struggle for Palestine* (Haymarket Press), edited *Terrorism and War,* a collection of new interviews with Howard Zinn (Seven Stories Press), and is on the editorial board of *International Socialist Review.* Arnove is also a member of the Iraq Speaker's Bureau.

Naseer Aruri

Aruri is Chancellor Professor Emeritus of Political Science at the University of Massachusetts at Dartmouth and is chair of the board of the Trans-Arab Research Institute. His new book, *Dishonest Broker: The United States, Israel, and the Palestinians,* is forthcoming from South End Press. He has lectured and written widely on Middle East politics and history. He is also the editor of *Palestinian Refugees: The Right of Return* (Pluto) and co-editor of *Revising Culture, Reinventing Peace: The Influence of Edward W. Said* (Interlink).

Barbara Nimri Aziz

An anthropologist and journalist, Aziz has written extensively on Iraq since her first visit there in 1989. Her articles have appeared in the *Christian Science Monitor, Toward Freedom,* and several anthologies, including *Food for Our Grandmothers* (South End Press). She has contributed essays on Iraq to *Metal of Dishonor* (1999) and *Genocide by Sanctions* (1998), both published by the International Action Center. Aziz hosts a weekly radio public affairs magazine on Pacifica WBAI Radio from New York. She is also executive director of the Radius of Arab American Writers, Inc.

David Barsamian

Barsamian lives in Boulder, Colorado, and is the producer of the award-winning syndicated radio program, Alternative Radio. A regular contributor to *The Progressive* and *Z Magazine*, Barsamian is the editor of *Eqbal Ahmad: Confronting Empire* (South End Press/Pluto), the editor of *Propaganda and the Public Mind,* a collection of interviews with Noam Chomsky (South End Press/Pluto), and author of *The Decline and Fall of Public Broadcasting* (South End Press).

Phyllis Bennis

Bennis is a fellow of the Institute for Policy Studies in Washington, DC. She is an author and journalist and has written about UN and Middle East issues for almost twenty years. Her most recent books include *Calling the Shots: How Washington Dominates Today's UN,* second edition (Olive Branch Press) and *Before and After: US Foreign Policy and the September 11th Crisis* (Olive Branch Press). She also co-edited *Beyond the Storm: A Gulf Crisis Reader.*

George Capaccio

Capaccio is a writer, storyteller, and teacher based in Arlington, Massachusetts. He has traveled to Iraq on eight delegations to document the impact of sanctions. Capaccio has written on Iraq for *The Progressive* and other publications. His poetry collection, *While the Light Still Trembles,* won the 1999 Peace Writing Award from the University of Arkansas. Capaccio is a member of Voices in the Wilderness.

Noam Chomsky

Chomsky is Institute Professor in the Department of Linguistics and Philosophy at the Massachusetts Institute of Technology. He has published fouteen books with South End Press, including *Pirates and Emperors, Old and New: International Terrorism in the Real World, Rogue States: The Rule of Force in World Affairs*, and *Propaganda and the Public Mind* (in the UK by Pluto Press).

Robert Fisk

Fisk is an award-winning reporter for *The Independent* newspaper in London (www.independent.co.uk). He served as Middle East correspondent for the *Times* (London) from 1976 to 1987 and for *The Independent* since 1987. Fisk received the 1998 Amnesty International UK Press Award. He is a seven-time winner of the British International Journalist of the Year Award (most recently in 1995 and 1996). Fisk currently lives in Beirut. His writing appears in *The Nation, The Independent,* and other publications worldwide. His classic book *Pity the Nation* was released in a third edition by Oxford Paperbacks in 2001.

Denis J. Halliday

Secretary-General Kofi Annan appointed Halliday to the post of United Nations humanitarian coordinator in Iraq in September 1997. He resigned the post in protest of sanctions in fall 1998. Prior to that, Halliday served in the UN for thirty-four years, including as assistant secretary-general for human resources management and as director of the division of personnel in the United Nations Development Program.

Kathy Kelly

An activist based in Chicago, Illinois, Kelly helped initiate Voices in the Wilderness, a campaign to end the sanctions against Iraq. For bringing medicine and toys to Iraq in open violation of the sanctions, she and other campaign members have been notified of a proposed $163,000 penalty for the organization and threatened with twelve years in prison. Kelly has been to Iraq numerous times. She has taught in Chicago-area community colleges and high schools since 1974, and is active with the Catholic Worker movement.

Rania Masri

Masri is a human rights advocate, writer, researcher, and environmental scientist. Masri is the director of the newly formed Southern Peace Research and Education Center at the Institute for Southern Studies. Masri has a doctorate from North Carolina State University. She is a national board member of Peace Action, the Arab Women's Solidarity Association's representative to the United Nations, and the coordinator of the Iraq Action Coalition. She is a contributor to *The Struggle for Palestine* (Haymarket Press).

Dr. Peter L. Pellett

Pellett is Emeritus Professor of Nutrition at the University of Massachusetts at Amherst. He served on four United Nations Food and Agriculture Organization missions to Iraq. He has served as a consultant to the World Health Organization, Unicef, US Department of Agriculture, World Food Program, and National Academy of Sciences. Pellett is a board member of the International Nutrition Foundation for Developing Countries. He is the Editor in Chief of *Ecology of Food and Nutrition*.

John Pilger

Pilger is a documentary filmmaker, journalist, and author. He has twice won Britain's highest award for journalism, Journalist of the Year. He has been named International Journalist of the Year and his documentaries have won Academy awards in the United States and United Kingdom. His most recent documentaries for London-based Independent Television (ITV) include *Paying the Price: Killing the Children of Iraq* and *Palestine Is Still the Issue*. Pilger's documentary *Death of a Nation: The Timor Conspiracy* has been shown in theaters internationally. A regular contributor to the *Guardian* and *New Statesman*, he is the author of *Hidden Agendas* (New Press), *Heroes* (South End Press), and *The New Rulers of the World* (Verso).

Sharon Smith

Smith was the national coordinator of the signature ad campaign to end sanctions. A leading member of the International Socialist Organization in Chicago, she was active in building opposition to the 1991 Gulf War. A member of the National Writers Union, she is a regular columnist for the *Socialist Worker* newspaper, as well as a frequent contributor to the *International Socialist Review*. She is author of the forthcoming *End of the American Dream* (Haymarket).

Voices in the Wilderness

Since March 1996, Voices has led numerous delegations to hospitals and clinics in Iraq, breaking the siege imposed by the sanctions. Voices advocates nonviolence as a means for social change. The organization opposes the development, storage, and use—in any country—of any weapons of mass destruction, be they nuclear, chemical, biological, or economic.

Howard Zinn

Zinn is professor emeritus at Boston University. He is the author of numerous books, including *A People's History of the United States,* the plays *Emma* and *Marx in Soho* (South End Press), *The Zinn Reader,* and the autobiographical *You Can't Be Neutral on a Moving Train*. He lives with his wife, Roslyn, in Massachusetts and lectures widely on history and contemporary politics.

Index

A

B

C

D

I

J

K

L

M

N

O

S

T

U

V

W

Y

Z

About South End Press

South End Press is a nonprofit, collectively run book publisher with more than 200 titles in print. Since our founding in 1977, we have tried to meet the needs of readers who are exploring, or are already committed to, the politics of radical social change.

Our goal is to publish books that encourage critical thinking and constructive action on the key social, economic, ecological, and political issues shaping life in the United States and in the world. In this way, we hope to give expression to a wide diversity of democratic social movements and to provide an alternative to the products of corporate publishing.

Through the Institute for Social and Cultural Change, South End Press works with other political media projects—*Z Magazine;* Speak Out, a speakers bureau; and Alternative Radio—to expand access to information and critical analysis.

To order books, please send a check or money order to: South End Press, 7 Brookline Street, #1, Cambridge, MA 02139-4146. To order by credit card, call 1-800-533-8478. Please include $3.50 for postage and handling for the first book and 50 cents for each additional book.

Write or email southend@southendpress.org for a free catalog or visit our website at www.southendpress.org.

Related Titles from South End Press

Dishonest Broker
The United States, Israel, and the Palestinians
By Naseer Aruri
$18.00 paper; $40.00 cloth

Live From Palestine
International and Palestinian Direct Action Against the Israeli Occupation
Nancy Stohlman and Laurieann Aladin
$15.00 paper; $40.00 cloth

Fateful Triangle
The United States, Israel, and the Palestinians
Updated Edition
by Noam Chomsky
$22.00 paper; $40.00 cloth

Collateral Damage
The "New World Order" at Home and Abroad
edited by Cynthia Peters
$16.00 paper; $40.00 cloth

Eqbal Ahmad
Confronting Empire
Interviews with David Barsamian
$16.00 paper; $40.00 cloth

Imperial Alibis
Rationalizing U.S. Intervention After the Cold War
by Stephen R. Shalom
$19.00 paper; $25.00 cloth

The Real Terror Network
Terrorism in Fact and Propaganda
by Edward S. Herman
$16.00 paper; $35.00 cloth

Intifada
The Palestinian Uprising Against Israeli Occupation
edited by Zachary Lockman and Joel Beinin
$15.00 paper; $35.00 cloth

Food for Our Grandmothers
Writings by Arab-American and Arab-Canadian Feminists
edited by Joanna Kadi
$16.00 paper; $40.00 cloth

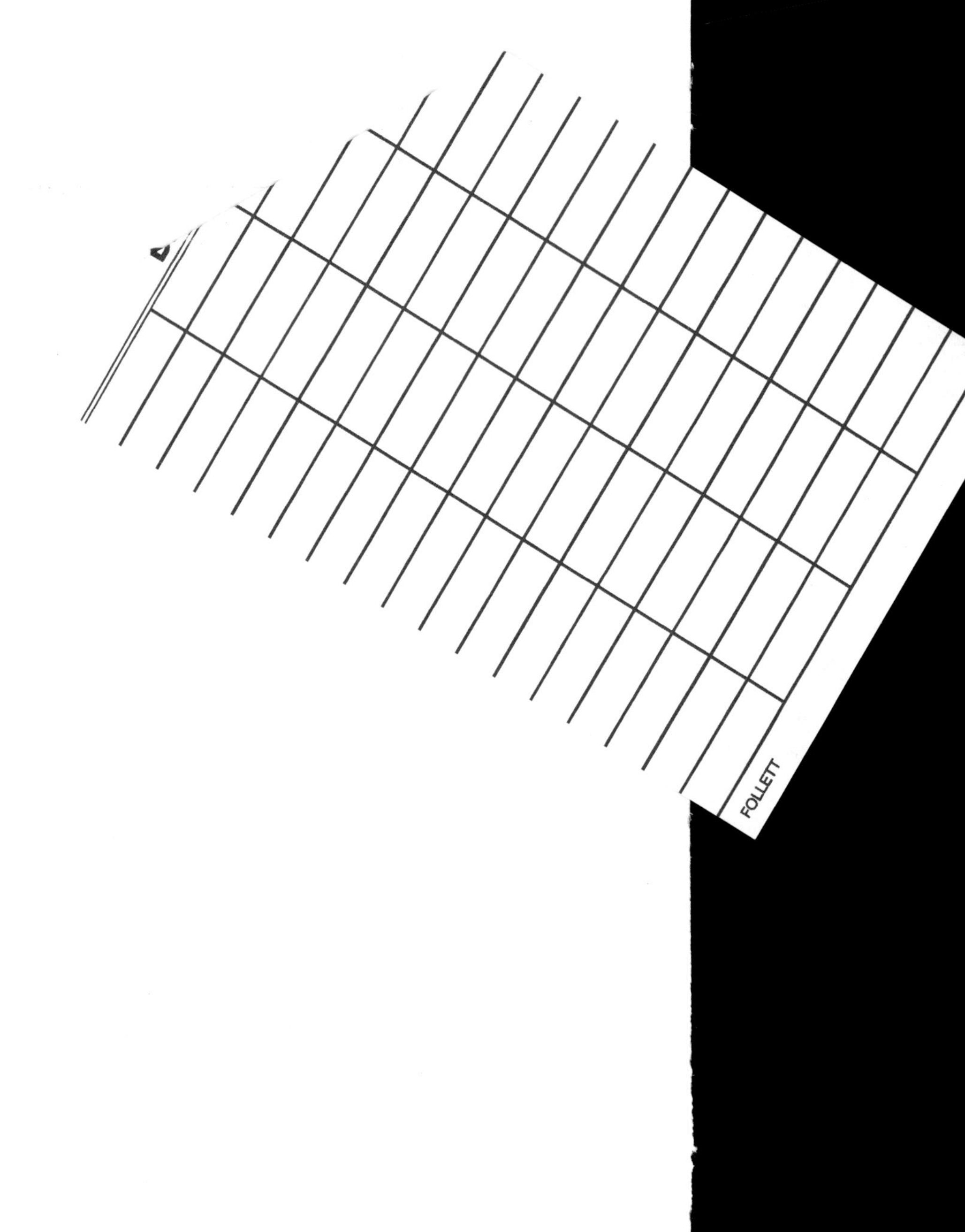
FOLLETT